JOURNAL FOR THE STUDY OF THE NEW TESTAMENT
SUPPLEMENT SERIES
63

Executive Editor
David Hill

JSOT Press
Sheffield

POWER
AND POLITICS
IN PALESTINE

The Jews and the
Governing of their Land
100 BC–AD 70

James S. McLaren

Journal for the Study of the New Testament
Supplement Series 63

For
Mary-Rose

Copyright © 1991 Sheffield Academic Press

Published by JSOT Press
JSOT Press is an imprint of
Sheffield Academic Press Ltd
The University of Sheffield
343 Fulwood Road
Sheffield S10 3BP
England

Typeset by Sheffield Academic Press
and
Printed on acid-free paper in Great Britain
by Billing & Sons Ltd
Worcester

British Library Cataloguing in Publication Data

McLaren, James S.
    Power & politics in Palestine: the Jews
    and the governing of their Land, 100BC–AD70.–
    (JSNT supplements, 0143-5108; 63).
    I. Title II. Series
    933.05

    ISBN 1-85075-319-9

CONTENTS

Acknowledgments

There are many people whose guidance, example and expertise have been important in the writing of this book, the text of which was originally submitted for a doctorate at the University of Oxford in Hilary Term, 1990. I had the privilege of working under the auspices of Professor Ed Sanders and Dr Martin Goodman. Ed was instrumental in guiding my research, giving direction, criticism and encouragement when necessary. I benefitted greatly from his support, generosity and enthusiasm for the subject. Martin was also generous in offering focus and direction in the latter stages of my research. My thanks are due also to Professor Fergus Millar and Dr Philip Davies, who examined the thesis and offered encouragement and suggestions regarding the work. I take this opportunity to mention also Mr Ron Ridley who encouraged me to pursue my interest in this period of history as an undergraduate and graduate at the University of Melbourne. Dr Geoff Jenkins kindly undertook to read the first section of the manuscript, for which I am grateful. Naturally, I take full responsibility for any omissions or errors of judgment that may remain in the work. During my time in Oxford I had the good fortune to be a member of Pembroke College. I am grateful for the friends I made there, for the pleasant setting it provided, and for the financial assistance the College offered. I also wish to thank the staff at Sheffield Academic Press, and especially Andrew Kirk, for the assistance they have provided in the publication of the book. Their speed and efficiency have been greatly appreciated.

I am especially aware of the numerous occasions when my family, in particular my mother, have provided support and encouragement; to them my thanks. Finally, and undoubtedly, the person to whom I am most grateful is my wife. Few words could express how much I have depended on her love and support—to her I dedicate this book with my deepest gratitude.

ABBREVIATIONS

AB	Anchor Bible
Ant.	Josephus, *Antiquities of the Jews*
Apion	Josephus, *Against Apion*
b.	Babylonian Talmud
BARev	*Biblical Archaeology Review*
Bib	*Biblica*
BTB	*Biblical Theology Bulletin*
CBQ	*Catholic Biblical Quarterly*
CCER	*Cahiers du Cercle Ernest Renan*
CQ	*Classical Quarterly*
CRIANT	Compendium Rerum Iudicarum ad Novum Testamentum
HTR	*Harvard Theological Review*
HUCA	*Hebrew Union College Annual*
IBS	*Irish Biblical Studies*
IEJ	*Israel Exploration Journal*
JBL	*Journal of Biblical Literature*
JES	*Journal of Ecumenical Studies*
JJS	*Journal of Jewish Studies*
JQR	*Jewish Quarterly Review*
JR	*Journal of Religion*
JRA	*Journal of Roman Archaeology*
JRS	*Journal of Roman Studies*
JSJ	*Journal for the Study of Judaism*
JSS	*Journal of Semitic Studies*
JTS	*Journal of Theological Studies*
Leg. Gai.	Philo, *Legatio ad Gaium*
Life	Josephus, *Life of Josephus*
m.	Mishnah
NovT	*Novum Testamentum*
NTS	*New Testament Studies*
SBL	Society of Biblical Literature
SBT	Society of Biblical Theology
War	Josephus, *The Jewish War*
ZNW	*Zeitschrift für die neutestamentliche Wissenschaft und die Kunde des Urchristentums*

Certain specific terms in the text that have been translated are accompanied by the original Greek the first time they appear in each section.

Chapter 1

INTRODUCTION

There has been a long-standing scholarly interest in the political and social organization of Palestine in the first centuries BC and AD. In Jewish circles this examination has focused on the underlying reasons for the AD 66–70 revolt. From the Christian perspective, interest has centred on the question of who was responsible for the death of Jesus. The few classical scholars who discuss the events in Palestine do so because the extant narratives provide one of the most detailed accounts of a Roman province in the first century AD. These, and other underlying concerns, have resulted in a large amount of general discussion of the administration with some detailed investigation of a few specific issues.

In this study the emphasis does not fall exclusively on any one of the three branches of scholarship. It is a historical examination of the administration and differs from previous work in two aspects: what it seeks to establish and the approach that will be taken. In a broad sense this study seeks to determine the extent to which the Jews were self-governing. It examines which people and/or institutions are recorded as actually making decisions for the Jewish community. The majority of the study focuses on detailed case studies of incidents recorded in the sources. On the basis of observations drawn from these case studies we shall be in a position to assess who held authority in Palestine and how this authority was used in decision-making and understood by the Jews.

The following analysis of the main scholarly approaches to the administration in Palestine displays the ways in which these have often rested on theoretical ideas of government rather than on a close examination of the contemporary sources. I will then outline the approach used in this study, highlighting the ways in which it differs from previous works. The final section of this introduction is devoted to several comments regarding the nature of the sources being used.

1. *Survey of Main Scholarship*

Despite interest in the functioning of the administration, a survey of present scholarship indicates that there has yet to be a comprehensive assessment of which Jews participated in administration and the extent to which they were able to do so. Furthermore, although scholars rely on the same source material,they reach extremely diverse conclusions.

Interest in administrative affairs in Palestine has been incorporated into three distinct types of work: studies specifically devoted to the issue of self-government; works by scholars in which observations regarding the administration are made within the context of another interest; and studies that address in detail one particular aspect of the administration in Palestine. An assessment of these works indicates the concentration of thought on formal institutions of power. It also highlights the need for a study that seeks to establish who actually held power as opposed to who should have held power or who it is believed should have done so.

Three scholars, S. Safrai, Z.W. Falk and E. Schürer, have specifically addressed the issue of Jewish self-government between 100 BC and AD 70. It is notable that not one of these scholars devotes more than a section of a large introductory text on the Second Temple period as a whole to the administration. Safrai claims that the Jews held a 'considerable degree of autonomy' throughout the first centuries BC and AD.[1] The main instruments through which this autonomy was expressed were the office of high priest and the sanhedrin. They remained separate institutions, with the latter playing the greater role. At the beginning of the Second Temple period a national assembly was the most important element in the government. In time this function was taken over by the sanhedrin, which was also known as the *boule* and *gerousia*. These different titles reflected the changing status of the sanhedrin throughout the period. There was, however, only one council in existence at any point in time during the Second Temple period.

---

1.   S. Safrai 'Jewish Self-Government', in S. Safrai and M. Stern (eds.), *The Jewish People in the First Century*, I (CRIANT; Assen: Van Gorcum, 1974), pp. 377-419.

On the assumption that all source material is of equal relevance, Safrai proceeds to outline what he considers to be the powers and areas of jurisdiction of the sanhedrin, the 'principal element of government'. Here Safrai is largely dependent on tannaitic literature. The sanhedrin was Jerusalem's city council and the legislative, judicial and executive authority for all Jews in Palestine. It was also the central place for the study of Torah, and it supervised the national religion and acted as the supreme authority in all disputes regarding Torah. Although some legislative duties were delegated to courts of seven and three, capital cases were judged by the sanhedrin. The right to inflict capital punishment was removed at some stage before AD 70 but Safrai makes no attempt to suggest when this might have happened. The high priest and the leading Pharisaic sage shared the leadership of the sanhedrin, whose members were appointed for life. Claiming a distinction between political and religious matters, Safrai states that the high priest ruled over the former while the leading sage presided over religious affairs. He concludes by stating that the power of the sanhedrin was dependent on its relationship with the Romans in the first century AD. Whenever a disruption to public order threatened, the Romans intervened, thus restricting the extent of Jewish autonomy.

Three brief comments need to be made regarding Safrai's contribution. First, he assumes that whatever power the Jews had was connected with particular formal institutions. In part this may be the result of separating discussion of the historical surroundings from that of Jewish self-government. Secondly, despite the fact that Safrai argues for equality amongst the sources, he relies almost entirely on tannaitic literature. Thirdly, he assumes a distinction between political and religious affairs. It is notable, however, that no examples are given to indicate what came under which heading. In effect, by limiting the discussion primarily to the sanhedrin and relying almost entirely on tannaitic literature for the description of it, Safrai presents a generalized outline of what should, according to one source, have been the instrument of Jewish administration.

Although primarily interested in describing the Jewish legal system of the Second Temple period, Z.W. Falk[1] devotes a specific chapter to

---

1. *Introduction to Jewish Law of the Second Commonwealth*, Part 1 (Leiden: Brill, 1972).

discussing the Jewish elements of government. In a similar way to Safrai, Falk begins from the premise that all available sources are equally relevant to a discussion of Jewish self-government. Three aspects of the administration are of interest to Falk: the high priesthood; the council at Jerusalem; and the local level of administration. Falk states that Pompey designated the high priest as the official Jewish leader, responsible to the Romans for the maintenance of law and order. When Judaea became a Roman province this practice was re-instituted.

Most of Falk's interest lies in a discussion of the second aspect, the council in Jerusalem. Early in the Second Temple period the council was called *gerousia*. At the end of the Hasmonaean period the council became known as the sanhedrin. What role this institution played in the administration was entirely dependent on its relations with the existing head of state. For example, early in the Hasmonaean period the sanhedrin was an advisory body, dealing with public affairs. Under Herod, however, the original sanhedrin was not involved in state matters. Rather, the king sought advice from a personal council.

Falk states that the leadership of the sanhedrin was shared by the serving high priest and the leading sage. This claim is justified by accepting the notion that there was a distinction maintained between religious and political matters from the time of Alexander Jannaeus. The leading sage presided over religious issues while the high priest chaired meetings that pertained to political affairs. The reign of Alexander Jannaeus also marked the beginning of a special Pharisaic council. Unfortunately Falk does not indicate the relative functions fulfilled by the sanhedrin and the Pharisaic council in the administration, although he does suggest that Herod restricted the sanhedrin's role to the extent that it became primarily an 'institution of religious instruction'.

The third aspect of the administration that Falk discusses pertains to local affairs, the town councils and rulers. Although Falk draws almost entirely on Old Testament source material he appears to imply that it reflects the situation until AD 70. In each town there was a 'plenary assembly'. Above this assembly stood the district council of elders, which dealt with minor legal cases. All important cases were referred to one of the three small sanhedrins or the sanhedrin in Jerusalem.

Although Falk seeks to place the material contained in the tannaitic literature within a plausible historical setting, it is notable that he fails to provide many examples of how the constitution actually functioned. Furthermore, despite his statement that all the source material is historically relevant and several references to Josephus, there is a strong reliance on tannaitic literature for his information.

The third work addressing the issue of Jewish self-government is the revised edition of Schürer.[1] On the local level, reference is made to the existence of town councils, and, in larger towns, to courts of twenty-three. Much attention is paid to the sanhedrin which allegedly functioned in Jerusalem. It is suggested that this institution was responsible for the collection of taxes throughout the Jewish region of Palestine. It is also described as holding *de facto* authority in terms of Jewish law. During the first century AD the sanhedrin's area of control only incorporated Judaea and when Palestine became a Roman province the idea of 'political unity' became inappropriate. There was only ever one sanhedrin in existence in Jerusalem at any given point in time. Throughout its lifetime, probably from the fourth century BC to AD 70, this council had a number of titles, including *gerousia* and sanhedrin. The large number of cases that had to be dealt with, however, probably indicates that other courts operated under the supervision of the sanhedrin.

According to Schürer it was the high priest alone who presided over the sanhedrin. The references in the tannaitic literature to the *nasi* as leader are viewed as being historically inaccurate. Although it is acknowledged that the extent of the sanhedrin's power depended on the Romans' decisions, Schürer concludes by claiming that the sanhedrin held a 'high degree of autonomy'. Civil jurisdiction in Jewish law and criminal law came under its control. The sanhedrin was also empowered to arrest people but it was probably not able to inflict the death penalty.[2]

---

1. E. Schürer, *The History of the Jewish People in the Age of Jesus Christ* (2 vols.; rev. trans. G. Vermes, F. Millar and M. Black; Edinburgh: T. & T. Clark, I, 1973, II, 1979).

2. There is also some discussion of the meaning of the term 'chief priests' (οἱ ἀρχ'ερεῖς) (*History*, II, pp. 232-36). Whereas J. Jeremias (*Jerusalem in the Time of Jesus* [trans. F.H. and C.H. Cave; London: SCM Press, 1969], pp. 175-81) concludes that the term refers to the priestly aristocracy, Schürer confines the term to individuals or families that could claim some link to the high priesthood but agrees that the priestly aristocracy were in fact most probably also close

Schürer marks a break from the approach of Falk and Safrai by suggesting that the information contained in the tannaitic literature is inaccurate. Schürer favours the idea of there being only one leader of a single national council. It is notable, however, that Schürer maintains a basic premise, that is, the existence of at least one formal national 'institution' which was the cornerstone of the Jewish realm of administration.

The studies of Safrai, Falk and Schürer display a tendency to separate analysis of Jewish autonomy and administration from the narration of events in Palestine during the Second Temple period. This division results in the discussion focusing on the theory rather than what may, in fact, have been the practice. These studies do not claim to be comprehensive of all aspects of Jewish history. They do, however, reflect an accepted approach in which particular aspects of the Second Temple period are isolated for the purposes of clarification and amplification. It is notable that there remains a certain degree of difference between these three works, despite the fact that they do not attempt to go beyond a basic outline of the administration. In the main, this division can be explained by the approach taken regarding the available source material. It is apparent from the assessment of these three works that some analysis of the relative value of the sources is necessary.

The second type of scholarly discussion is found in those works which comment on the administration within the context of other interests. Included in this category are works by G. Alon, E.M. Smallwood, D. Rhoads, C. Roth, E.P. Sanders and T. Rajak. Alon makes several observations regarding the administrative system in Palestine prior to AD 70.[1] His main interest, however, is in presenting information which he considers relevant to his purpose, the study of post AD 70 Jews who lived in Palestine. In this context Alon begins from the basis that the tannaitic literature and non-rabbinic material are all of equal relevance to his discussion. Commenting on the local level of administration Alon states that within the districts there were courts of twenty-three and courts of seven in each town. The leadership of towns was under the control of the elders, from

relatives of the high priest.
1.   G. Alon, *The Jews in Their Land in the Talmudic Age* (trans. G. Levi; Jerusalem: Magnes Press, 1980).

probably three rulers were chosen to act as an executive.

Alon focuses much of his attention on the national level of administration. He suggests that from the time of Herod, Jewish Palestine came under the judicial control of Jerusalem. The two main elements of the administration were the high priest and the sanhedrin. These were separate institutions, and the remaining discussion is focused on problems regarding the actual composition of the sanhedrin. It became operative in the fourth century BC and, although several titles were used to describe the sanhedrin, there was always only one such institution.

The duties and powers of the sanhedrin are outlined, based almost entirely on the tannaitic literature. The sanhedrin was the highest authority in religion and law, acting as the 'representative national body' of the Jews. It settled disputes in Jewish law and imposed religious discipline on all Jews. The sanhedrin supervised the temple cult, fixed the calendar and held executive jurisdiction in capital cases. There was a division of control: in all religious and internal matters the *nasi* presided, while in state and public matters the high priest was president of the sanhedrin. Of these two leaders, Alon believes that only the high priest held official status; the *nasi's* position was gained *de facto* through the increasing influence of the Pharisees.

There are two significant features of Alon's observations that require comment. First, he accepts that there was a permanent official instrument of government commonly known as the sanhedrin. As a result, his comments regarding the control of affairs in Palestine are based on the notion that a permanent council must be included. The second feature is the fact that his observations are general—few examples are included. In the same way as Falk and Safrai, Alon relies on tannaitic literature for his remarks on the national level of administration.

In 1976 E.M. Smallwood published the first detailed examination of the political relations between the Jews and the Romans to be undertaken by a classical historian.[1] Included in this study are a number of comments regarding the Jewish participation in the administration of Palestine. Smallwood states that the degree of Jewish political independence depended on the identity of the head of state. She accepts the

---

1. E.M. Smallwood, *The Jews under Roman Rule: from Pompey to Diocletian* (Leiden: Brill, 1976).

existence of two sanhedrins, one political and judicial, the other religious and legislative. The former is referred to in the works of Josephus and the New Testament, the latter in the tannaitic literature. No detailed information is provided regarding the actual role played by these two sanhedrins. It was the political sanhedrin that had its power affected by the head of state. Gabinius reduced the sphere of influence of the political sanhedrin to Jerusalem and its environs, while after AD 6 it became 'the real ruler under the aegis of the Roman resident governor'. The high priest, who was subject to the Romans, was the leader of this sanhedrin. In effect, therefore, the sanhedrin came under Roman control. Because it was Roman practice to channel as much responsibility for the administration as possible into the hands of locals, the political sanhedrin was used 'as the administrative and judicial body for local Jewish affairs'. Although unable to inflict the death penalty in political cases, the Jews were probably able to try such cases and were able to try and execute people for religious offences. During the revolt, it is suggested that a popular assembly held 'ultimate authority'.

Although hers is an extensive study, much of what Smallwood states is taken verbatim from Josephus. Furthermore, there is little attempt made to examine any link between the political sanhedrin and actual events as narrated by Josephus. Rather than investigate the role of this political sanhedrin in practice and the extent of its power, she accepts the view that there were two sanhedrins and that a distinction was maintained between political and religious affairs.

In his discussion of the causes of the revolt in AD 66–70, D. Rhoads presents a brief outline of the administration during the first century AD.[1] The two features he highlights are the high priest and the sanhedrin. The former became the 'primary political head of state' when Judaea became a Roman province, while the sanhedrin acted as the 'principal institution of self-government', whose members were elected for life. When Judaea was a province, the Jews there had greater autonomy than they did during the Hasmonaean period, when the high priest and sanhedrin were 'nominal institutions'. Contrary to many scholars, Rhoads makes no distinction between political and religious affairs and does not suggest that there was more than one

---

1.   D. Rhoads, *Israel in Revolution: 6–74 CE: A Political History Based on the Writings of Josephus* (Philadelphia: Fortress Press, 1976).

sanhedrin. He does note that although the Romans did not interfere in matters pertaining directly to the Jews, the prefect/procurator held ultimate authority in all legal matters.

While concentrating on the Jewish administration during the revolt, C. Roth makes several general observations regarding the administration during the first centuries BC and AD.[1] It was only during AD 66–70, when a republic was established, that the Jews were completely independent. With the intervention of Pompey, the government of Judaea changed from being a hierarchic monarchy to indirect Roman rule through the Herodian family and later, to direct rule. Only three institutions of the traditional Jewish constitution remained intact under the Romans: the high priesthood, the state council (sanhedrin) and the king. Although the high priest held some prestige, his political power diminished when Judaea became a Roman province.

Roth suggests that the sanhedrin began in AD 6. Although acknowledging that the mishnaic account may be partly idealized, Roth accepts that a Pharisaic council probably developed as a religious court which operated independently from the formal sanhedrin. The latter was the official council whose functions were restricted by the Romans to mainly religious and judicial matters. It is possible that the *boule* was identical with the sanhedrin. During the revolt, ultimate authority lay with 'the people at large', represented by a general assembly. Leading citizens, possibly from the sanhedrin, acted as the executive 'deliberative' council, and the serving high priest was the main head of state in AD 66–68. Because the king was pro-Roman he was not given a share in the administration. After AD 68 this system became increasingly disputed and eventually personal dictatorship became the means of administering affairs. At no stage, however, was there mob rule in Judaea.

Two more recent studies referring to Jewish involvement in the administration of affairs in Palestine contain important insights regarding the possible approach required in the assessment of the source material. T. Rajak and E.P. Sanders point to the need to scrutinize the available sources carefully. In her examination of Josephus's life and works, Rajak comments on the administration in

---

1.   C. Roth, 'The Constitution of the Jewish Republic of 66–70', *JSS* 9 (1964), pp. 295-319.

Judaea during Josephus's lifetime.[1] Although the Romans held 'ultimate control', some leading Jews played a part in the administration. In fact, it is stated that the actual outbreak of revolt in AD 66 can be connected to the failings of both the Roman procurators and the Jewish leaders. There were ten leading citizens who were 'active as representatives and organizers' for the populace. The Roman procurator held judicial authority but he relied 'upon a body of co-operative local aristocrats' to support him. These aristocrats included Josephus and at their head was the serving high priest. Rajak acknowledges that many questions regarding the nature of the sanhedrin remain unclear, especially the part it actually played in the decision-making process. It was presided over by the serving high priest and most of its membership was drawn from the priesthood. Rajak questions (like Rhoads) both the basis on which a distinction can be made between political and religious functions for the sanhedrin, and the idea that there was more than one such institution.

More recently E.P. Sanders has made several comments regarding the administration of Palestine in the context of his discussion on the trial of Jesus.[2] Sanders notes that, according to Josephus's narrative, a few leading citizens, especially 'the chief priests' (οἱ ἀρχιερεῖς), played a major part in the interaction between the Romans and the populace in the pre-war events. He suggests that these men were an important element in the actual functioning of government in Palestine during the mid-first century AD. It should be noted that E.P. Sanders addresses each source separately and seeks to proceed from an analysis of specific passages to determine the role of governmental groups and individual officers in concrete events.

The third type of discussion to consider is presented by those scholars who examine specific administrative aspects and/or events. The majority of this work falls into three categories: the existence of the sanhedrin; the depiction of Jerusalem as a polis; and the role of the Jewish upper class. The studies devoted to the sanhedrin concentrate on the number of sanhedrins, the identity of the leader(s), and the competence of the sanhedrin(s). The first and third of these issues have been considered primarily in terms of the sanhedrin's

---

1.   T. Rajak, *Josephus: The Historian and his Society* (London: Duckworth, 1983).

2.   E.P. Sanders, *Jesus and Judaism* (London: SCM Press, 1985).

responsibility for the trial and death of Jesus.

Rather than attempt to discuss all that each scholar has stated regarding the sanhedrin, it is sufficient to outline the major contributions and innovations since the work of A. Büchler.[1] He was perplexed by the fact that Josephus and the New Testament refer to the high priest as leader of the sanhedrin, while in the Mishnah the *nasi* is leader. Believing that each of these sources accurately reflected a historical situation in the Second Temple period, Büchler sought a solution to the discrepancy by way of a novel idea which has since been adopted by a number of scholars. He claims that there were, in the first century AD, two permanent courts. One was political, as depicted by Josephus and the New Testament; it was led by the high priest, who himself had no political standing, and was primarily a criminal court. The other court was religious, led by the *nasi*: it is depicted in the Mishnah. Büchler also argues that there was a third institution, the *boule* , which was responsible for the administration of Jerusalem. The religious court had its origins during the Hasmonaean period, while the political court was a Roman creation. Since the publication of this thesis, many scholars have engaged in a discussion centred on whether there were one, two, or even three courts operating at the same time.

In several studies, S. Zeitlin presents his reasons for accepting the existence of two separate courts, one religious, the other political.[2] This division began in 141 BC when Simon allegedly lost control of religious affairs. A new court was required, that is, the *bet din*. Only this new religious court was permanent: the political council became a tool of the state ruler who invoked it simply when he believed there was a need. Furthermore, *synedrion* was a common term—it was not intended as a term applying to one specific council. Not until after AD 70 did *synedrion*, as used by Josephus, refer to the Jewish religious court in the Hebraized form sanhedrin.[3] The leader of the political

1. A. Büchler, *Das Synedrion in Jerusalem und das grosse Beth-Din in der Quaderkammer des Jerusalemischen Tempels* (Vienna: Alfred Holder, 1902).

2. S. Zeitlin, 'The Political Synedrion and the Religious Sanhedrin', *JQR* 36 (1945–46), pp. 109-40 and 'Synedrion in Greek Literature, the Gospels and the Institution of the Sanhedrin', *JQR* 37 (1946–47), pp. 189-98.

3. This view is restated by Zeitlin ('Synedrion in the Judeo-Hellenistic Literature and Sanhedrin in the Tannaitic Literature', *JQR* 36 (1945–46), pp. 307-15) in response to H.A. Wolfson ('Synedrion in Greek Jewish Literature and Philo', *JQR* 36

court, the high priest, became subject to Roman interests after 63 BC, while the religious court, dominated by Pharisees, maintained its independence. Zeitlin concludes that the Jews had no jurisdiction in political offences and that the ability to inflict capital punishment lay in the hands of the Roman prefect/procurator.

S. Hoenig's study elaborates upon the powers, nature and characteristics of the 'traditional Great Sanhedrin'.[1] Hoenig suggests that greater emphasis should be placed upon the use of the Mishnah rather than on Josephus. Although the latter wrote during the Second Temple period, the Mishnah has the advantage of being compiled later, enabling it to take an overview of the entire period. From 141 BC the 'administrative techniques' employed in Judaea altered. Political and religious matters were separated and a new institution was created to deal with the latter. It was called the Great Sanhedrin. This body remained intact until AD 66 and held the right to try religious offenders on capital charges. Because the Great Sanhedrin was a religious institution, and the Romans were not interested in religious affairs, there was no conflict between it and the Romans regarding areas of jurisdiction. Under Herod, political matters were dealt with by an advisory council, while under the Roman administrators the high priest and priestly aristocracy fulfilled this task.

H. Mantel begins from the basis that the tannaitic literature is relevant to a historical study of the first centuries BC and AD.[2] As a result he concludes that the position of *nasi* was operative during the Second Temple period. Mantel follows Büchler's basic concept of two permanent courts, one political and the other religious. Contrary to Büchler, however, Mantel believes that the political sanhedrin was not primarily a criminal court. Rather, it was a royal court that dealt with a number of criminal cases and had a relatively small membership. Mantel also argues that the Great Sanhedrin, the *bet din*, pre-dates the political sanhedrin. Alexander Jannaeus deprived the Great Sanhedrin

---

(1945–46), pp. 303-305), who argues that *synedrion* was understood to mean council and court. H. Mantel (*Studies in the History of the Sanhedrin* [Harvard Semitic Series, 17; Cambridge, MA: Harvard University Press, 1961], p. 92) follows Wolfson while S.B. Hoenig (*The Great Sanhedrin* [Philadelphia: Dropsie College, 1953], pp. 8-9) adheres to Zeitlin's definition of the term in Jewish literature.

1. Hoenig, *Great Sanhedrin*.
2. Mantel, *Studies*.

of its political powers and, although these were briefly restored by Salome Alexandra, Herod permanently rid the Great Sanhedrin of its political role. Under the Roman administrators, the high priest and the political sanhedrin were responsible for Jewish administration, with former high priests being consulted, but holding no official authority. Finally, according to Mantel, the Jews were able to try people for capital offences during the first century AD.

A different approach is taken by J.S. Kennard in an attempt to define what he describes as the characteristics of the sanhedrin.[1] He argues that to understand the history of the sanhedrin we must view it within the context of Roman provincial policy. He rejects the idea that the sanhedrin should be perceived in terms of a political sanhedrin or as an advisory council in the mould of the Hellenistic model. Rather, the sanhedrin depicted in Josephus and the New Testament was an adaptation of the Hasmonaean priestly assembly that the Romans devised as part of their general provincial policy. This policy was to use the local wealthy ruling class to act as a national administrative body in the guise of a council. The references to the sanhedrin, especially in terms of the trial of Jesus, indicate that Judaea was not an exception to this practice. Kennard refers to this body as the 'ethnic assembly' and suggests it was a national organization that met annually.[2] Its executive, which dealt with day-to-day matters, was called the sanhedrin and could judge capital cases. The ethnic assembly was introduced by Julius Caesar. After AD 40 its importance began to wane as the status of the Roman emperor in the eyes of most Jews began to decline. Each city had a *boule* that was responsible for the administration of that particular city. Finally, Kennard believes there was a separate Pharisaic council which is depicted in the Mishnah. He considers the importance of this council, however, to have been vastly exaggerated in the Mishnah.

More recently, E. Rivkin, working from a similar perspective to that of Zeitlin, has argued for the existence of two separate councils.[3]

1. J.S. Kennard Jr, 'The Jewish Provincial Assembly', *ZNW* 53 (1962), pp. 25-51.

2. This term (κοινόν) is translated as 'common council' in this study. It is notable that Kennard associates much power with this assembly (pp. 43-44) but does not relate it in operation to the events narrated by Josephus.

3. E. Rivkin, 'Beth Din, Boulé, Sanhedrin: A Tragedy of Errors', *HUCA* 46 (1975), pp. 181-99. Also see E. Rivkin, *What Crucified Jesus?* (Nashville:

From what he describes as some 'methodological...sequential thought steps', theoretically devoid of knowledge of the secondary sources, Rivkin states that Josephus and the New Testament refer to a political sanhedrin. This was a loosely organized group that dealt with public and state matters under the presidency of the high priest. It was this sanhedrin, acting as the 'stooge' for the Romans during the first century AD, that was responsible for the trial of Jesus. The Mishnah, on the other hand, refers to the religious council which adjudicated in internal Jewish affairs under the leadership of the *nasi*. Furthermore, this religious council would be more appropriately entitled *bet din* which should, in turn, be equated with *boule* in Greek, not *synedrion*.[1] There was a clear distinction between religious and political affairs. The high priest and his supporters aided the Romans in administering the latter, while the *nasi* and his Pharisaic associates controlled the former through the *bet din*/sanhedrin.

According to J. Efron the pictures of the sanhedrin presented by Josephus and the Mishnah are idealizations of how it operated.[2] Furthermore, the New Testament picture of the sanhedrin cannot be supported from the information contained in the other source material.[3] In the context of his discussion, Efron states that Josephus depicts a formal institution of government called the *boule*.

This survey of the main scholarly contributions to the discussion of the sanhedrin prompts two pertinent observations. First, and probably the most fundamental, is the assumption in the studies that at least one sanhedrin always functioned in Judaea. Little attention is paid to the question of whether in fact there is evidence for a permanent institution that actively participated in the administration and was referred to as sanhedrin.[4] The second observation relates to the use of source

Abingdon Press, 1984), pp. 16-18, 75.

1. Note, however, that Rivkin ('Beth Din, Boulé, Sanhedrin', p. 198) does argue that sanhedrin should be equated with *bet din*.

2. J. Efron, *Studies in the Hasmonean Period* (trans. N. Handeliman; Leiden: Brill, 1987).

3. This argument suffers somewhat from Efron's statements elsewhere that little value can be found in the portraits of the sanhedrin provided by Josephus and the Mishnah (*Studies* pp. 337-38).

4. It is notable that in his discussion of recent scholarship on Second Temple period Jewish history Cohen does not question whether a permanent institution actually existed. See S.J.D. Cohen, 'The Political and Social History of the Jews in

material. There is only limited discussion of the relative value of the sources in terms of describing actual events. The majority of scholars accept the tannaitic literature as being a vital witness to the events pertaining to the sanhedrin in the Second Temple period. Only Efron explicitly queries the material in terms of examples where 'the sanhedrin' participated in the administration.

There has been a limited amount of discussion of the idea that Jerusalem could be regarded as a polis. Avi-Yonah argues that Jerusalem was a Hellenistic city from the reign of Herod onwards.[1] The notion that Jerusalem was a polis is addressed directly by Tcherikover.[2] He claims that the reference to the *boule* is the main reason for regarding the city as part of the Hellenistic system. This *boule*, however, was merely a different way of referring to the traditional Jewish council. Furthermore, there is no evidence for the existence of an active demos or gymnasium. Tcherikover also states that Herod did not replace the sanhedrin with a new Greek-style city council in Jerusalem.

The other specific issue discussed by scholars is the role of the Jewish upper class in the administration. Buehler examines Josephus's writings as a means to clarify the early history of the Sadducees and Pharisees.[3] He considers the possible situation in Judaea from the perspective of the social structure in Rome. There is much detailed assessment of the use of particular terms in Josephus's works to describe the various classes in Jewish society. Buehler concludes that the aristocracy of Judaea was divided into two basic groups, those who held their status because of birth, and those who attained it through

---

Greco-Roman Antiquity: The State of the Question', in G.W.E. Nickelsberg and R.A. Kraft (eds.), *Early Judaism and Its Modern Interpreters* (Philadelphia: Fortress Press, 1986), pp. 39, 44-46.

1. M. Avi-Yonah, *The Holy Land* (Grand Rapids: Baker Book House, 1966), p. 94. Schürer (*History*, II, pp. 213-14) also notes a strong Greek influence, referring to the use of *boule* and the probable existence of a committee of ten men in Jerusalem.

2. V.A. Tcherikover, 'Was Jerusalem a Polis?', *IEJ* 14 (1964), pp. 61-78. Safrai ('Self-Government', p. 389) supports the view that Jerusalem should not be regarded as a Greek polis.

3. W.W. Buehler, *The Pre-Herodian Civil War and Social Debate. Jewish Society in the Period 76–40 BC and the Social Factors contributing to the Rise of the Pharisees and the Sadducees* (Basel: Friedrich Reinhardt, 1974).

wealth. The former of these groups was pro-oligarchic and connected with the Pharisees, while those powerful because of their wealth were pro-monarchic and associated with the Sadducees. Although no attempt is made to assess the possible role of the men described by Josephus as 'the powerful men' (οἱ δυνατοί), 'the notable men' (οἱ γνώριμοι), 'the first men' (οἱ πρῶτοι) and 'the leading men' (οἱ ἐν τέλει) outside pre-existing notions of governmental institutions or accepted social divisions, the work highlights the need to examine the role of the upper class as a group in the administration of Judaea.

Smallwood has discussed the role of the high priest and his associates.[1] She notes that the office was held by only a small number of families in the first century AD. They fulfilled a major role in the administration of Judaea. In the main, Smallwood argues that the high priest was required to work for the interests of the Jews and Romans simultaneously, a task they completed with a certain amount of success. However, from the late AD 50s it is probable that the high priest engaged in anti-Roman activities. As a result Smallwood believes that Josephus idealized the high priest as a peace maker in *The Jewish War*.

Largely in response to Smallwood's arguments, R.A. Horsley examined the relationship between the high priest and the Romans.[2] Horsley, however, also includes in his study the activities of the Jewish aristocracy as a whole. He commences by arguing that it is not possible to understand the relationship until the available evidence is viewed within the context of the Roman imperial system. The Roman practice was to use the existing local aristocracy in provincial administration. In Judaea the high priest had been the ostensible leader of the Jews, and he was a leading element of the Jewish aristocracy, which consisted of wealthy, priestly families. Expecting the high priest and the aristocracy to control society, the Romans placed them in charge of Judaea. The natural result of this situation was the collaboration of the aristocracy with the Romans. Although there

---

1. E.M. Smallwood, 'High Priests and Politics in Roman Palestine', *JTS* ns 13 (1962), pp. 14-34.

2. R.A. Horsley, 'High Priests and the Politics of Roman Palestine', *JSJ* 27 (1986), pp. 23-55. Horsley notes that Smallwood's approach has been accepted by other scholars, namely G. Theissen (*Sociology of Early Palestinian Christianity* [trans. J. Bowden; Philadelphia: Fortress Press, 1978]), thus warranting a response (p. 23).

were occasional tensions between the interests of the Romans and those of the aristocracy, at no stage did the latter engage in, or encourage, anti-Roman activities. Even after the defeat of Cestius, the aristocracy remained in command, seeking a peaceful end to the conflict. Horsley briefly analyses several incidents described by Josephus in the process of reaching his conclusions. He claims that the sources he uses, including Josephus, must be neutral or actually critical of the ruling elements in Judaea because these elements were pro-Roman. There is no recognition, however, that Josephus was a representative of the wealthy priestly families.

More recently, M. Goodman has undertaken a major study of the role of the Jewish upper class in the administration.[1] His work focuses on the possible significance of the upper class in the outbreak of the revolt against Rome in AD 66. Within this framework Goodman is the first scholar to examine in any detail Josephus's account of the make-up of the ruling class, especially for the period after AD 44. Like Horsley, Goodman outlines the Roman imperial context, noting the tendency for the Romans to call upon the local aristocracy to assist them in governing the territory. Goodman's main argument is that there was no such natural aristocracy in Judaea, leading inevitably to a break-down in trust and communication which culminated with the revolt in AD 66 when the Romans perceived the existing ruling class as being openly rebellious. Goodman's work does much to highlight the fact that apart from specific institutions of government, it is necessary to consider the possible involvement of particular social groups, often associated with the high priesthood, in the administration. This obser-vation is clearly made in Goodman's detailed examination of

---

1. M. Goodman, *The Ruling Class of Judaea. The Origins of the Jewish Revolt against Rome AD 66–70* (Cambridge: Cambridge University Press, 1987). The substantial part of the research for my study had been completed before the publication of Goodman's book. His text is of major importance to the field of late Second Temple period Jewish history and it deals with material of direct relevance to this study. Consequently a number of Goodman's conclusions will be addressed in the course of this work. See also P.A. Brunt, 'The Romanization of the Local Ruling Classes in the Roman Empire', in D.M. Pippidi (ed.), *Assimilation et résistance à la culture gréco-romaine dans le monde ancien. Travaux du VIe Congrès International d'Etudes Classiques, Madrid, Septembre 1974* (Bucharest: Editura Academiei, 1976), pp. 161-73. He argues in detail that the local ruling elite co-operated with the Romans in the governing of provincial territory.

Josephus's narrative of the events in Jerusalem during the AD 50s and 60s.

The discussion focusing on the role of the upper class highlights the possibility of non-formal participation in the administration. Although the high priest is viewed as a leading figure within the aristocracy, it has been pointed out that he did not act alone. Furthermore, there is still much debate about the intentions of this aristocracy, especially in terms of whether it represented Roman or Jewish interests. It is important to acknowledge the Roman approach to local government in relation to the administrative structure which was implemented in Palestine. Understanding that context, however, does not necessarily explain how the Jewish aristocracy perceived its role in Judaea during the first century AD, nor clarify the contribution of that aristocracy.

The preceding survey of secondary sources indicates a tendency towards discussing possible institutions of government. Foremost among these institutions are the high priesthood and the sanhedrin. The possible involvement of particular social groups is considered only in a few instances. It is apparent that most scholars believe that there was an established system of government which operated with varying degrees of success depending on the identity of the head of state.

Paramount to this system of government, to the majority of scholars, is the acceptance of a formal institution normally called sanhedrin. Although some scholars have expressed doubt regarding the permanency of this sanhedrin, the general view has been to accept that the Jews had a permanent formal institution that was their 'national representative council'.[1] Debate remains, however, on the exact number of sanhedrins and the functions it/they fulfilled. Opinions range from there being one permanent council with the other unofficial advisory bodies, to there being three official councils during the first century AD. Many of these differences of opinion relate to how particular sources are employed. A further factor in this discrepancy is the absence of the provision of examples. Few scholars present concrete events which reflect the administrative structure which they favour. This situation is especially prevalent amongst those scholars who focus their attention on the Mishnah. In fact, apart from

---

1. There are several exceptions to this view. For example, see E.P. Sanders (*Jesus and Judaism*, p. 314) and Efron (*Studies*, p. 290).

the comments made in the studies of E.P. Sanders and Goodman, modern scholarship appears to neglect a detailed assessment of actual events where decisions are made in Judaea.

Incorporated in the discussion of the institutions of government has been a general assumption that the Jews distinguished between religious and political matters. Furthermore, this distinction was apparently recognized by the Romans. Such a view is fundamental to the approach taken by Rivkin in his assessment of the Jewish involvement in the death of Jesus. Accompanying this division in affairs has been the perception that Josephus portrays political action while the Mishnah deals with religious affairs. Related to the belief that two separate councils existed, one for political, the other for religious affairs, is the debate surrounding the relative importance of the Pharisees and the priesthood. The assumption that religious and political affairs were distinguished has resulted in a number of scholars arguing that control of affairs was divided between the priesthood and the Pharisees.[1]

It is clear from this survey that there is a lack of consensus regarding the relative emphasis that should be placed on the source material. The majority of scholars acknowledge the tannaitic literature as relevant to describing events in the Second Temple period. The same is true of Josephus and, generally, of the New Testament. It is notable, however, that scholars have then tended to deal with each source as a complete entity, either accepting its entire contents, or rejecting it in total, irrespective of whether there is internal unity in any one source. Hoenig, for example, favours the tannaitic literature, rejecting the works of Josephus. Conversely, some scholars occasionally incorporate different accounts without any clear explanation being offered for such synthesis.[2] Such scholars as Mantel and Safrai present a further example of the way sources are sometimes used. They claim all the sources are relevant, yet rely heavily on the Mishnah.

---

1.   This state of affairs is reflected in the existence of several texts devoted to a discussion of the prominence of the Pharisees and related topics. See, for example, E. Rivkin, *A Hidden Revolution* (Nashville: Parthenon Press, 1978). For a more balanced approach see A.J. Saldarini, *Pharisees, Scribes and Sadducees in Palestinian Society* (Edinburgh: T. & T. Clark, 1989).

2.   Schürer tends to follow one of Josephus's accounts if his texts are at variance without stating a reason for such a preference. See, for example, the narration of the trial of Herod under Hyrcanus II (*History*, I, pp. 275-76).

2. *Outline of the Approach Taken in this Study*

The lack of examples to support much of what is claimed regarding the administration and the differences regarding the relative value of the source material indicate the need for an effective means to examine the issue of Jewish involvement in administration. I believe that case studies of incidents will fulfil this need. The essential aim of the following cases is to establish who was actually involved in the decision-making process and political manoeuvring in Palestine, according to the narrative of each incident. This approach has the value of fostering an examination of real-life situations as opposed to theoretical constructions. Further, it will not begin from the premise of confirming or rejecting what appears to be said in any one particular source. Rather, it provides the opportunity to draw on a variety of materials narrating specific incidents in which the administration of Palestine is implicitly or explicitly discussed.

By undertaking case studies we can address a number of issues that arise in terms of scholarly discussion of the administration of Palestine: whether there was a system of Jewish government, and whether it included a sanhedrin; whether there is evidence that political and religious affairs were separated; whether the Jews were able to convict and execute people for capital offences in the first century AD; what roles, if any, were played by individuals or social groups in the administration; and what the motivations of those involved in the administration may have been. We may then be in a position to conclude by commenting on the extent to which the Jews were self-governing under the various heads of state of the first centuries BC and AD. The nature of this study will also enable us to stand outside existing perceptions of the appropriate way to examine the administration of affairs in Palestine.

Some explanation of the case-study approach is necessary. The cases are drawn from incidents recorded in the sources which can be linked to a certain chronological point in time during the first centuries BC or AD. Each case is assessed separately and observations regarding their contents are drawn together only after all the cases have been considered. The major tasks in undertaking this approach are to establish who was perceived to be, and who actually was involved in the administration, and to determine how matters were resolved. I shall also consider any possible references which identify particular people or institutions, the methods by which certain people believed that they could express their authority and the basis on which this authority was perceived to operate.

A number of the incidents are recorded in more than one source. On such occasions the accounts are initially considered separately, irrespective of whether they come from the hand of the same author. The intention is to examine any possible differences that exist, establishing where there is common ground and where there may be irreconcilable differences. A basic outline of the incident is then presented but this will not necessarily accommodate all aspects of every account. If certain points of detail appear to be historically inaccurate or uncertain they are not incorporated into the historical reconstruction simply for their own sake. For example, we can accept that Herod was called to Jerusalem to answer charges regarding his conduct by Hyrcanus II and that Herod escaped unharmed. The versions in *Antiquities of the Jews* and *The Jewish War*, however, contain certain details that are difficult to reconcile and which must be questioned. Similarly, Jesus was arrested, formally convicted under the prefectship of Pilate, and was executed. The historical accuracy of details regarding the people who opposed Jesus and the timing of the trial before the Jews, however, are difficult to establish.

The origin of the information in each narrative is treated with some caution as we cannot always distinguish whether it comes directly from actual eyewitnesses, the author, written accounts, or oral tradition. Obviously, if there is only one account of an incident we can only be discerning regarding the details if there is any internal division to suggest the need for such caution. For example, the account in Acts of how Stephen met his death appears to incorporate different versions of the event. As a result, it is appropriate to query the details of the entire account in an effort to seek an outline of the historical event.

Rather than assume that we can always establish a historical account of each incident, it is accepted that in some instances we may only be able to establish an outline with details that reflect the perception of particular interests. I have, however, proceeded by accepting each narrative as being essentially historically accurate. Details are regularly questioned by the study of parallels where they exist and of such internal evidence as consistency and inherent plausibility. While it is possible that individual narratives may have been invented, an assumption of the general authenticity of the events recorded, if not the details of the narrative, must normally be upheld as an essential basis on which historical study can proceed.[1]

It is important to note that this study is not intended as an attempt to establish any one particular version of an incident as being a more accurate reflection of the historical events than any other version. As a result, the use made of the available sources in each instance is not on the basis that one particular source is generally considered to be more or less accurate than another, for whatever reason.

One further comment concerns the relative value of the narratives and speeches in some of the sources. In the narratives, certain pertinent pieces of information may be ignored, or included in a particular position within the account to enhance a point the narrator wants to make. However, the author's narration usually describes things which actually happened. An author writing at length who attempts to record history, as did Josephus, and who draws on sources to write this narrative, would find it difficult to manufacture event after event.[2]

In general, the speeches probably reflect the narrator's perception of the person to whom they are attributed as much as what was actually said. Speeches are relatively easy for the historian to control,

---

1.   In a review article ('Rules of Evidence', *JRS* 68 [1978], pp. 178-86, reviewing F. Millar, *The Emperor in the Roman World 31 BC–AD 337* [London: Duckworth, 1977]), K. Hopkins drew attention to a number of important issues for the practice of ancient history. Underlying the review is the tension between restricting our understanding of material to that of a literal level where the facts as quoted in the sources are all important and the other extreme of approaching the source material thematically in an attempt to bring the period alive. I have indicated some of the problems regarding the administration in Palestine that have arisen because actual events have not been addressed in any detail. Therefore, it is essential that this study is based on contemporary accounts of what happened. Limits of space require that I restrict my attention to clarifying the decision-making process and the identity of the participants to provide a basis for future study of other aspects of the sociopolitical history of the Jews in first centuries BC and AD.

2.   For example, Josephus summarizes the Pharisees as a group who did not express insurgent tendencies (*War* 2.166; *Ant.* 18.12-15). The narrative of events during the reign of Salome Alexandra, however, suggests that at least some Pharisees actively participated in the fighting to overthrow Alexander Jannaeus. See below, Chapter 2, section 2.

and the current conventions of historiography suggest that authors put a good deal of effort into the composition of speeches which were suitable to the time and place.[1] Because we cannot know precisely the relationship between the speeches and what was actually said, however, I have sought to establish a reliable version of each incident from the basis of the narratives.

Twenty-one cases form the kernel of this study. Some of these cases deal with individual incidents while others incorporate several events that are directly related in time and content. Three main elements formed the basis of selection. The first of these elements was chronology. I commence with the reign of Alexander Jannaeus. This date was chosen for two main reasons: first, and most importantly, certain events associated with the reign of Alexander Jannaeus have been regarded by modern scholarship as suggesting that the administrative structure in Palestine underwent significant change, especially in terms of the role of the Pharisees and the national representative council, the sanhedrin; secondly, there is a general increase in the amount of information pertaining to events in the first century BC. I conclude the study with the destruction of the Temple in AD 70. Despite the fact that the available source material for events in Jerusalem becomes increasingly sketchy after AD 67, it is possible to reconstruct an outline of the administration of the city until the final submission of the Jews to the Romans commanded by Titus.[2]

Working within this chronological period, the second basis for selection was in terms of the people involved. In general, incidents

1. On speeches in Greek literature, see F.W. Walbank, 'Speeches in Greek Historians', in *Selected Papers, Studies in Greek and Roman Historiography* (Cambridge: Cambridge University Press, 1985), pp. 242-61. Basing the discussion primarily on Polybius, Walbank argues that although fabrication was not common, historians did develop the art of presenting a personalized rendition of speeches (p. 259). See also D.E. Aune, *The New Testament and its Literary Environment* (Philadelphia: Westminster Press, 1987), pp. 91-93, 124-28. The two speeches of Eleazar at Masada recorded by Josephus may reflect the mood of what was said in the fortress but it is difficult to claim that Josephus was aware of the full details, let alone the actual wording.

2. As indicated by Cohen ('Political and Social History', pp. 38-39), these dates should not be assumed to mark the chronological confines of Jewish interest in independent government. Rather, they act as a convenient confine for the limits of this study.

have been excluded where the head of state is clearly established. There are certain exceptions to this guideline. Although the Roman prefect/procurator was officially in full control of the province I have included incidents where he interacts with the Jews to reach a decision. Other events where he acts alone are not discussed in any detail in the text of this study.[1] Similarly, when there was a Jewish leader acting as head of state, events will not be subject to any detailed examination. The narrative of events provided by Josephus indicates that although Hyrcanus II, Antigonus, Herod, Archelaus, Philip, Antipas, Agrippa I and Agrippa II were subject to certain interests, they were in command within their territories. For example, Herod gave military assistance to the Romans. In return his kingdom was increased on several occasions (*War* 1.396-98; *Ant.* 15.217, 343). Herod was aware of the need to obtain Roman backing in any proposed military campaign against neighbouring territories (*Ant.* 16.335-55). In internal affairs he was also aware of the need to allow Roman intervention in issues that were of concern to them. For example, in the cases against his main heirs, Herod consulted with the relevant Roman authority (*War* 1.452, 537-43, 617-40; *Ant.* 16.90-126, 356-72; 17.91-145). In all other trials, however, he is portrayed as being able to do as he wished (*War* 1.433, 443, 544-49, 648-55; *Ant.* 15.87, 173-77, 229, 231-36; 16.393-94; 17.156-67). Furthermore, Herod ordered the death of the man he appointed as high priest (*War* 1.437; *Ant.* 15.50-56). He undertook major building programmes (*War* 5.238; 7.172-77; *Ant.* 15.331-41, 380-425, 16.142-45), introduced a law allowing thieves to be sold into foreign slavery (*Ant.* 16.1-5) and altered the level of taxation as he deemed

1.   The terms 'prefect' and 'procurator' are understood to refer to the same office in the province of Judaea, the former being more common during the reigns of Augustus and Tiberius. See Schürer, *History*, I, pp. 358-60, and A.H.M. Jones, *Studies in Roman Government and Law* (Oxford: Basil Blackwell, 1960), pp. 117-25. As a result, in this study the Roman appointees prior to Agrippa I will be referred to as prefect and those men appointed after the death of Agrippa I will be described as procurator. One of the main actions fulfilled by the prefect which will not be discussed in any detail was the appointment of the high priest (*Ant.* 18.34-35). Note, however, that there were also occasions when the legate of Syria took responsibility for the appointment of the high priest, normally at a time when there was no prefect in office (*Ant.* 18.123) or when the legate was carrying out a specific order (*Ant.* 18.26).

appropriate (*Ant.* 15.365; 16.62-65).

Archelaus's position in Judaea was decided by Augustus (*War* 2.94-98; *Ant.* 17.317-21) as was his removal (*War* 2.111-17; *Ant.* 17.342-44). Only with Archelaus was it expressly stated that his position was dependent on his ability to rule the territory without causing too much hardship for the inhabitants. Even within the tetrarchies it is apparent that the Jewish head of state was in control. Herod Antipas decided the fate of John the Baptist without reference to anyone else (Mt. 14.10; Lk. 3.20; 9.9; Mk 6.17; *Ant.* 18.116-19). Further evidence of the internal dominance of the Jewish head of state can be found during the reign of Agrippa I. Appointed by Gaius, Agrippa I dealt with several Christians as he deemed appropriate (Acts 12.2, 19), decided the tax levels (*Ant.* 18.299) and made several appointments as he liked (*Ant.* 19.297, 299, 313-16). When Agrippa I decided to increase the height of the city wall, however, the Romans intervened and ordered all work to cease (*War* 2.218; *Ant.* 19.326-27). It is possible that the heads of state called upon the assistance of certain groups or individuals but they were not subject to other Jews. As long as these men appeased the Romans after 63 BC they were allowed to govern their kingdoms.[1]

There are three notable exceptions to this guideline. The first of these is during the reign of Alexander Jannaeus, when there was a dispute regarding his right to control Palestine. The second is in reference to the division of authority under Salome Alexandra and the third is the trial of Herod while Hyrcanus II was ethnarch and high priest. These incidents relate to the issue of which Jews were involved in deciding how the country was administered and as such warrant detailed examination.

The third principle underlying the final selection of incidents was the desire to obtain as broad a representation of 'types' of incidents as was possible. There are four categories into which the material in the available sources may be placed. The first of these categories includes incidents where a decision is made in which the Jews as a whole are

---

1. The one exception to this was Antigonus, who owed his appointment as king to Parthian assistance (*War* 1.269; *Ant.* 14.365). This action, however still brought Antigonus into contact with Rome because of Antony's willingness to support Herod in reclaiming the throne as an ally of Rome (*War* 1.282-85; *Ant.* 14.381-85).

successful in obtaining their aim, irrespective of other factors. Occasions when certain Jews were not able to achieve their aim constitute the second category. The third category includes occasions when one Jewish viewpoint is successful in achieving its aim above another claim. The final category broadly incorporates incidents that illustrate the division of power and/or clarify the possible avenues by which an aim could be fulfilled at particular times in Palestine. These incidents reflect aspects of the other categories.

There are a number of other incidents narrated, especially by Josephus, which may be considered relevant. For example, the intervention of Pompey (*War* 1.120-57; *Ant.* 14.4-79), the actions of Gabinius in the context of the relations between Hyrcanus II and Antipater's family (*War* 1.158-70, 171-74, 176-78; *Ant.* 14.79-91, 92-97, 100-103), the institution of Judaea as a province in AD 6 (*War* 2.117-18; *Ant.* 18.2), Vitellius's actions in Jerusalem (*Ant.* 18.85-124), trouble under the procuratorship of Cumanus (*War* 2.223-31; *Ant.* 20.105-17), the request by Herod of Chalcis to control the Temple (*Ant.* 20.15-16), the request made by the Levites to Agrippa II (*Ant.* 20.216-17), and the trouble in Caesarea during the procuratorship of Felix (*War* 2.266-70; *Ant.* 20.162-78). To ensure that this study is both comprehensive and thorough, it is necessary to limit the number of incidents discussed in detail, yet acknowledge all possible relevant material. On this basis, incidents not presented in the text are referred to within discussions on similar or related incidents. They are also referred to in the final section of this study where I draw together the information derived from the case studies.

3. *Comments regarding the Sources Used*

There is no new source material that can be added to that already discussed by modern scholars. I have, however, noted a disparity in the treatment of that source material. In this chronological and event-based study the emphasis is on the narratives that include historical events. At the same time I believe that other material which is not event-based can be of value in establishing the accuracy of particular narratives. Here I give an outline of the sources that are available. In so doing, I have considered both the contents of the literary works and any apparent thematic developments in them which may indicate that care is necessary when using these sources. In turn, I have attempted to reflect on how the sources might be expected to provide information relevant to the Jewish administration in the first centuries BC and AD.

There are five literary sources and two other types of source material, numismatic remains and archaeological findings. The literary sources—Josephus, Philo of Alexandria, the New Testament Gospels and Acts of the Apostles, Tacitus and tannaitic literature—incorporate the interests of different cultural and religious groups. Each source requires specific attention.

The information we have regarding Josephus's life is obtained solely from his writings. We are, therefore, only told what Josephus wants his reader to know. Certain points are clear. Josephus was born in AD 36–37 (*Life* 5), he was related to the Hasmonaean line (*Life* 2) and was the son of a priest (*Life* 4). He was educated in Jerusalem and apparently became acquainted with several of the Jewish schools of thought early in his life (*Life* 9–12). In public affairs, Josephus went to Rome to plead the case for several Jewish priests, returning to Palestine immediately before the revolt (*Life* 13–16). Having been sent to Galilee as commander (*War* 2.568; *Life* 28–29), he found acceptance in the Roman camp after the fall of Jotapata (*War* 3.392-408, 5.362-419; *Life* 417–21). After the destruction of the Temple, Josephus lived in Rome under the patronage of Vespasian and his children (*Life* 414–16, 422–24). At some point he apparently proclaimed an allegiance to Pharisaic teachings (*Life* 12).

There is much debate regarding the relative importance of certain events and interests to the way Josephus lived. It is important to consider how the events connected with Josephus's life may have affected his perspective, as they may subsequently be reflected in personal bias or apologetic interests in his writings.

It is difficult to assess the character of Josephus and the nature of his works, not only because he provides a selective amount of material about himself, but also because all his works were undertaken in Rome. As a result much interest has been focused on determining the point where Jewish and Roman interests meet in what he wrote. At one end of the scale is the approach which perceives Josephus merely as a Roman propagandist who may have acquired certain nationalistic feelings late in his life.[1] The other extreme views Josephus as a

---

1. This view is favoured by S.J.D. Cohen, *Josephus in Galilee and Rome* (Leiden: Brill, 1979), pp. 144-51. W. Weber (*Josephus und Vespasian: Unter-*

pragmatic opportunist. In the midst of these extremes most work is
focused on drawing a balance between personal interests and political–
religious apologetics.[1] It is apparent that Josephus would want to
acknowledge the sponsorship he received from Vespasian, especially
in his early work. It is also plausible that Josephus had to orientate his
work in a manner that might attract interest from readers in his
immediate surroundings, the Graeco-Roman world.[2] As a Jew who
had received a Jewish education, yet who was aware of Greek
language and culture, Josephus's cultural heritage was Palestinian
Judaism located within a Graeco-Roman context. Whether he was a
Pharisaic Jew from early in his life is a matter of some debate. It
does appear that in the later texts a preference for Pharisaism is
noticeable.[3]

It is not possible to categorize all of Josephus's works in any one
particular manner. It is apparent that an interplay of personal defence,
apologetic for his people and religious ideology in a changing world
combine to affect the value of particular passages.

Josephus's Greek version of *The Jewish War*, dating from the late
AD 70s in its present form, centres around the destruction of
Jerusalem. The work describes the events that led up to the revolt and

1921]) argues that *War* was actually based on a Flavian text and that it was intended
to be propaganda that would help safeguard the first non-Italian emperor. Other
scholars rate propaganda for the Romans as one of the main themes of *War*. See, for
example, H.St J. Thackeray, *Josephus the Man and the Historian* (New York:
Jewish Institute of Religion Press, 1929), p. 27, and G.A. Williamson, *The World
of Josephus* (London: Secker & Warburg, 1964), p. 305.

1.   Here the work of Rajak (*Josephus*, pp. 78-103, 185-222) and P. Bilde
(*Flavius Josephus Between Jerusalem and Rome* [JSPSup, 2; Sheffield: JSOT
Press, 1988], pp. 173-206) is important.

2.   This point applies to the Greek edition of *War*. We are unable to determine
what alterations, if any, were considered necessary between the production of the
Aramaic and later extant Greek version of the text.

3.   For example, see *Life* 10–12, 191. Rajak (*Josephus*, pp. 11-45) argues that
Josephus remained loyal to Pharisaic teachings from his youth; cf Cohen (*Josephus*,
pp. 144-51). For a discussion of Josephus's relationship to Pharisaism, see Bilde
(*Flavius Josephus*, pp. 189-91). Note also S.N. Mason ('Was Josephus a Pharisee?
A Re-Examination of Life 10–12', *JJS* 30 [1989], pp. 40-44), who questions
whether Josephus was an active Pharisee, suggesting that he merely proclaimed
allegiance so that he could enter public affairs. Note that Josephus referred to the
Essenes with a certain degree of respect (*War* 2.120-61; *Ant.* 18.18-22).

Jerusalem. The work describes the events that led up to the revolt and culminated in the destruction of Jerusalem and its immediate aftermath. Writing thus, Josephus sought to explain why the Jews eventually went to war. The information contained in *The Jewish War* appears to be derived from several sources: personal memory, eyewitness accounts, and Nicolaus of Damascus (*War* 1.18; *Apion* 1.47-49). The brevity of the text regarding the early years of the first century AD may indicate that Josephus had no detailed written source for that period. Obviously in the events leading up to the revolt and during the war Josephus could draw upon the information of associates and his own experiences.

The emphasis on the events prior to the destruction of the Temple appears to indicate that they were closely connected with Josephus's motivation for writing *The Jewish War,* Josephus states that he believed it was appropriate that an accurate account of the war be written (*War* 1.1, 4-5). He acknowledges the difficulty in objectively narrating events of which he had first-hand experience, yet he claims to present an accurate account of what happened (*War* 1.9-12, 13-16). The contents of *The Jewish War*, however, indicate that in order to determine Josephus's underlying interests in writing it, we must look beyond his alleged desire to present an objective account of the war and destruction of the Temple.

In describing events both prior to and during the revolt Josephus concentrates his discussion on certain episodes which he believes to have been of prime importance. Josephus's reasons for including certain material may be discerned from the reasons he provides for the outbreak of the revolt: Jewish–Greek tension, the failings of the Roman administrators, and the political aspirations and criminal actions of the brigands. It is evident that Josephus seeks to explain the revolt and apportion blame for its beginning. Analysis of the text also indicates that it was influenced by his concern to honour the Flavians and to justify his personal position during and after the war. Central among Josephus's concerns was a desire to accommodate the disaster in both Jewish and Roman terms. It appears that Josephus believed the Temple was destroyed because God was punishing the Jews for internal dissension and disregard for the laws (*War* 1.10). This was encapsulated in the actions of a vague and undefined group of brigands. Furthermore, these brigands could be used by Josephus to lay blame for the revolt at the feet of a non-representative section of the Jewish community (*War* 1.10). As a result, Jews with whom Josephus associated were innocent and should be seen as such by the Roman overlords. The way forward for the Jews was to co-operate with the Romans. Vespasian and his troops had been instruments of God's divine punishment of the Jews.

Although Josephus was also concerned to honour those Romans who had offered him a new life in Rome, *The Jewish War* should not be viewed simply as a text dedicated to pro-Flavian propaganda. Josephus does acknowledge, and in part admires, the strength and importance of the Roman empire (*War* 3.70-109), but other important apologetic interests, like those noted above, also appear to have influenced what he wrote. Josephus narrates his role in the war distantly, yet appears to be aware of the need to explain his change in allegiance. In part, this is achieved by the implicit notion that the Romans should be seen as a legitimate part of God's world plan.

These influences combine to help structure *The Jewish War* in general, and organize specific material within the text. The significance of these influences may vary in particular passages. What is apparent is that, while the narrative may generally adhere to recounting historical events, the details highlighted may primarily reflect Josephus's underlying aims. One example of this is provided by the suggestion that the Roman administrators were at fault in the events leading up to the revolt (*War* 2.277, 283). On occasions when Josephus mentions individual Romans who favoured the Jews, this serves essentially to present a contrast to the later, disliked procurators (*War* 2.271-76). Romans who respected the Jews are not positively mentioned for their own sake. Josephus admonishes certain procurators, but does not acknowledge that any Jews involved may have also failed to do as they should in a particular situation.

Josephus's second main text was *Antiquities of the Jews*, completed in the early AD 90s. This work covers a history of the Jewish people and their religion from the time of Adam until AD 66. Josephus includes a number of incidents that were recorded in *The Jewish War* as well as other material. In part this may reflect the use of different sources and/or different requirements in writing *Antiquities of the Jews*. Whereas the style of *The Jewish War* is generally uniform, there is some variation in *Antiquities of the Jews*. Where Josephus does not draw directly on sources this change may indicate that he had less assistance with the production of the Greek text in

Antiquities of the Jews than he did with *The Jewish War*.[1]

It appears that Josephus perceived his audience to be primarily Graeco-Roman, but it is also conceivable that he believed the Jews could benefit from what he wrote. The subject matter of *Antiquities of the Jews* was important to Josephus but it was not directly related to him personally. In essence *Antiquities of the Jews* appears to be an apologetic text.[2] Its main aim was to present Judaism and the Jewish people as an ancient and honourable race. As a result, the Jews should be recognized as having a legitimate place in world history.

The *Life of Josephus* first appeared as an appendix to *Antiquities of the Jews*.[3] The text does not present a full account of all Josephus's activities, but narrates in detail certain periods of his life. Of these the most important is the time when he was sent from Jerusalem to command Galilee in AD 66. In the narrative of these events it is notable that there are several differences between the *Life of Josephus* and *The Jewish War*. One of the most fundamental of these is the assertion in *The Jewish War* that Josephus was sent to command the preparations for war, while according to *Life of Josephus* he was sent to stop Galilee joining the revolt against Rome. This and other related differences, and the concentration of the *Life of Josephus* narrative on events in Galilee, highlight the question of Josephus's motivation in writing the text.[4]

The *Life of Josephus* was in part a personal apology. Details regarding Josephus's activities in Galilee are presented in an effort to show that he was an honest and diligent, if reluctant, soldier (*Life* 28–29, 204–207). Furthermore, the reference to Justus of Tiberias and his supposedly inaccurate account of the revolt in Galilee suggests that Josephus believed it was necessary to defend himself (*Life* 336–37). This idea of personal apology, however, should not be over-estimated. The narrative of the *Life of Josephus* presents Josephus in a positive

1. For an assessment of the assistance Josephus received in the production of his Greek version of *War* see Rajak, *Josephus*, pp. 233-36.

2. This approach is clearly expressed by Bilde (*Flavius Josephus*, pp. 99-103).

3. For a discussion of the relationship between the *Life* and *Ant.* see Schürer (*History*, I, pp. 53-54), Rajak (*Josephus*, pp. 236-37) and Bilde (*Flavius Josephus*, pp. 104-106).

4. Cohen (*Josephus*, pp. 67-83) presents a detailed examination of the *Life* and *War* account of Josephus's time in Galilee. See Chapter 5, section 4 for further discussion of this aspect of Josephus's narrative.

light throughout. The text is not, therefore, merely a response, but a positive affirmation of Josephus's character and position. It is apparent that certain features are highlighted: Josephus's high family status (*Life* 1–6), his prowess as a military leader (*Life* 114–21, 399–404), and his ability to comprehend the forces at work at any particular moment and to decide the appropriate action he should take (*Life* 385–89). As a result, any differences that exist between the narratives of the *Life of Josephus* and *The Jewish War* may not necessarily be explained simply by proclaiming that one text is historically accurate throughout. Both texts have differing immediate aims, but are possibly based on similar underlying principles.

The final text written by Josephus, *Against Apion*, does not present a historical narrative. Rather, it is a work that addresses questions regarding disputes between Greeks and Jews as to the status of the Jewish people (*Apion* 1.1-5, 42-46; 2.65-78). In arguing his case, however, Josephus includes some information that may be relevant to this study. When responding to arguments, Josephus presents his understanding of the political and spiritual status of Judaism in the world at large. As in *Antiquities of the Jews*, Josephus appears concerned to assert the importance of the Jews and their religion, and to encourage Jews to appreciate their value within the Graeco-Roman world.

This survey of Josephus's life, activities and works results in two important observations. First, there is a continual interplay between several factors that affect the tone and type of detail that Josephus records in his narrative. Nowhere is this interplay as apparent as in *The Jewish War*. Secondly, despite a possible change in emphasis, especially in terms of his attitude toward the value of Pharisaism, there is a consistency in Josephus and his works. He appears to develop a concern for the fate of Judaism, to explain how it came to be in the state that it was after the revolt and to assess how it could adjust. The vast amount of information that Josephus records, especially in *The Jewish War* and *Antiquities of the Jews*, makes him an extremely important source regarding the events of Palestine in the first centuries BC and AD. By examining each text separately where appropriate in the following cases, we shall be able to consider if any particular details reflect a concern above and beyond those of historical narrative.

The other main Jewish author whose work has been used in

discussion of administrative affairs in Palestine is Philo of Alexandria. Like Josephus, Philo was contemporary with the main historical events that he narrates. He visited Palestine, and was aware of certain events that took place there. Despite the large corpus of his extant literature, however, only the *Legatio ad Gaium* is of direct relevance to the study of the administration in Palestine. Although the *Legatio ad Gaium* pertained mainly to the embassy sent by Alexandrian Jews to Rome seeking recompense for the riots between the Jews and Greeks in the city, there are within the narrative accounts of Gaius's attempt to have his statue erected in Jerusalem and an action undertaken by Pilate. It is possible that Philo was aware of other administrative decisions made in Palestine, but it was only these two specific events that were relevant to his interests. The positioning and use of these two incidents within the *Legatio ad Gaium* reflect the major theme of the text.

Philo's work proclaims to the reader that the enemies of the Jews cannot restrict God's ability to preserve his people. Justice will triumph in the form of divine providence. Such a view was appropriate because the riots had ended and the Jews of Alexandria now lived in peace. Philo not only used the events associated with the embassy to present this theme, but he also used the character of Gaius to good effect. Philo begins by praising Gaius (*Leg. Gai.* 8-13), greeting his accession with enthusiasm, only to record the change in Gaius's personality mirrored by his attempt to have power over Judaism (*Leg. Gai.* 114-19). In a sense, therefore, the text is both a historical and ideological treatise, fulfilling both aims, but primarily the latter.[1]

The New Testament texts, the Gospels and the Acts of the Apostles, record a number of events involving decision-making from the mid-first century AD. This literature generally pertains to the interests of Christian beliefs and practices. The Gospels attributed to Matthew, Mark, Luke and John primarily relate events connected with the teachings and actions of Jesus of Nazareth. Acts relates events concerning early Christians and some of their leaders' activities and teachings in Palestine and the surrounding region.

There are three aspects of the New Testament material that indicate

---

1. Note that Philo probably intended to finish *Legatio ad Gaium* with a commentary regarding the death of Gaius (*Leg. Gai.* 373). If so, this would further emphasize the polemical nature of the text.

the need for care when using the texts: the question of when the texts were written; their use of source material; and the purpose of the texts. These are important factors affecting the value of the New Testament material as sources for an examination of the administration in Palestine. The first two aspects are in part related and neither issue can be conclusively determined.

The dating of the texts, and the degree of oral tradition preceding the written accounts, are not possible to ascertain. The texts are obviously directly relevant to the first century AD, especially the early to middle part of the century. For the Gospels the earliest date of composition is the mid-AD 30s and for Acts, the late AD 50s. How long after the final events narrated in the Gospels and Acts the texts were written is a matter of debate. It is difficult to claim that there is any allusion in the Gospels to events after the death of Jesus. In a sense, this is of some surprise considering the fate that befell the Jerusalem Temple in AD 70.[1] Such ostensible silence, however, does not necessarily indicate that the Gospels pre-date AD 70.[2] At best we can state that the Gospels were probably written from the latter half of the first

1.   Some scholars argue that Mk 13.1-27; Mt. 24.1-31; and Lk. 19.32-44; 21.5-28 (especially the latter) refer to the events of AD 70. For example, see J. Fitzmyer, *The Gospel according to Luke X–XXIV*, II (AB, 28a; New York: Doubleday, 1985), pp. 1254-1255, 1329; J.D.G. Dunn, *Unity and Diversity in the New Testament* (London: SCM Press, 1977), p. 331; and G.W.H. Lampe, 'AD 70 in Christian Reflection', in E. Bammel and C.F.D. Moule (eds.), *Jesus and the Politics of His Day* (Cambridge: Cambridge University Press, 1984), p. 163. See also J. McLaren, 'Jerusalem to Pella—the Evidence in Question' (unpublished MA Thesis, University of Melbourne, 1985), pp. 90-110.

2.   J.A.T. Robinson (*Redating the New Testament* [London: SCM Press, 1976]), and B. Reicke ('Synoptic Prophecies on the Destruction of Jerusalem', in D.E. Aune [ed.], *Studies in New Testament and Early Christian Literature* [NovTSup, 33; Leiden: Brill, 1972], pp. 121-34) argue that the Gospels should be dated before the destruction. Note also that J.A.T. Robinson (*The Priority of John* [ed. J.F. Coakley; London: SCM Press, 1985], p. 122) and M. Hengel (*The Johannine Question* [trans. J. Bowden; London: SCM Press, 1989], pp. 105-32) argue that the author of John was from Palestine, that he knew Jesus and may have been John, the son of Zebedee. Another approach is taken by S.G.F. Brandon (*The Fall of Jerusalem and the Christian Church* [London: SPCK, 2nd edn, 1968], pp. 186-87), who argues that Mark was written as a propaganda text after the war. Any argument that is based on the revolt as a means of determining the date of the Gospels is difficult to substantiate.

century AD onwards, if not later, possibly in the order Mark, Matthew, Luke and finally John. It is important to note, however, that even if the generally accepted order for the writing of the Gospels is adopted, it is not necessarily true that in every instance the earliest Gospel includes the most original or historically accurate account of particular events or sayings linked with Jesus.

The second aspect of the texts to consider is the use of source material in the Gospels and Acts and the possible implications of the use of sources for the relationship between specific Gospels. It is plausible that some of the sayings associated with Jesus and the meaning, if not the actual words, of certain speeches recorded, reflect historical situations. Unless the texts were written at the time of the events they narrate, however, it is likely that oral tradition as much as written accounts played a major part in the production of the speeches. It is probable that Luke was responsible for many of the speeches included in Acts.[1] It may be appropriate to accept the gist and intention of the speeches as reflecting what was commonly believed to have been spoken. We should, however, take care not to assume that the words recorded are verbatim on every occasion.

In Acts some of the events may have been derived from first-hand experience or eyewitnesses. In the Gospels, however, it is difficult to establish such a view. The repetition in Mark, Matthew and Luke indicates a link between the Gospels, presumably in terms of the traditions they called upon. The individual touches and independent aspects of the Gospels suggest the existence of more than one basic tradition and the willingness of certain people to highlight particular events or sayings. Differences that exist between the Gospels may indicate contradictory accounts or the individual licence taken by the authors to present certain incidents in a manner that best suited their needs.[2]

---

1. See H. Cadbury, *The Making of Luke–Acts*, (London: SPCK, 2nd edn, 1958), pp. 184-93; E. Haenchen, *Acts of the Apostles* (rev. trans. R. McL. Wilson; Oxford: Basil Blackwell, 1971), pp. 103-110; and Aune (*New Testament*, pp. 124-28) for a discussion of the speeches that appear in Acts.

2. There is a great deal of scholarly debate regarding the relationship between the Gospels. Of the more recent literature examining a number of aspects of the topic, see B. Reicke, *The Roots of the Synoptic Gospels* (Philadelphia: Fortress Press, 1986), pp. 1-23; and E.P. Sanders and M. Davies, *Studying the Synoptic Gospels* (London: SCM Press, 1988), pp. 51-119.

This leads to the third aspect to note, the purpose of the New Testament texts. The Gospels and Acts were written by Christians. Whether they were Jewish converts or Gentile Christians is a matter of debate. They were aware of the fact that Christianity arose from within the boundaries of Judaism in Palestine. The contents of the texts indicate a concern to provide information for Christians, and to the world, of the good news.

Although the majority of events and sayings recorded in the Synoptic Gospels are the same, the existence of certain variations and differences suggests that not all the details about Jesus' life are recorded. Several periods from Jesus' lifetime are not mentioned. The same situation is found in Acts regarding the early Christians. It appears, therefore, that a process of positive selection took place in the construction of the New Testament texts. This selection was primarily the result of what information regarding Jesus and the early Christians survived or was known by the various authors. Of most importance here is the process of positive selection, namely, the decision by each author to include certain material and the means by which the available material was organized. There appear to be four interests which were most influential in dictating what was included in the Gospels and Acts. First, and foremost, the proclamation that Jesus was the saviour of all humanity: every person had to turn to him if they were to receive salvation or eternal life. This theme was treated with varying degrees of sophistication and elaboration. From this premise each author proceeded to consider the three other interests, the relationship of Christianity to various other groups, namely the Romans, the Jews, and the Greek-speaking world. It is evident that the authors were concerned to indicate that Christianity could hold a respected position under Roman rule, that the Christians were to perceive themselves as God's chosen people, and that the Jews had rejected Christ. These concerns were addressed by each author in varying degrees of detail by his recording of particular deeds and words and by the way each text was constructed.

In this context it appears we should not believe that every event recorded in the New Testament is necessarily an accurate account of the historical situation. Conversely, it does not follow that the events described did not take place. Rather, the requirement is to consider each incident, and then each detail within the narrative, on its own merit.

The final major source material to consider is the tannaitic literature. This large corpus, especially the earliest text, the Mishnah,
contains information relevant to the Second Temple period, the First
Temple period and the post-AD 70 period. It includes a tractate specifically devoted to describing a permanent institution, *m. Sanhedrin*.
The Mishnah also incorporates the majority of other tannaitic
literature passages that are relevant to this study.

Two aspects of the Mishnah present us with some difficulty: its
purpose, and the history of its formulation. On both points there is
much scholarly discussion. For example, Neusner argues that the
Mishnah contains material from different chronological periods. He
also believes it reflects a single world-view that was determined at the
time of Judah, the final redactor.[1] Albeck states that the Mishnah was
merely a collection of sayings which Judah alone gathered and that it
was not intended to be regarded as a law code.[2] Goldberg also describes the Mishnah as a collection of views regarding halakah.[3]
Epstein suggests that several stages in the development of the Mishnah
can be distinguished, as Judah used earlier collections which he altered
to construct its final form.[4]

It appears that the Mishnah was gathered into its present form
around AD 200. The references made to individual rabbis suggest that
much of the information belongs to the second century AD.[5] Major
questions remain as to whether Judah collected, edited or compiled the
Mishnah and whether it was intended specifically to be a law code.

1. See, for example, J. Neusner (ed.), *The Study of Ancient Judaism*. I.
Mishnah, Midrash, Siddur (New York: Ktav, 1981), pp. 21-22 and *Method and
Meaning in Ancient Judaism* (Missoula, MT: Scholars Press, 1979), pp. 3, 5.
2. See G.G. Porton, 'Hanokh Albeck on the Mishnah', in J. Neusner (ed.),
The Modern Study of the Mishnah (Leiden: Brill, 1973), pp. 209-24.
3. See W.S. Green, 'Abraham Goldberg', in Neusner (ed.), *Modern Study*,
pp. 225-41.
4. See B.M. Bokser, 'Jacob N. Epstein's *Introduction to the Text of the
Mishnah*', and 'Jacob N. Epstein on the Formation of the Mishnah', in Neusner
(ed.), *Modern Study*, pp. 13-36, 37-55. Halivni indicates that there was probably
some debate about the value and purpose of the Mishnah when it was formu-
lated. See D.A. Halivni, 'The Reception Accorded to Rabbi Judah's Mishnah', in
E.P. Sanders with A.I. Baumgarten and A. Mendelson (eds.), *Jewish and Christian
Self-Definition*. II. *Aspects of Judaism in the Greco-Roman Period* (London: SCM
Press, 1981), pp. 204-12.
5. See the summary of references presented by Schürer (*History*, I, pp. 74-76).

Rather than argue that the Mishnah was either merely a collection or
heavily edited by Judah, a certain degree of compromise appears to be
necessary. It is plausible to view the Mishnah as a record which
elaborates upon the written law. It also appears that Judah, following
the initiative of Akiba and Meir, intended the Mishnah to be more
than an academic reference work recording the sayings of particular
rabbis. Accepting the theory that the Mishnah reflects adaptations and
variations to the oral law indicates the possibility of contradictions
within the text. Furthermore, it may make difficult the task of determining to what period particular statements are related.

As a whole, the Mishnah appears to present a guideline for correct
Jewish behaviour. Certain accepted principles are presented and
applied to particular situations by the rabbis.[1] Consequently it is
plausible to suggest that the Mishnah does, in part, reflect the historical world rather than just an idealized vision of it.

There is, however, a further dimension to the material included in
the Mishnah. Not only does it provide a practical outline in the
present, but it may also hold a polemical interest for the future of
Judaism. In an era when the Jewish people did not hold much worldly
influence it is an idealized outline of what should be the true state of
affairs. In this context it was appropriate to refer to practices relevant
when the Temple stood and to describe the institution presented in
m. Sanhedrin as though it were still active.[2]

Uncertainty remains regarding the period to which the Mishnah
actually bears relation and to the antiquity of the sources used. This
uncertainty is enhanced by the likelihood that the Mishnah incorporates diversity derived from its long process of development. There
is, however, a sense of unity provided by the effort of Judah to
present the Mishnah as a unified text. Despite the probability that oral
traditions from the pre-AD 70 period are located in the Mishnah, it
remains the latest of all the available sources in its written form.

The tractate *m. Sanhedrin* is primarily devoted to describing the
legal structure that existed amongst the Jews in Palestine. The text
outlines the activities of the sanhedrin/*bet din* of seventy-one which

---

1. This approach is taken by M. Goodman in *State and Society in Roman
Galilee, AD 132–212* (New Jersey: Rowman & Allanheld, 1983), p. 6.
2. On this point see H. Maccoby, *Early Rabbinic Writings* (Cambridge:
Cambridge University Press, 1988), p. 33.

was located in the chamber of hewn stone in Jerusalem. We are informed that there were three types of courts, numbering seventy-one, twenty-three and three (*m. Sanh.* 1.1; 5). The correct legal procedure used by these courts is described in detail along with the areas of jurisdiction each of the courts held (*m. Sanh.* 4.1). There was only one court of seventy-one, the one located in Jerusalem. There was, however, a large number of courts of at least twenty-three and three, on the basis that any community with more than one hundred people was entitled to a court of at least twenty-three (*m. Sanh.* 1.6). All the courts dealt with legal matters and with the interpretation of the written law. The courts of three were only empowered to assess non-capital cases (*m. Sanh.* 1.1; 4.1). Disputes were placed before the courts of three in the first instance. Where a decision could not be reached a court of twenty-three was to decide the case (*m. Sanh.* 4.1). In turn, if the court of twenty-three could not resolve the dispute the matter was placed under the jurisdiction of the court of seventy-one (*m. Sanh.* 4.1). The tractate also outlines the appropriate forms of punishment that were to be administered (*m. Sanh.* 7.1).

The court of seventy-one in Jerusalem was the pinnacle of the entire legal system (*m. Sanh.* 11.2). It was, however, also the centre of the administration. Proclamations regarding laws to be enforced throughout the nation were sent forth from the court of seventy-one (*m. Sanh.* 11.2). Furthermore, this court was responsible for trials of false prophets, high priests and tribes (*m. Sanh.* 1.5; 2.1). It was also responsible for declaring war, proclaiming a city to be an apostate city, giving approval for changes to be made to the Temple courts and city and for establishing sanhedrins for particular tribes (*m. Sanh.* 1.5). In effect, the entire administration was centred around this court of seventy-one.

The other important feature of the tractate is the distinction it maintains between the positions of king and high priest. Although the former was separate from the court and could not be tried by it, the high priest could take part in trials and could also be tried by the court of seventy-one (*m. Sanh.* 2.1). This assumed distinction raises the issue of when this legal structure was in practice. Apart from the reference to Simeon b. Shetah who possibly dates from the time of Alexander Jannaeus (*m. Sanh.* 6.4),[1] it is difficult to establish overt

---

1. See Maccoby, *Early Rabbinic Writings*, p. 119.

chronological references to the Second Temple period. If anything, the tractate appears to be written with the understanding that the system outlined was ever-present since its inauguration by Moses. Such a notion, however, is difficult to accept, especially as the office of king and high priest were united for a time under the Hasmonaeans. The reference to the tribal organization also appears to contradict other Mishnaic records regarding the second temple period (*m. Sanh.* 1.1; *m. Šebu.* 2.2; *m. Hor.* 1.5).

Although *m. Sanhedrin* may appear to present a clear, ordered account of the Jewish legal structure of Palestine, headed by an apparently permanent national institution in Jerusalem, there are some doubts raised by the text's internal structure, and the absence of any consistent references to the events of the Second Temple period. These doubts are clearly evident in the one event narrated in *m. Sanhedrin.* Reference is made to the execution by burning of a priest's daughter (*m. Sanh.* 7.2). There are two significant problems with the recording of this incident. First, we are unable to confirm any details. It is possible that the account is simply a re-narration of the law quoted in Lev. 21.9. If, however, it is a historical event, we are unable to locate it chronologically and establish the identity of those responsible for the decision. Second, the method by which the adultress is executed contradicts the theory of how execution by burning should take place (*m. Sanh.* 7.2). The rabbinic explanation that the executioners of the adultress were ignorant of the correct procedures highlights the question of when, if ever, the legal system described in *m. Sanhedrin* was actually practised.

One approach taken by scholars who consider the Mishnah to be of historical value for the pre-AD 70 period is to state that the Mishnah presents an idealized version of the sanhedrin. Several of its functions as described, however, were factual and relevant to the period of the Second Temple (*m. Sanh.* 2.1; *m. 'Ed.* 7.4; *m. Pe'ah* 2.6; *m. Mid.* 5.4).[1]

The more common approach by those scholars giving credence to the Mishnah is to view *m. Sanhedrin* as a historically accurate document, written on the basis of a reliable oral tradition. The detailed knowledge of legal proceedings and seating arrangements are thus

---

1. See, for example, A. Guttmann, *Rabbinic Judaism in the Making* (Detroit: Wayne State University Press, 1970), pp. 24-25.

explained. For Falk, *m. Sanh.* 2.1 indicates that until the time of Alexander Jannaeus the king could be tried, and 11.2 shows that the chief function of the sanhedrin/*bet din* was to provide religious instruction for the nation.[1] Hoenig claims that there is clear evidence to show that the sanhedrin existed prior to AD 70.[2] He suggests that *m. Sanhedrin* provides us with important details regarding where the sanhedrin/*bet din* sat and its duties, and argues that the *nasi*, the title associated with the head of the sanhedrin/*bet din*, was an office instituted before AD 70.[3]

In his detailed assessment of scholarship on specific issues associated with the sanhedrin, Mantel also concludes that the office of *nasi* began before AD 70, and certainly as early as the first zugot.[4] Interpreting *m. Sanhedrin*, Mantel argues that the sanhedrin/*bet din* was primarily a legislative body; only in exceptional instances was it a judicial institution.[5] In practical terms the sanhedrin/*bet din* acted as an 'appellate' court that defined particular laws for the inferior courts of twenty-three and three.

Zeitlin does not see the need to assert the validity of *m. Sanhedrin*. Rather, much of his attention is devoted to matters of terminology. He argues that before AD 70 *bet din* was used to describe the institution, whereas after AD 70 *bet din* and sanhedrin, the Hebraized form of *synedrion*, were interchangeable.[6] Zeitlin links this alteration to the duties that were carried out by the sanhedrin/*bet din*. Prior to AD 70 it was a religious law court which held no civic authority. After AD 70, however, it took on responsibility for civil matters and acquired the term sanhedrin because the Romans referred to it by a term they readily understood, *synedrion*.[7]

Rivkin follows Zeitlin but also argues that the institution was more commonly referred to as *bet din*.[8] He does not doubt the account of

1. Falk, *Jewish Law*, p. 55.
2. Hoenig, *Great Sanhedrin*, pp. 12-15.
3. Hoenig, *Great Sanhedrin*, pp. 38, 147; citing *m. Hag.* 2.2
4. Mantel, *Studies*, pp. 49, 53.
5. Mantel (*Studies*, p. 96) cites *m. Sanh.* 11.2 and *Sifre Deut.* 152. An example of when the sanhedrin was a judicial institution was any case brought against the high priest.
6. See Zeitlin, 'Synedrion in the Judeo-Hellenistic Literature', p. 315.
7. See Zeitlin, 'Synedrion in Greek Literature', p. 198.
8. See Rivkin, 'Beth Din, Boulé, Sanhedrin', p. 198.

m. Sanhedrin. Rather he stresses the idea that the sanhedrin/*bet din* was the 'generative' source for all aspects of the legislative, judicial and executive features of the Jewish administration, in which it was responsible for the making and rescinding of all laws. In this sense, it is appropriate to equate the sanhedrin/*bet din* with the Greek term *boule*.[1]

The approach of these scholars accepts that the Mishnah provides us with an accurate account of the central administrative institution for Jewish religion. Where the Mishnah differs from other sources, it is believed that it speaks of a separate institution. It is also assumed that the mishnaic account is relevant to the late Second Temple period rather than this being confirmed by close examination. Although we should not expect the entire Mishnah to present a coherent account, it appears that to accept the existence of a permanent institution given in *m. Sanhedrin*, some corroborative evidence from that tractate or from other tannaitic literature is important.[2] An enquiry seeking confirmation that a permanent institution can be connected with a chronological period, however, fails to find any reference to the sanhedrin/*bet din* in actual decisions taken.

According to rabbinic views there appears to be some evidence to suggest the existence of an institution of some sort in the First Temple period (*b. Git.* 57b; *b. Sanh.* 16b, 49a). After the return the successors of Ezra are the zugot (*m. Hag.* 2.2). It appears that these men held the title of *nasi* and *ab bet din*, the former being the superior position. These officers appear to have acted in their own right rather than being the representatives of a particular institution (*m. Ned.* 5.5; *m. Ta'an.* 2.1; *m. 'Ed.* 5.6). The powers of these zugot were apparently extensive in terms of religious instruction and certain legal proceedings. They gave rulings, judged capital cases and made other decisions without any reference being made to a sanhedrin/*bet din* (*m. Ab.* 1.8-11; *m. Sanh.* 6.4; *m. Hag.* 2.2; *b. Git.* 57b). Following the zugot the few references to decisions become more restricted to aspects of Jewish religion. Without there being an overt connection with the sanhedrin/*bet din* there is reference made to certain sages gathering on the temple mount to discuss some issues (*m. 'Ed.* 7.3-4; *m. Miq.* 5.5). What is most notable from the Second Temple period is

---

1. See Rivkin, 'Beth Din, Boulé, Sanhedrin', p. 192.
2. The following section is, in part, based on Efron (*Studies*, pp. 293-96).

that the disputes between Hillel and Shammai and their followers are not referred to the sanhedrin/*bet din* for arbitration (*m. 'Ed.* 1.1-14; *m. Yeb.* 1.4; *m. Ket.* 1.5; 13.1-2; *m. Pes.* 8.8).

It is apparent that for the few instances in the Mishnah where we can locate events that took place in the Second Temple period, there is a general silence regarding the involvement of the institution described in *m. Sanhedrin.* Some sort of legal system did exist; whether it remained constant is uncertain. Eminent Jews also gathered on certain occasions to discuss issues. *M. Sanhedrin,* however, presents us with a tradition that there was a permanent institution, the sanhedrin/*bet din* of Jerusalem, which controlled the legal system. There is no consistent reference to this institution even in the remainder of the Mishnah where decisions are made. We are unable, therefore, to find a chronological home for the sanhedrin/*bet din* in the late Second Temple period. As a result it is possible that we should look elsewhere for the origin of this institution. It may be that *m. Sanhedrin* reflects events after AD 70, the pre-Second Temple period, a combination of both, or simply the idealized picture of the post-AD 70 period.

The evidence from the tannaitic literature tends to suggest that the sanhedrin/*bet din* of the Mishnah has no practical application, or even existence, in the Second Temple period. The final assessment of the historicity of the sanhedrin/*bet din* as it is recorded in *m. Sanhedrin,* however, should be reserved until the twenty-one cases have been examined. For the moment we should note the mishnaic portrait of a permanent institution and the lack of consistency in the tannaitic literature. Furthermore, it must be emphasized that this theoretical outline of the Jewish legal system, the latest of all the written sources in the form it survives, is not by its very nature relevant for this incident-based study.

There are three other sources that may prove to be relevant: the writings of Tacitus, numismatic remains, and archaeological findings. A brief comment regarding each of these sources is necessary. The Roman historian Tacitus included in his *Histories* and *Annals* several references to the Jews. Of the two texts, the *Annals* is probably the more important for this study, referring indirectly to the trouble between Galilaeans and Samaritans. Tacitus's primary interest lay in internal Roman affairs—describing the decline of the Julian and Claudian dynasties and the fortunes of the senatorial order. From the fragments of the work that survive, it is apparent that Tacitus's information regarding the Jews lacks details. His relevance for this study, therefore, is limited.

In a few specific instances coinage and archaeological remains may help clarify or confirm what can be gleaned from the literary sources. They are used as supplementary evidence in such cases as the trouble under Alexander Jannaeus and the events in Jerusalem during the revolt.

A final point to note in the use of the sources relates to the nature of the incidents recorded. The authors employed a certain degree of selection; not everything that happened in Palestine between 100 BC and AD 70, for example, is recorded by Josephus. This raises the issue of whether the incidents to be examined should be viewed as routine and reflecting everyday situations, or as reflecting what happened only on special or abnormal occasions. Most of the incidents reflect times when effective decisions were required. They do not, therefore, necessarily represent the ordinary everyday pattern exactly.[1] The events recorded present conflicts of interests, between Romans and Jews, between Jews, and between Jews and other groups living in Palestine, whether Christians, Greeks or Samaritans. They are occasions where the administrators had to take action. When something had to be done we are provided with information regarding who was perceived as actually acting. These events, therefore, indicate what had to be done in practical terms, irrespective of any notions of a desired ideal. As a result we can obtain an insight, not so much into the theoretical organization as into the practical situation. It is also possible that the examination of the twenty-one cases may establish whether or not a routine practice existed for occasions when decisions were required at short notice. Our study may also indicate whether there was a difference between those regarded as important in a crisis situation and those regarded as important in supposedly routine events.

We have seen that most accounts of the administration in Palestine deal with legal discussions based on the Mishnah and that this discussion is not set in the context of historical description. An examination of individual incidents and closely related events in the form of separate case studies will enable us to establish what actually

---

1. On this issue see A.N. Sherwin-White, *Roman Society and Roman Law in the New Testament* (Oxford: Oxford University Press, 1963), p. 8.

happened in Palestine in the view of the available sources. My study, therefore, is primarily based on examples which occur in narratives. The intention here is to determine who participated in the decision-making process in Palestine and in what manner they did so. The insights obtained from the assessment of these cases are drawn together in the final section of this study in an effort to reconstruct the historical situation.

Chapter 2

HASMONAEAN RULE: 100 BC–40 BC

1. *Trouble under Alexander Jannaeus*

War 1.85, Alexander Jannaeus becomes king, 88, Jews rebel at festival,
mercenaries quell uprising, 89, 6,000 Jews killed, 90, Jews rebel again
after Obedas defeats Alexander Jannaeus, 91, lasts six years, 50,000
Jews die, 92, Demetrius aids rebels, 95, and defeats Alexander Jannaeus,
Jews turn to support the king, Demetrius leaves, 96, rebels captured, 97,
king executes 800 and their families, 98, 8,000 Jews flee, Alexander
Jannaeus lives in peace.

Ant. 13.320, Alexander Jannaeus becomes king, 372, Jews rebel at
festival, claiming he is descended from a slave, 373, 6,000 Jews die,
375, Alexander Jannaeus defeated by Obedas, Jews rebel again, 376,
lasts six years, over 50,000 Jews die, rebels aided by Demetrius, 378,
who defeats Alexander Jannaeus, 379, 6,000 Jews turn to support him,
Demetrius leaves, king defeats rebels, 380, 'the most powerful' (οἱ
δυνατώτατοι) rebels captured, 800 executed with their families, 383,
8,000 Jews flee, Alexander Jannaeus lives in peace, 399, on deathbed, he
talks to his wife, 401, suggests that she should yield some power to the
Pharisees, they would tell the Jews to favour her as they had so much
influence over the nation, 402, the king's conflict with the nation caused
by his poor treatment of the Pharisees, 403, Salome Alexandra advised to
tell them that she would not act without their consent.

After the death of Aristobulus I in 103 BC his widow released
Alexander Jannaeus from prison and aided him in obtaining control of
the country. Alexander Jannaeus was then forced to defend his position as head of state against Jewish protest. The first signs of revolt
were linked with the festival of Tabernacles when Jews apparently
threw lemons at the king while he performed the sacrifices.[1] In the

---

1. There is much debate as to whether *b. Yom.* 22b and *b. Suk.* 48b should be
equated with Josephus's narrative. Although Alexander Jannaeus is not the central

version in *Antiquities of the Jews*, the 32 protestors also taunt Alexander Jannaeus with the claim that he was descended from a slave, and, therefore, was not fit to be high priest.[1] Alexander Jannaeus reacted violently and some 6,000 Jews were killed.

A more significant outbreak of trouble followed Alexander Jannaeus's military setback against Obedas. On this occasion there was prolonged and bloody fighting in which Josephus claims that 50,000 Jews died in six years. Whatever the real number of the dead, Alexander Jannaeus's control of Judaea was seriously threatened. The change of allegiance by some Jews, and Demetrius's departure, enabled Alexander Jannaeus to recommence hostilities against the rebels.

character, a number of scholars believe it is a reflection of what happened to him: for example, Schürer, *History*, I, p. 223 n. 16, and Mantel, *Studies*, p. 100; cf. G. Alon ('Did the Jewish People and its Sages Cause the Hasmonaeans To be Forgotten?', in G. Alon (ed.), *Jews, Judaism and the Classical World* [trans. I. Abrahams; Jerusalem: Magnes Press, 1977], p. 8) who links it to a priest of Herod's reign, and S. Zeitlin (*The Rise and Fall of the Judaean State*, I [Philadelphia: The Jewish Publication Society of America, 1962], p. 327), who opposes the linking of the talmudic story with Alexander Jannaeus. A. Schalit ('Domestic Politics and Political Institutions', in A. Schalit (ed.), *The World History of the Jewish People*. 1st series, VI. *The Hellenistic Age* [Jerusalem: Massada Publishing House, 1972], p. 295 n. 75) may be correct in claiming it is not possible to establish whether the accounts should be equated. Irrespective of the conclusion drawn, the talmudic version bears no special significance in terms of the incident.

1. Several scholars believe that *b. Qid.* 66a should be associated with Alexander Jannaeus as he is the principal character named. The opposition of the Pharisees, therefore, is specifically directed against Alexander Jannaeus; it was not a general policy. See I. Friedländer ('The Rupture between Alexander Jannai and the Pharisees', *JQR* 4 [1913/14], pp. 443-48) and G. Alon ('Did the Jewish People?', p. 8 and 'The Attitude of the Pharisees to Roman Rule and the House of Herod', in *Jews, Judaism and the Classical World*, pp. 23-24), who also argues that the Pharisees were opposed to Alexander Jannaeus because he was king. E.E. Urbach ('Jewish Doctrines and Practices in the Hellenistic and Talmudic Periods', in S.W. Baron and G.S. Wise (eds.), *Violence and Defence in the Jewish Experience* [Philadelphia: The Jewish Publication Society of America, 1977], p. 79) links *b. Qid.* 66a with Josephus's account, while S. Hoenig ('*Dorsh Halakot* in the Pesher Nahum Scrolls', *JBL* 83 [1964], p. 136) and M.J. Geller ('Alexander Jannaeus and the Pharisee Rift', *JJS* 30 [1979], p. 211) argue that *b. Qid.* 66a pre-dates Josephus's version of the incident; cf. Schürer, *History*, I, p. 214 n. 30; and Marcus, *Josephus*, VII [Loeb], p. 258. It is not possible to prove conclusively one way or the other whether *b. Qid.* 66a relates to Alexander Jannaeus or John Hyrcanus, although Schürer's point concerning the confusion of names makes it more plausible to reject a link between the story and the events of Alexander Jannaeus's reign.

The version in *Antiquities of the Jews* provides the greater detail, stating that Alexander Jannaeus besieged 'the most powerful' rebels in Bethoma/Bemeselis.[1] These men were captured and taken to Jerusalem where Alexander Jannaeus had 800 of the captives crucified and their wives and children killed in their presence.[2] In fear, a further 8,000 people fled Judaea and remained in exile until the end of Alexander Jannaeus's reign. The remaining years of Alexander Jannaeus's life were free from internal conflict. All these events probably took place between c. 96–95 BC and 87–86 BC.

The rebellion was marked by serious fighting between Alexander Jannaeus and the rebels. The reaction to the offer of peace, and the willingness to involve a Syrian king, indicate the rebels' degree of opposition to the king. Furthermore, the vengeance exacted on the rebels by Alexander Jannaeus indicates that he wished to put an end to the dispute once and for all.

Despite the bitterness of the fighting there was not an insurmountable division between the antagonists. When Alexander Jannaeus was defeated by Demetrius many Jews apparently chose to desert the rebel cause in favour of a Jewish king. Josephus claims that this was done because the Jews did not want a foreigner ruling over them. If this was the only reason, some explanation for the fact that Alexander Jannaeus continued to be supported when he attacked the rebels, devoid of foreign aid, is necessary. Moreover, after Alexander Jannaeus executed some of the rebels and 8,000 fled, he was to remain free from internal trouble for another ten years in spite of further military setbacks. Presumably all those opposed to Alexander Jannaeus

1. It is not possible to determine the exact identity of the town to which these rebels fled, as indicated by Schürer (*History*, I, p. 224). Buehler (*Civil War*, p. 41) appears to be correct in interpreting 'the most powerful men' as a description of the most determined and influential rebels.

2. Most scholars accept this part of the narrative without question. See, for example, H. Jagersma, *A History of Israel from Alexander the Great to Bar Kochba* (trans. J. Bowden; London: SCM Press, 1985), p. 91; and Schürer, *History*, I, p. 224. For the possible link between Pesher Nahum and the execution of Alexander Jannaeus's opponents see Y. Yadin, 'Pesher Nahum/4QpNahum', *IEJ* 21 (1974), pp. 1-22; and Schürer, *History*, I, p. 224 n. 22. Doubt remains as to whether these men were condemned by a trial or simply executed on the king's orders. J. Le Moyne (*Les Sadducées* [EBib; Paris, 1972], p. 244) states that many Pharisees were among the 6,000 killed by Alexander Jannaeus's troops.

had either died, fled the country, or decided to accept his jurisdiction.[1]

There is no apparent reason to suggest either that the link between the festival and the outbreak of violence is of special significance, or that the timing of the complaint was especially significant in religious terms. It is notable that Alexander Jannaeus had been high priest for some eight to ten years before this incident took place. Therefore, if the question of Alexander Jannaeus's legitimacy as high priest was the source of the grievance it is difficult to explain why there was such a delay before the complaint was vocalized.[2] All that can be stated is that this particular festival was the occasion for a public display of anger toward Alexander Jannaeus as the leader of the Jews. The harshness of his reaction suggests that Alexander Jannaeus considered

1. A number of scholars suggest that the retributions exacted by Alexander Jannaeus were not as severe as Josephus presents, claiming that they were the result of Pharisaic distortions. For example, see J. Klausner, 'Judah Aristobulus and Jannaeus Alexander', in Schalit (ed.), *The Hellenistic Age*, p. 233, and Urbach, 'Jewish Doctrines', p. 80. Although it may be appropriate to reduce the numbers and the extent of cruelty, Alexander Jannaeus did deal effectively with the rebels. Furthermore, we have no positive evidence that Josephus drew on a Pharisaic source for his account of these events.

2. The timing of the revolt has been the subject of some debate. Central to this is Alon ('Attitude of the Pharisees', pp. 16 n. 16, 24-26), who claims that the revolt erupted because Alexander Jannaeus attacked the sanhedrin, which was the power base of the Pharisees in the administration. According to Alon this attack is clearly marked by the change in wording on Alexander Jannaeus's coinage. Mantel (*Studies*, p. 96) also argues that the Pharisees lost control of the religious sanhedrin under Alexander Jannaeus. Other scholars, while acknowledging the decrease in power associated with the sanhedrin, highlight the tendency towards Hellenism displayed by Alexander Jannaeus. See Klausner, 'Judah Aristobulus', pp. 229-30; Zeitlin, *Rise and Fall,* I, p. 322; and Schalit, 'Domestic Politics', pp. 279, 288, 293-94. A major problem with these interpretations is the lack of evidence to indicate the active participation of a body called sanhedrin in which the Pharisees played a part. Regarding the meaning of the absence of *hever* on the coinage, Y. Meshorer (*Ancient Jewish Coinage*, I [New York: Amphora Books, 1982], p. 47, 77) indicates that there is no positive reason to follow either a specific or general application of the term. Even Alon ('Attitude of the Pharisees', p. 24) acknowledges the lack of conclusive evidence for his interpretation. Certainly Alexander Jannaeus desired influence and power in the region. The narrative pertaining to Salome Alexandra indicates that there were men associated with Alexander Jannaeus who assisted him, implying that he was not a despot who ruled without advisors. If, as Alon and others suggest, Alexander Jannaeus did change the men close to him it does not necessarily follow that he neglected the role of any institution, as they imply. Rather, it was a change of personnel.

the matter serious and that he wished to prevent it from spreading. It is conceivable that the high priesthood and the occasion of the festival acted as a rallying point for a number of divergent groups to voice their opposition against a common foe. If we accept a link between the two outbreaks of protest, the tactical delay before the second assault suggests that Alexander Jannaeus's opponents were not driven by a fanaticism that required immediate action.

Josephus's explanation for this major internal conflict over the control of Judaea is contained in Alexander Jannaeus's death-bed speech in *Antiquities of the Jews*. It was the poor treatment of the Pharisees that caused the nation to rise against the king: to go against the wishes of the Pharisees was to provoke retribution because they controlled the masses. As a result Alexander Jannaeus implored his wife to obtain Pharisaic support for the administration. We should not, however, be too quick in accepting Josephus's statement regarding the Pharisees as applicable to the situation narrated.[1] It is only in *Antiquities of the Jews* that the Pharisees feature. Moreover, although some Pharisees participated in the rebellion, the statement regarding the extent of Pharisaic influence is questionable. Josephus makes his claim that the Pharisees were influential with the masses without providing supporting evidence.[2] In fact, Josephus's claim is contradicted

1. This reference has been incorrectly taken as the cornerstone to explaining the revolt. For example see V. Tcherikover, *Hellenistic Civilisation and the Jews* (trans. S. Applebaum; Philadelphia: The Jewish Publication Society of America, 1959), p. 253; Smallwood, *Jews under Roman Rule*, p. 18; E. Bickerman, *From Ezra to the Last of the Maccabees* (New York: Schockern Books, 1947), p. 169; and Rivkin, *Revolution*, pp. 37, 44-45. Some scholars do amplify the account, such as Klausner ('Judah Aristobulus', pp. 231-32), who claims it was extremist Pharisees that rebelled and Zeitlin (*Rise and Fall*, I, pp. 335-36), who argues that it was a political struggle between the Pharisees and Sadducees. Schürer (*History*, I, p. 222) suggests that Josephus's reference reflects a rift between the Pharisees and Hasmonaeans over the office of high priest. W.S. McCullough (*The History and Literature of the Palestinian Jews from Cyrus to Herod, 550 BC to 4 BC* [Toronto: University of Toronto Press, 1975], p. 137), W.R. Farmer (*Maccabees, Zealots and Josephus* [New York: Columbia University Press, 1956], p. 48) and Buehler (*Civil War*, pp. 40, 63, 73-76) argue that it was a revolt involving religious authority. It is notable that only C. Rabin ('Alexander Jannaeus and the Pharisees', *JJS* 6 [1956], p. 58) actually questions whether or not the speech should be connected to the revolt narrative. He, however, follows other scholars by accepting the speech as being historically relevant to the reign of Alexander Jannaeus.

2. Some comment is necessary on Josephus's account of the incident involving John Hyrcanus and the Pharisees (*War* 1.66-69; *Ant.* 13.288-98). Alon ('Attitude of

by several aspects of the narratives in *The Jewish War* and *Antiquities of the Jews*. For example, although the Pharisees controlled the masses, it took some eight years for the conflict to begin. Josephus's implicit linking of the cause of the rebellion to Alexander Jannaeus's treatment of the Pharisees also poses a further problem. After the execution and flight of approximately 9,000 people, Alexander Jannaeus lived in peace. The fact that the Pharisees were dead or in exile, and the populace content to settle under Alexander Jannaeus, should have removed the necessity for the death-bed speech. The speech seems to have been used by Josephus to proclaim the alleged antiquity of the Pharisees' importance and to provide a background for the events that were to follow. It may be more appropriate, therefore, to associate the contents of the speech with the reign of Salome Alexandra rather than that of her husband.[1]

Alexander Jannaeus was faced with a serious rebellion. He dealt with the rebels harshly but suffered no further open opposition. Alexander Jannaeus may have been questioned regarding his legitimacy as high priest and his assumption to the throne.[2] In effect, some

the Pharisees', p. 26) and more importantly, M.J. Geller ('Alexander Jannaeus', pp. 205-208), argue that the incident should not be connected with John. Others, such as Jagersma (*History*, p. 90) and Schürer (*History*, I, pp. 213-14), follow the narrative of Josephus. Instead of changing the participants it is more appropriate to acknowlege the authorial licence employed by Josephus. It is only in *Ant.* that the incident involving John occurs. The story of Eleazar was used by Josephus to indicate the importance of the Pharisees and their influence over the populace. The incident however, is an example of Josephus re-interpreting events, presenting his current perspective on Jewish affairs. It is possible that Josephus made other such alterations and extensions to his narrative in *Ant.* which are not necessarily relevant to the period he narrates. See M. Smith ('Palestinian Judaism in the First Century', in H.A. Fischel (ed.), *Essays in Greco-Roman and Related Talmudic Literature* [New York: Ktav, 1977], pp. 183-87) regarding the emphasis on Pharisees in *Ant.*

1. Smith ('Palestinian Judaism', pp. 192-93) takes this approach. For acceptance of the death-bed speech as a sign of reconciliation between Alexander Jannaeus and the Pharisees see Klausner, 'Judah Aristobulus', p. 233; Jagersma, *History*, p. 93; Geller, 'Alexander Jannaeus', p. 209; and J. Naveh, 'Dated Coins of Alexander Jannaeus', *IEJ* 18 (1968), p. 25. Also see Urbach, 'Jewish Doctrines', p. 79, for a possible parallel between the speech and that made by Alexander the Great. It is notable that Rivkin (*Revolution*, p. 49) inadvertently supports the notion that Josephus doctored the narrative regarding the role of the Pharisees.

2. There is some debate regarding the identity of the first Hasmonaean to use the title king. For example, Zeitlin (*Rise and Fall*, I, p. 318) and Geller ('Alexander Jannaeus', p. 208 n. 32), accept Josephus, while Schalit ('Domestic Politics',

Jews disputed his right to rule. It is not possible to establish whether
the rallying point was religious in nature or purely in terms of administrative power, if such a distinction is valid. Nor is it apparent why
the revolt arose when it did. Whatever the case, those who opposed
Alexander Jannaeus but survived the rebellion were willing to bide
their time in exile or under his rule.

Pharisees were probably involved in the rebellion as the opponents
of Alexander Jannaeus.[1] The claim regarding the Pharisees' extensive
influence over the populace, however, does not reflect the events of
the period being narrated. In this instance Josephus used the
Antiquities of the Jews to impose later perceptions and interests on his
history of the Jews. Furthermore, there is no evidence for the
involvement of a representative national body, nor of its existence in
this incident.

2. *Affairs of State under Salome Alexandra*

War 1.107, Salome Alexandra bequeathed the throne by her husband,
109, appoints Hyrcanus high priest, 111, Salome follows the Pharisees,
they do as they please, 112, Salome doubles size of army, employs more
mercenaries, 113, Pharisees kill Diogenes and others, friends of
Alexander Jannaeus, 114, Aristobulus speaks for 'the most respected
men' (οἱ προύχειν δοκοῦντε), they leave Jerusalem, 115, Salome
sends troops to Damascus, 116, she befriends Tigranes, 117, Aristobulus
and friends take fortresses when Salome is ill, 118, Hyrcanus asks
Salome to act against Aristobulus.

Ant. 13.407, Salome Alexandra bequeathed the throne by her husband,
populace love her, 408, appoints Hyrcanus high priest, people told to
obey Pharisees and their regulations, 409, Pharisees do as they like,
Salome doubles the size of the army, employs more mercenaries, 410,
Pharisees ask Salome to execute those responsible for the death of the 800
under Alexander Jannaeus, 411, they kill Diogenes and others,
Aristobulus speaks for 'the powerful men' (οἱ δυνατοί), 417, Salome
allows them to take control of some of the fortresses, 418, Salome sends

p. 288 and *König Herodes, Der Mann und Sein Werk* [Berlin: de Gruyter, 1969],
pp. 743-44) claims that Alexander Jannaeus was first to do so. There is, however,
no evidence to support the claim that we should alter Josephus's narrative.

1.   Apart from the reference in the death-bed speech there are two other hints that
Pharisees oppposed the king. See *Ant.* 13.296, where Josephus refers to the trouble
faced by John Hyrcanus and his sons, and *War* 1.113: *Ant.* 13.410, where Pharisees
seek revenge on the advisors of Alexander Jannaeus.

Aristobulus as commander of army to Damascus, 419, she befriends
Tigranes, 422, Aristobulus begins rebellion when Salome is ill, 423, he is
assisted by Palaestes, one of 'the powerful men' at Agaba, 428, 'the
elders' (οἱ πρεσβύταεροι) and Hyrcanus ask Salome to act against
Aristobulus, 429, she gives these men a free hand.

When Alexander Jannaeus died in 76 BC he bequeathed control of the
territory to his wife. The account of Salome Alexandra's reign
between 76–68 BC appears to indicate Pharisaic domination of the
Jewish administration. The situation, however, is not quite that
straightforward. Several aspects of *The Jewish War* and *Antiquities of
the Jews* require examination before we can combine the narratives
and make any statement regarding the division of power during
Salome Alexandra's reign.

The account in *The Jewish War* is divided into four parts. The first,
107–112, summarizes the character of Salome Alexandra's reign,
while the other three describe specific events. According to the summary, Salome Alexandra was a good ruler, primarily because of her
piety. Due to a mutual respect for the observance of religion, Salome
Alexandra came under the guidance of the Pharisees to the extent of
being controlled by them. In this summary Josephus refers to three
specific actions. They are the appointment of Hyrcanus as high priest,
the recruitment of Jews to the army, and the hiring of mercenaries, all
performed by Salome Alexandra. Therefore, although Josephus claims
that the Pharisees were in control, the queen fulfils the few tasks
mentioned in the summary.[1]

The remaining narrative in *The Jewish War* is divided into three
examples of administrative decisions. In all of these Salome Alexandra
is in command. The first example is the treatment of Alexander
Jannaeus's advisors. Here the Pharisees were able to seek revenge for

---

1. Few scholars acknowledge this distinction. Rather, the majority accept the
general tenor of the summary without question, as with *Ant.*. For example, see Alon,
'Attitude of the Pharisees', p. 23, who describes the relationship in political rather
than religious terms; Bickerman, *Ezra*, p. 170; and Mantel, *Studies*, p. 30 n. 175.
D. Schwartz ('Josephus and Nicolaus on the Pharisees', *JSJ* 14 [1983], p. 170,
claims that *War* 1.111-14 is the only political passage in the text that survived
editing. Smith ('Palestinian Judaism', p. 185) is correct in concluding that anti-
Pharisaic comments are located in *War,* which he links with the hand of Nicolaus.
What he does not state is that Josephus appears to have partially edited these
comments, interpreting the references to the Pharisees in a positive light.

past events.[1] They influenced the queen in that she consented to the punishment of the advisors. The fact, however, that Salome Alexandra was able to release many of the men targeted by the Pharisees is inconsistent with the notion that they ruled her.

The second example concerns external relations when Salome Alexandra sent troops to Damascus and then greeted Tigranes with gifts and offers of a treaty. Here, it is the queen who decided upon the appropriate action, not the Pharisees.

The third example is Aristobulus's attempt to seize control of affairs when Salome Alexandra became seriously ill. Aristobulus instigated the incident, Hyrcanus and 'the elders' complained to Salome Alexandra of what Aristobulus was doing, and the queen proceeded to take action, but died before anything significant could be done. Nowhere in this incident do the Pharisees appear as an identifiable group.[2]

In the three incidents Salome Alexandra is the active head of the administration and the legal authority. A division existed between the advisors of Alexander Jannaeus and the Pharisees, among others. The latter appear to have gained the confidence of the queen and were given public standing while their opponents, initially in physical danger, lived in the country districts of Judaea. In this context the part of the summary where the Pharisees are described as all-powerful appears to have been Josephus's personal attempt to highlight their role in the administration.

The version in *Antiquities of the Jews* of Salome Alexandra's reign can also be divided into summary sections and descriptions of incidents. The one point on which the two versions agree is that the Pharisees were all-powerful. Although Salome Alexandra held the title of queen it was the Pharisees who were the real administrators. The major summary in *Antiquities of the Jews*, the eulogy, appears to contain two sections. The first speaks of Salome Alexandra in positive terms while the second is extremely critical of her. The first part refers to her ability to carry out her objectives. The implication is that Salome Alexandra was the leading authority. Conversely, the view of Salome Alexandra expressed in the second part of the eulogy is

---

1. Zeitlin (*Rise and Fall*, I, p. 337) relates the vengeance of the Pharisees to their developing a 'political mind'.
2. It is conceivable that these men could be 'the elders' (*Ant.* 14.428).

critical. She allowed justice to be ignored and desired power when she had two sons fit to rule. Furthermore, Salome Alexandra sided with the Pharisees, people who were opposed to her family. Finally, and most regrettably, Salome Alexandra left the country divided.

The other summary statements present a similar divergence. The restlessness of the Pharisees, the ineptitude of Alexander Jannaeus's friends in allowing Salome Alexandra to control affairs, and the defensive explanation of Aristobulus's revolt may complement the view expressed in the second part of the eulogy. The other statements indicating the importance attached to Alexander Jannaeus's funeral and the claim that the Pharisees were all-powerful possibly relate to the first half of the eulogy. These comments regarding Salome Alexandra's reign probably derive from two different sources, both of which date long after the events they record.[1]

Antiquities of the Jews has two details which do not appear in *The Jewish War* which indicate the importance of the Pharisees. First, the funeral of Alexander Jannaeus. The primary purpose of the funeral narrative is to highlight the influence of the Pharisees. In return for Salome Alexandra's adherence to the Pharisees they were able to ensure a favourable public memory for Alexander Jannaeus.

The second addition is the reintroduction of regulations proposed by the Pharisees which had been abandoned by John Hyrcanus. Josephus also states that Salome Alexandra ordered the populace to obey the Pharisees. The probable explanation of this statement is that Salome Alexandra orientated public regulations according to Pharisaic teaching. As a result the populace were placed in a position where they were legally bound to follow the Pharisees.

As in *The Jewish War* the other incidents indicate the prominence of Salome Alexandra. In external relations the queen decided to send troops to Damascus to fight Ptolemy. Significantly, Aristobulus commanded the army.[2] Assuming Josephus is accurate here, we are faced

---

1. J. Klausner ('Queen Salome Alexandra', in Schalit (ed.), *The Hellenistic Age*, p. 243) acknowledges the presence of two summaries, one drawn from a Jewish-Pharisee source, the other either from a hostile Greek or anti-Pharisee source. He favours the pro-Pharisee account in describing the administration. Note Rivkin, *Revolution*, p. 46, who argues that there is not a pro-Pharisaic source.

2. There is no reason to doubt that the absence of this reference from *War* indicates that Josephus is not historically accurate in naming Aristobulus as general. This additional information may be the result of the use of an extra source by

with two complications. First, it is strange that Aristobulus was chosen if the Pharisees completely dominated Salome Alexandra. Aristobulus had defended the friends of Alexander Jannaeus against persecution by the Pharisees. The second complication is that Aristobulus is alleged to have sought public attention and power too vigorously for the liking of Salome Alexandra. In this context it is odd that she should appoint him commander of an army.[1] The queen also employed mercenaries and doubled the size of the Jewish army. Furthermore, Salome Alexandra took decisive action to protect Judaea from encroachment by Tigranes, sending envoys to him bearing gifts and overtures of friendship.

In the persecution of the Jews friendly to Alexander Jannaeus the Pharisees are central but not all-powerful. The Pharisees attempted to convince Salome Alexandra that the advisors of Alexander Jannaeus should be put to death. That the Pharisees eventually took matters into their own hands and murdered Diogenes and several others suggests that Salome Alexandra did not entirely consent to the punishment requested. Fearing for their lives, these men pleaded with Salome Alexandra through Aristobulus.[2]

Josephus relates at some length the arguments of these men. They were willing to leave Jerusalem, a major concession which would restrict their ability to influence affairs. They did, however, request some compensation, successfully obtaining the control of most of the fortresses. We cannot tell whether the Pharisees approved of this concession. What we do know is that Salome Alexandra decided their fate and that, although they were not condemned by her, physical pressure from the Pharisees resulted in their departure from Jerusalem.

Josephus in compiling *Ant*.

1. It is possible that Josephus's depiction of Hyrcanus and Aristobulus was an idealized polarization of two moral characters rather than an accurate description of the two men.

2. Note the variation between *War* and *Ant*. regarding the punishment of Alexander Jannaeus's friends. In *War* Salome Alexandra gives her consent to the attack, while in *Ant*. no such explicit consent is mentioned. This difference suggests a slight alteration in the bias of the account from being pro-Pharisaic in *War* to a more neutral stance in *Ant*., possibly due to a change in the sources employed by Josephus. Note S.N. Mason ('Josephus on the Pharisees Reconsidered: A Critique of Smith/Neusner', *Studies in Religion* 17 [1988], pp. 455-69), who argues that Josephus was actually critical of the Pharisees, with this opinion being best expressed in *Ant*. (p. 469).

The attempt to gain power by Aristobulus reinforces the view that Salome Alexandra controlled the administration. Those people opposed to Aristobulus called upon the queen to take action, despite her illness. The general identity of the opposing forces is discernible. Aristobulus drew his support from the men he had defended before Salome Alexandra, the friends and advisors of Alexander Jannaeus. Aristobulus's alleged motivation was the preservation of his family's status. Hyrcanus was due to succeed Salome Alexandra, but Aristobulus believed that the Pharisees would manipulate his older brother's incapacity to govern. In these circumstances it is possible that the appointment of Hyrcanus as high priest, although made by Salome Alexandra, may have been made at the instigation of the Pharisees. Hyrcanus is listed as one of the key figures representing the group opposing Aristobulus. It is probable that some of the men who exacted punishment on Alexander Jannaeus's friends were among this group, presumably Pharisees. The reference to 'the elders' is unclear. If Josephus intended leading Pharisees it is puzzling that he did not say so.[1]

There are several points pertinent to the administration of Palestine in the accounts of Salome Alexandra's reign.[2] Despite any comments to the contrary, it appears that Salome Alexandra was the effective head of state. Alexander Jannaeus bequeathed the throne to her and there was no opposition to that proposal. In subsequent events it is Salome Alexandra who decides what is to be done. She appoints Hyrcanus high priest. With this position Hyrcanus does not appear to hold any separate authority, but remains subordinate to Salome Alexandra and her system of command. Hyrcanus's ineffectiveness may, in part, be due to his character as described by Josephus. It is

1. Klausner ('Salome', p. 245) assumes that Aristobulus was rebelling against Hyrcanus and the Pharisees. Buehler (*Civil War*, p. 77) implies that 'elders' should be understood to mean a council. Although the men may have belonged to a council, there is no reason to conclude that 'elders' here is a synonym for council.

2. Klausner's argument ('Salome', p. 243) that Salome Alexandra was prominent in external affairs because the Pharisees were not interested in 'diplomatic and military affairs' is not convincing, even if he admits that foreign and domestic affairs cannot be divided. Note that Rivkin (*Revolution*, p. 48) does not deny Salome Alexandra's central role in foreign affairs. A. Schalit ('The Fall of the Hasmonean Dynasty and the Roman Conquest', in M. Avi-Yonah (ed.), *The World History of the Jewish People*. 1st series, VII. *The Herodian Period* [Jerusalem: Massada Publishing House, 1975], p. 26) accepts Josephus at face value; there was a division of power between external and internal matters.

apparent that Pharisees participated in public affairs for several years. This is consistent with their previous prominence. Under John, regulations based on Pharisaic principles had been in use for some years. Then, under Alexander Jannaeus it appears that at least some of the 800 men executed were linked with the Pharisees. During Salome Alexandra's reign Pharisees were given a prominent public role in the administration.

It is evident that a division existed between the friends and advisors of Alexander Jannaeus sponsored by, and in turn supporting Aristobulus, and the Pharisees with their temporary allies being Salome Alexandra and Hyrcanus.[1] When the associates of Alexander Jannaeus left Jerusalem, the Pharisees were the main influential group in the city. There is no suggestion of these two groups sharing power, nor of any council being active in the administration.[2] The success of the Pharisees in forcing their opponents to leave Jerusalem, however, should not be overstated. Salome Alexandra allowed the Pharisees' opponents to take control of many of the country's fortresses. At the opportune moment Aristobulus called on these men to support him in a rebellion against the present administration.

Finally, Josephus used both texts to proclaim that the Pharisees were

1. Alon ('Attitude of the Pharisees', p. 23) notes the political nature of the alliance between Salome Alexandra and the Pharisees. Zeitlin (*Rise and Fall*, I, p. 340) states that many of Aristobulus's allies were Sadducees and military men. See also E. Bevan, *Jerusalem under the High Priests* (London: Edward Arnold, 1904), p. 133, and Buehler, *Civil War*, pp. 39-40, who describes the allies of Aristobulus as aristocrats who obtained their status by wealth and arms. Josephus names one such ally, Palaestes, one of 'the powerful men' of Agaba. Schalit ('Hasmonean Dynasty and Roman Conquest', p. 28) describes Aristobulus's allies as Sadducees.

2. There is no evidence in Josephus to support any of the claims made by scholars regarding a formal institution in operation under Salome Alexandra and the alleged changes that it underwent. See, for example, Jagersma, *History*, p. 96, and Bickerman, *Ezra*, p. 170, who claim that Salome Alexandra introduced 'scribes' to the council. Buehler (*Civil War*, p. 77) proposes that the increase in the status of the Pharisees in the council resulted in Josephus using *synedrion* because the aristocratic character was now diminished. Mantel (*Studies*, pp. 30, 56, 61, 96), reflecting on other scholars' opinions, writes of the Pharisees' complete control of the religious sanhedrin. Le Moyne (*Les Sadducées*, pp. 244-45) argues that the Pharisees dominated the sanhedrin. They used their influence with the queen to oppose the Sadducees (p. 244). See also Klausner ('Salome', p. 243), Schürer (*History*, I, p. 230 n. 5) and McCullough (*History and Literature*, p. 137). Saldarini (*Pharisees*, pp. 91-92) argues that the Pharisees only held limited power under the queen.

all-powerful within the Jewish community. It is clear that Pharisees participated in public affairs during Salome Alexandra's reign. Aware of this, Josephus decided to emphasize the role of the Pharisees as best he could. This bias appears in *The Jewish War*. In *Antiquities of the Jews*, however, extended praise of the Pharisees is slightly muted by the presence of at least one view to the contrary.[1]

3. The Trial of Herod

War 1.204, Herod captures and executes Ezekias and followers, 205, Syrians pleased, 206, Phasael a good administrator in Jerusalem, 208, Hyrcanus envious of Antipater's prestige, malicious men at court angered, 209, they claim Hyrcanus no longer held authority, Herod executed men without permission of Hyrcanus, a man must be tried, 210, Hyrcanus summons Herod, 211, Sextus orders Hyrcanus to find Herod not guilty, Hyrcanus does so happily, 212, Herod joins Sextus, Hyrcanus requested to recall Herod, 213, Sextus appoints Herod commander of Coele-Syria and Samaria, 214, Herod, reminded of his 'acquittal', (ἀφέσεως) decides not to attack Jerusalem.

Ant. 14.159, Herod captures and executes Ezekias and followers, 160, Syrians pleased, 161, Phasael a popular administrator in Jerusalem, 163, 'the leading' (οἱ ἐν τέλει) Jews angered by Antipater's growing prestige, 164, Antipater claims monetary gift to Romans was from him, 165, 'the first' (οἱ πρῶτοι) Jews accuse Antipater and family of taking power, 167, Herod killed men without a trial by the *synedrion*, he did not have the permission of Hyrcanus, 168, mothers of dead men request Herod be judged in the *synedrion*, 169, Herod summoned to Jerusalem by Hyrcanus, 170, Sextus urges Hyrcanus to acquit Herod, adding threats, Hyrcanus uses the letter to prevent the *synedrion* from harming Herod, 171, Herod in the *synedrion*, 172, Samaias speaks, mentions others seeking mercy before this *synedrion*, 175, later, Herod kills Hyrcanus and all the members of the *synedrion* except Samaias, 177, members of the *synedrion* intent on killing Herod, Hyrcanus postpones the trial, Herod flees, 178, to Sextus, 179, members of the *synedrion* ask Hyrcanus to recall Herod, 180, Sextus appoints Herod commander of Coele-Syria, 182, reminded of his 'acquittal' Herod decides not to attack Jersualem.

The trial of Herod took place while Hyrcanus II was ethnarch and

---

1.   Smith ('Palestinian Judaism', p. 192) correctly emphasises the *Ant.* account as lauding the Pharisees. He does not, however, acknowledge that Josephus allowed strong pro-Aristobulus tendencies to exist in *Ant.* over and above any re-interpreted criticism of the Pharisees located in *War*.

high priest of the territory left in Jewish hands by Pompey. While Hyrcanus remained the official head of state, Antipater was formally recognized by the Romans as an important figure in the administration. Antipater then appointed Phasael and Herod as commanders of Jerusalem and Galilee respectively. Early in his term as commander of Galilee, Herod performed an action that attracted much attention. The accounts of the death of Ezekias and his followers in *Antiquities of the Jews* and *The Jewish War* agree on a few points. There are, however, many differences in the narrative of the trial and several unparalleled details included in *Antiquities of the Jews*.[1]

The texts agree on most aspects of the incident before and after what happened in Jerusalem. A similar context for the incident is provided in each text. The appointments of Phasael and Herod are included as part of an outline of Antipater's rising stature in Palestinian affairs.[2] Within this framework the account of Herod's capturing and killing of Ezekias and his followers is presented. This action received favourable attention from the Syrians and Sextus Caesar and apparently ignited a desire for fame in Phasael.[3] He achieved this aim by

---

1. The differences are seldom explained. See, for example, Schürer, *History*, I, pp. 275-76, and A. Schalit, 'Rise of Herod', pp. 48, 50, and *König Herodes*, pp. 43-48. Falk (*Jewish Law*, p. 182) and Alon ('Attitude of the Pharisees', p. 35) equate parts of *War* and *Ant.* where no parallel exists.

2. It is argued by Schalit ('Rise of Herod', p. 43 and *König Herodes*, p. 41) and Smallwood (*Jews under Roman Rule*, p. 45) that Antipater made these appointments in his capacity as a Roman official. See *War* 1.199 and *Ant.* 14.143 regarding Antipater's Roman recognition. Uncertainty regarding Sextus's motivation does not allow us to support or deny this contention categorically. It is clear, however, that Hyrcanus was able to order Herod to journey to Jerusalem, implying some degree of control over Herod, irrespective of the capacity in which he was appointed. See Schürer, *History*, I, p. 275 n. 29, and Smallwood, *Jews under Roman Rule*, p. 44 n. 1, for a discussion of the likely age of Herod when he was given control of Galilee.

3. The idea that Ezekias was a nationalistic leader of the Hasmonaean family is without foundation. There is no reason to doubt that a bandit was the cause of considerable concern and a destabilizing factor to the local community. See F. Loftus, 'The Anti-Roman Revolts of the Jews and the Galileans', *JQR* 68 (1977–78), p. 82; A.H.M. Jones, *The Herods of Judaea* (Oxford: Oxford University Press, 1938), p. 29; M. Grant, *Herod the Great* (London: Weidenfeld & Nicolson, 1971), p. 38; W. Farmer, 'Judas, Simon and Athronges', *NTS* 4 (1957–58), pp. 150-52; M. Hengel, *Die Zeloten* (Leiden: Brill, 1961), p. 321; and S. Freyne, *Galilee from Alexander the Great to Hadrian, 323 BC to 135 CE* (Wilmington, DE: Michael Glazier, 1980), p. 63.

controlling Jerusalem in a manner that pleased the inhabitants. As a result of Herod and Phasael achieving notoriety, Antipater began to be treated like a king.[1]

The texts also agree in the criticisms registered against Antipater's family. People complained that Antipater and his sons were being allowed to control affairs; Hyrcanus was only a figurehead. Antipater and his sons should administer affairs on behalf of Hyrcanus, as his stewards, not as outright rulers.

Antiquities of the Jews and *The Jewish War* agree that Hyrcanus alone summoned Herod to stand trial. It appears, therefore, that Herod, although appointed by Antipater, was responsible to Hyrcanus. Furthermore, Antipater recognized the authority of Hyrcanus, advising Herod to answer the charges laid against him.

After leaving Jerusalem, Herod went to Damascus to seek the protection of Sextus Caesar. While under his protection Herod was able to strengthen his position, being appointed commander of Coele-Syria. According to the version in *The Jewish War*, Samaria was also part of the territory allocated to Herod's area of jurisdiction.

Finally, Josephus records the advice given to Herod by Antipater and Phasael when Herod proposed to attack Jerusalem. They agreed that Herod was justified in being angered at the summons to trial, but that he should also remember that he had been 'acquitted'. In other words, Herod answered the charges in a formal hearing and was formally released. Furthermore, it is suggested that Herod should be thankful to Hyrcanus because it was he who allowed Herod to obtain such high status. The implication here appears to be that regardless of how much Antipater and his sons believed they could attain power, it was legitimized only by Hyrcanus. Antipater and Phasael also suggest to Herod that Hyrcanus was influenced in this instance by bad counsel. Hyrcanus may have summoned Herod to stand trial at the beckoning of some influential people.

It is apparent from the information where there is little or no deviation that Hyrcanus was responsible for summoning Herod to

---

1. Note that Hyrcanus's formal title was ethnarch and high priest, (*War* 1.153, 194; *Ant.* 14.73, 184). Josephus's use of king to describe Hyrcanus (*War* 1.203, 241) may reflect a personal preference, a description used by the Jewish community or a combination of the two. The change in Hyrcanus's position instituted by Gabinius was short lived (*War* 1.169-70; *Ant.* 14.90-91). Julius Caesar reinstated Hyrcanus in the position Pompey granted him (*War* 1.194; *Ant.* 14.143).

stand trial. Furthermore, Herod was formally released, probably by Hyrcanus. We also learn of some people expressing concern over the relationship between Hyrcanus and Antipater and his sons. These people believed that Hyrcanus no longer held authority. Antipater and his sons had ceased to be stewards of Hyrcanus and had begun to act as outright rulers. There is, however, no agreement in the texts on the identity of the plaintiffs, the charge(s) laid against Herod and the events in Jerusalem.

There are six occasions where the two narratives differ. The first difference is minor. In *The Jewish War*, Josephus depicts the men who complain to Hyrcanus in a derogatory manner, labelling them as 'malicious men at court'. In *Antiquities of the Jews*, however, they are 'the first men'. Unfortunately, we have no clue as to their actual identity. A further comment is necessary regarding the depiction of the plaintiffs in *Antiquities of the Jews*. Josephus's first reference to the people angered by the position of Antipater and his sons is to 'the leading men'. The men presenting the specific complaint regarding Herod's action were 'the first men'. Although it is conceivable that Josephus was referring to two distinct groups of people it is likely that he has employed two different descriptive phrases for the one group of people.[1]

A second difference lies in the specific complaint directed against Herod. According to the malicious men at court in *The Jewish War*, Herod had violated the law. To this point the version in *Antiquities of the Jews* is in agreement with that in *The Jewish War*. The malicious men at court then go on to state that if Herod was not a king, but a private citizen, he should appear in court to answer the charges. Herod was to address himself to the king and the laws, which state that no man is to be put to death without a trial. The implication is that Herod's status was within the law: he was answerable for his conduct.

---

1. Buehler (*Civil War*, p. 33) concludes that 'the first men' were 'men who held an official position in authority'. Unfortunately Buehler does not suggest what this position might have been. There are several suggestions as to the identity of these opponents of Antipater and Herod. Smallwood (*Jews under Roman Rule*, p. 45) describes them as members of the 'Sadducean aristocratic party'; Jones (*Herods*, p. 29) as Hasmonaeans who supported Antigonus; and, more generally, Schalit ('Rise of Herod', p. 48) as 'nobles of Jerusalem'. It is possible that some of these people can be connected with the men who expressed their support for Hyrcanus against Aristobulus on the encouragement of Antipater (*War* 1.242-43; *Ant.* 14.11, 43, 302, 324).

Hyrcanus was the representative of the law and the man before whom Herod had to plead his case. There is no suggestion that a specific council was involved. Certain people may have influenced and pressured Hyrcanus to act but it was only Hyrcanus who could ultimately decide what would happen.

In *Antiquities of the Jews*, on the other hand, the law Herod violated was the killing of a man without his first being condemned by the *synedrion*. This is the first reference to the *synedrion* in this incident.[1] By the use of the definite article Josephus appears to be referring to a specific body that held authority in terms of capital punishment. However, 'the first men' then state that Herod acted without Hyrcanus's permission. These two statements contradict one another. There is no explanation as to why Hyrcanus's approval was required if it was the *synedrion* that decided the matter. At this point it suffices to acknowledge the contradiction within *Antiquities of the Jews*. The *Jewish War* lays all authority and responsibility in the hands of Hyrcanus. *Antiquities of the Jews* agrees with this notion in one statement. This narrative, however, also indicates that the *synedrion* decided capital offences. It is apparent that Herod's action was not strictly legal. Furthermore, some people who opposed Antipater or his sons saw this as an opportune time to press their disapproval on a legal issue.[2]

The third difference pertains to Sextus Caesar's involvement in the trial. In *The Jewish War* Sextus explicitly ordered Hyrcanus to acquit

1. Earlier references in Josephus to *synedrion* are *Ant.* 12.103, the meeting at which the Bible was translated, and *Ant.* 14.91, Gabinius's division of the territory into administrative districts.

2. Jones (*Herods*, p. 28) and M. Grant (*Herod*, p. 38) acknowledge that Herod's action gave his opponents a legal cause to seek his downfall. Schalit ('Rise of Herod', p. 48) argues that Herod disrupted the accepted administrative practice in which Jerusalem was the central organization. Freyne (*Galilee*, pp. 63-64) believes that Hyrcanus was pressured into action by the members of the sanhedrin. Several scholars elaborate upon the basis of the *Ant.* version, linking the 'trial' with the sanhedrin's authority being threatened by Herod. Alon ('Attitude of the Pharisees', p. 35) and Schalit ('Rise of Herod', p. 48) speak of the sanhedrin as the national authority which caused the Pharisees (Alon)/Jerusalem nobility (Schalit) to demand that Herod be tried. Saldarini (*Pharisees*, p. 96) claims that it was the sanhedrin that ordered Herod to stand trial. See also M. Grant, *Herod*, p. 39, and Schürer, *History*, I, p. 275. These interpretations fail to account for differences between *War* and *Ant.* and assume the existence of an all-powerful national council called *synedrion*.

Herod. The account in *Antiquities of the Jews*, however, has Sextus urging Hyrcanus to acquit Herod, indicating his wishes by threatening Hyrcanus with retribution if Herod was not released.

Sextus wanted Herod to be formally released. Furthermore, it is implied that Sextus believed that Hyrcanus had the authority to fulfil his demand. Whether it was Hyrcanus or a particular court that would hear Herod's case, Hyrcanus was viewed as being able to determine what decision was reached.

Probably of equal significance is the belief of Sextus that he could intervene in Palestinian internal affairs. In one sense it is purely academic whether Sextus ordered Hyrcanus to release Herod or just encouraged him to do so. The former would enhance the argument for the Jews being a subject people. The latter would present Sextus as an astute legate who exerted his power by persuasion rather than force. Whatever the case, the fact is that Sextus did intervene to help Herod. By killing Ezekias, Herod had done no harm to the Syrians; rather he brought peace and security. It is possible that such an action, added to the friendship Antipater had previously shown to Sextus, may have encouraged the Roman legate to intervene.[1]

Sextus Caesar decided to call upon the existing authority in Judaea, as he understood it, to act on his behalf. Although he later appointed Herod commander of Coele-Syria he did not try to impose direct Roman control on affairs. Nor did he try to depose Hyrcanus. To the Romans, the situation may have been a happy one. Sextus Caesar intervened via the Judaean authority when he believed it was in Rome's interests. Otherwise, he left the Jews to their own devices.

The fourth difference between the narratives relates to events after Herod left Jerusalem. Some Jews request Hyrcanus to recall Herod. The difference lies in the description of these men. *The Jewish War* is derogatory, referring to 'the knaves at court' (οἱ πονηροὶ παρώξυνον). These men probably made the original complaint. In *Antiquities of the Jews*, the men who request the recall of Herod are

---

1. Friendship between Antipater and Sextus probably led to the latter's involvement rather than the direct request of Herod, as suggested by Jones (*Herods*, p. 30). The argument favoured by Mantel (*Studies*, p. 23) and Schalit ('Rise of Herod', p. 43 and *König Herodes*, p. 45) that Sextus intervened because he was dealing with a person subject to Roman jurisdiction is without foundation. Antipater had recognized the right of Hyrcanus to call Herod to Jerusalem to account for his actions.

members of the *synedrion*. Although it seems probable, I am not able to state conclusively that these men should be equated with 'the first men'/'leading men'. Again *The Jewish War* is critical of Herod's opponents, while *Antiquities of the Jews* holds no such bias. Herod's aggressive actions after he left Jerusalem, and a belief that Hyrcanus had not dealt with the issue properly due to the Roman pressure exerted on him, may have motivated demands for the recall. No matter how disappointed or angry these men were, they continued to channel requests for action through Hyrcanus.

The fifth point on which the texts differ may help explain the discontent of certain Jews. According to *The Jewish War*, Hyrcanus 'acquitted' Herod. In *Antiquities of the Jews*, however, we are informed that Hyrcanus postponed the trial and encouraged Herod to flee Jerusalem. In both accounts it is Hyrcanus who has the authority and ability to decide Herod's fate. If, as is stated in *Antiquities of the Jews*, Hyrcanus merely postponed the trial, it would be understandable that some people wanted Herod recalled. Josephus implies in *Antiquities of the Jews* that Hyrcanus had the power to decide when the trial took place, and so, in this case, when the *synedrion* met. The reference to Hyrcanus's postponing the trial, however, is contradicted by several other statements later in the narrative. Josephus records that Herod was 'acquitted'. Therefore, without the reference to the postponement, both versions agree that Hyrcanus acquitted Herod.[1]

The other difference concerns the role of Hyrcanus. In *The Jewish War*, Hyrcanus's inability to respond to Herod's threatening moves after the trial is explained by observing Hyrcanus's recognition of Herod's power. In *Antiquities of the Jews*, on the other hand, it is Hyrcanus's cowardice and folly that prevent him from taking any positive action. The same information is used to present a critical appraisal of Hyrcanus in *Antiquities of the Jews*.

The passages unique to one or other of the accounts require some explanation. The only reference peculiar to *The Jewish War* relates to the portrayal of Hyrcanus. Concerned by the increasing strength and fame of Herod, Hyrcanus was a willing receiver of the messages from the malicious men at court. Through these details a critical picture of

---

1. M. Grant (*Herod*, p. 39) and Marcus (*Josephus*, VII [Loeb], pp. 540-41) note that the narrative of Josephus does not state clearly whether Herod was formally tried.

Hyrcanus is presented in which he carries some blame for what happened.[1]

The first of the unparalleled passages in *Antiquities of the Jews* is the story that Antipater took money to the Romans as a gift. Originally done at Hyrcanus's instigation, Antipater claimed that he provided the gift. Informed of the action, Hyrcanus saw no harm arising, despite the fears of 'the leading men'. It is possible that financial interests were at stake as well as concerns regarding Antipater's prestige. This story is probably present in *Antiquities of the Jews* because of the interest to outline the rise in Antipater's power. We must note that the issue of the gift and the offence of Herod were not necessarily chronologically linked. It is possible that Josephus decided to link the two incidents in order to draw the criticism of Antipater and his family into one intensified block.

The next addition to the account is the reference to the mothers of the murdered men. These women called upon Hyrcanus and the people to bring Herod to stand trial in the *synedrion*. The women may have travelled to Jerusalem to influence what action was undertaken by making a public appeal. Its inclusion probably lies in its value in creating dramatic tension. Hyrcanus had already made up his mind, but these women intensify the situation and elevate its importance. It is noteworthy that Hyrcanus and the people, not a specific institution, are called upon to bring Herod to stand trial.

The third addition to the account in *Antiquities of the Jews* is the statement about Sextus's letter to Hyrcanus. Josephus claims that Hyrcanus wanted to use the letter from Sextus as a pretext to prevent the *synedrion* from harming Herod. Here Hyrcanus is only able to control what happens if he can present a plausible reason. The implication is that Hyrcanus does not have complete authority over the decisions this court makes. The explanation for this extra detail probably lies in the next two additions.

The description of Herod's appearance in the *synedrion*, including the speech of Samaias, is the most significant addition. Ostensibly, this part of the narrative indicates that Herod stood trial before a body known as the *synedrion*. Within this part of the text, the term

---

1. Note also the apparent contradiction within *War* between 1.209 where Hyrcanus is described as secretly fearing Herod and 1.211 where Hyrcanus is said to have loved Herod and wanted to free him.

synedrion refers to a criminal law court and its members. A distinction is drawn between Hyrcanus and the members of the *synedrion*. They may have been in the court together but they had separate identities. Furthermore, this *synedrion* is credited by Samaias as having the ability to decide whether or not it should release Herod for Hyrcanus's sake.

Many of the differences between and additions to *Antiquities of the Jews* and *The Jewish War* are related to the introduction of the *synedrion* into the narrative. The purpose of including this material appears to lie in the moral which Josephus wishes to project. Samaias warned of Herod's likely revenge, and, according to Josephus, he was proved right. The speech of Samaias showed the world that Herod was a man who triumphed over adversity, a man to be treated with respect. Because of the story associated with Samaias's speech it was necessary for Josephus to expand his account of the incident.[1]

The fifth addition to the account was necessary simply because of Samaias's speech and the response which followed it. We are told that Hyrcanus decided to postpone the trial because members of the *synedrion* intended to put Herod to death. To include the speech, Josephus required a link between it and the remainder of the narrative. Thus Hyrcanus intervened and ensured that Herod escaped from Jerusalem.[2]

The final addition to the narrative in *Antiquities of the Jews* is that Herod paid for his post as commander of Coele-Syria. It is conceivable that Sextus favoured Herod but there was little doubt that a bribe of some description would have enhanced his chances of attaining the office. Herod may have been keen to receive Roman recognition to help protect himself from further scrutiny by Jewish authorities. As a Roman official, even if only temporarily, any complaint would probably have to receive Roman approval.[3]

1. See Zeitlin, 'Political Synedrion', p. 158, and Schalit, 'Rise of Herod', p. 50 n. 9 and *König Herodes*, pp. 768-71, regarding the possible link between Samaias and Shammai.
2. The suggestion of Smallwood (*Jews under Roman Rule*, p. 45 n. 3) and Marcus (*Josephus*, VII [Loeb], pp. 540-41) that the speech should precede *Ant.* 14.170 does not resolve the confusion that is apparent in Josephus's versions of events.
3. It is in this context that Smallwood (*Jews under Roman Rule*, p. 46) and M. Grant (*Herod*, p. 40) may be correct in arguing that Sextus ordered Antipater to dissuade his son from seeking revenge.

I am now in a position to draw these three groups of material together. It is not possible to take the accounts of this incident at face value. *The Jewish War* and *Antiquities of the Jews* do not agree on the circumstances of the trial or its aftermath. It is possible, however, to present a general outline of what happened in Jerusalem. I have noted that Samaias's speech was probably included in *Antiquities of the Jews* for reasons not related to the trial. If we remove that and the related references to the *synedrion* from the account in *Antiquities of the Jews*, we are left with exactly the same details as are recorded in *The Jewish War*. Herod performed an action that was outside his official jurisdiction. Certain people in Jerusalem who feared for their status seized this opportunity to attack the increasing power of Antipater and his sons. Hyrcanus then summoned Herod to Jerusalem to answer the charges laid against him. Sextus decided to intervene on Herod's behalf, conceivably at the request of Antipater. Hyrcanus, in compliance with Sextus's preference, acquitted Herod of the charges. Herod left Jerusalem quickly, possibly fearing that some Jews were still not content. This view is supported by the requests made to Hyrcanus for Herod to be re-summoned. Herod was angered by the whole incident but was persuaded by his father and brother to let the matter rest.

Only when Josephus introduced the story of Samaias's speech and Herod's appearance in court were the extra details required. Thus, Josephus could not state in *Antiquities of the Jews* that Hyrcanus responded to Sextus's letter positively, nor that Hyrcanus acquitted Herod. Rather, we have the idea of Hyrcanus postponing the trial: an idea that is later contradicted by Josephus in the narrative in *Antiquities of the Jews* where he refers to Herod's 'acquittal'. A major motivation for including the speech lies in the references to Herod's actions once he became king: the killing of Hyrcanus and of the men who tried him.

It was Hyrcanus who made all the important decisions. There may have been a formal law court that Herod entered, as stated in *Antiquities of the Jews*, but the final say in all aspects of the incident lay in the hands of Hyrcanus. If a court case did take place, it did not affect the final outcome. It was Sextus and Hyrcanus who were the effective agents in determining what happened. The reference to a law court in *Antiquities of the Jews* was essential to provide an audience for the speech of Samaias. Josephus's decision to describe this institution as the *synedrion* should be understood as nothing more than an imposition in the narrative to meet a particular requirement. The story involving Samaias and the resultant inclusion of *synedrion* is an apocryphal anecdote which presumably draws its characteristics from real concepts. In other words, it is conceivable that a trial by court did take place. It is an entirely different issue, however, to claim that Josephus records a trial that involved the power of a supreme national council which acted as judge and jury. It is apparent from the differences in the language used to describe the participants that Josephus was subject to a changing emphasis in his use of sources. What was important was that Samaias had an audience and, therefore, Josephus could narrative his moral regarding Herod's action as king.[1]

There are a number of important points regarding the administration of affairs during the ethnarchship of Hyrcanus to be noted from this incident. It is clear that Hyrcanus made all the necessary decisions, summoning Herod to stand trial and then acquitting him of the charges.[2] Furthermore, it is implied throughout the narrative, especially in *The Jewish War*, that Hyrcanus had capital jurisdiction.

Secondly, Sextus Caesar intervened in the incident. Whether legally or not, Sextus decided to help Herod in an issue that did not specifically relate to a question of the leadership of the Jews. Hyrcanus was placed in a position where Herod's acquittal was the safest course of

1. The failure to consider all these factors has impaired much of the discussion on the identity of this *synedrion*, most of which attempts to determine whether or not it was 'the' sanhedrin. For example, Smallwood (*Jews under Roman Rule*, p. 45) says it is the political sanhedrin; Mantel (*Studies*, p. 96), states it was the Great Sanhedrin and that Hyrcanus was the defendant in a political trial (p. 275); cf. Hoenig (*Great Sanhedrin*, p. 7), who argues that it was not the Great Sanhedrin. Zeitlin ('Political Synedrion', p. 127) notes that *synedrion* is not used in *War* and that this is the only occasion in *Ant.* that the term is used in the 'sense of a court' (p. 114), but he believes that by AD 93 *synedrion* was used to describe a Jewish council and court and was thus the political *synedrion*. See also D.R. Catchpole, 'The Historicity of the Sanhedrin Trial', in E. Bammel (ed.), *The Trial of Jesus. Cambridge Studies in Honour of C.F.D. Moule* (SBT, II, 13; London: SCM Press, 1970), p. 59, who disputes the claim of Zeitlin that the trial of Herod was an example of a two session trial by 'the sanhedrin'.

2. There is no evidence to support other reasons proposed as to why Hyrcanus summoned Herod. For example, see Schalit, 'Rise of Herod', p. 58, who argues that Hyrcanus was in a position where he could not refuse the demands of the *synedrion*. Alon ('Attitude of the Pharisees', p. 35) claims, on the basis that the Pharisees dominated 'the' sanhedrin, that they charged Herod. Mantel (*Studies*, p. 23 n. 142) notes that whether it was advice or an order from Sextus, Hyrcanus followed his wishes.

action. It is notable that Sextus chose to express his request through the person whom he recognized to be the most appropriate Jewish authority, Hyrcanus. The implication is that Hyrcanus was capable of administering affairs amongst the Jews.

Such a notion is supported by the next point: the Jews acknowledged that Hyrcanus was the man to whom their requests were to be directed. The first complaints against Herod were addressed to Hyrcanus in the hope that he would undertake some appropriate action. After Hyrcanus had 'acquitted' Herod, and thus seemingly deserted the interests of the plaintiffs, these men continued to address their requests for action to him.

A further point to be observed is that Hyrcanus had jurisdiction over Herod in Galilee. This incident indicates that Hyrcanus held overall control of the Jews in Palestine. Although Herod, Phasael and Antipater were encouraged by Hyrcanus to engage in the day-to-day running of administrative affairs, they remained subject to him.[1] Some Jews viewed Herod's offence as an opportunity to attack Antipater's family. Irrespective of any desire for political influence, an offence had been committed for which official action could be requested. Hyrcanus may not have taken any action without the continual canvassing of certain people, but there is no doubt that he had the authority to call Herod to justice in both practice and theory.

There are two comments to be made relating to the language employed by Josephus. In *Antiquities of the Jews*, Josephus interchanges 'the first men' and the 'leading men' to describe the same group of Jews. We are given no clear details of their identity. It is conceivable that they held some influence with Hyrcanus, since, according to *The Jewish War*, they were connected to the royal court. It is also possible that they were wealthy men who stood to lose power and influence as the status of Antipater's family increased.

---

1. The prominence of Hyrcanus is indicated by the fact that the Romans continued to recognize him as the official head of state. They acknowledged his status and privilege as high priest and appointed him ethnarch (*Ant.* 14.194, 208-10). Hyrcanus participated in the administration primarily in terms of representing the cause and needs of the Jews, yet he also allowed Antipater to be an active participant. It is important to note that Antipater, his sons and Hyrcanus benefited from the relationship, yet the former remained loyal to Hyrcanus. The notion that Antipater and his sons fulfilled an executive function is supported by the attempts of others to usurp them in public prominence (*War* 1.223-32, 236-37; *Ant.* 14.277-92, 294-96).

This incident is the first occasion on which the *synedrion* is mentioned in a significant matter. Although confined to *Antiquities of the Jews* and not historically relevant to the trial, it is an example of how Josephus employed and understood the term *synedrion*. Throughout, it is a court of law that deals with a capital crime. Josephus implies in Samaias's speech that the *synedrion* had met before, in terms of a law court. We have no evidence of permanence nor of other areas of concern for the *synedrion*. Furthermore, it is separate from Hyrcanus but is summoned at his beckoning.

Chapter 3

DIRECT ROMAN RULE: AD 6–41

1. Samaritan Intrusion into the Temple

Ant. 18.29, Passover, 30, Samaritans place bones in the temple and porticoes, in response, measures taken [by priests] to protect the temple, including exclusion of people.

When Judaea was placed under the direct control of Rome in AD 6 the first prefect was Coponius. While he was in office some Samaritans placed human bones in the Temple at Jerusalem. Although a minor reference in *Antiquities of the Jews* this incident is important.

Some action was deemed appropriate to prevent a similar further sacrilege from being performed. Josephus indicates that security measures regarding the patrolling of the Temple and the exclusion of Samaritans from the Temple were implemented.[1] The text is corrupt and it is not possible to establish definitely who was responsible for the actions.[2] No widespread trouble is reported in connection with the Samaritan action. A possible implication is that the response was effective. It is also probable that it was priests who undertook

---

1. Several scholars believe that the 'Nazareth decree' which threatened tomb robbers with execution if captured was a result of this incident. See J. Carcopino, 'Encore le rescrit impérial sur les violations de sépulture', *Revue Historique* 156 (1931), pp. 83-89. M. Stern ('The Province of Judaea', in S. Safrai and M. Stern (eds.), *The Jewish People in the First Century*, I, p. 348 n. 1) states that such a link is 'no more than pure conjecture' while Smallwood (*Jews under Roman Rule*, p. 157 n. 53, p. 213) indicates that although the 'Nazareth decree' dates from the first half of the first century AD it post-dates the Samaritan incident because the edict related to Galilee, which came under direct Roman rule after the death of Agrippa I in AD 44.

2. The possibility of corruption or a lacuna in the text is noted by Feldman (*Josephus*, IX [Loeb], p. 27), and Smallwood (*Jews under Roman Rule*, p. 157). Jeremias (*Jerusalem*, p. 353) argues that Josephus neglects to tell his readers what Jewish action led to the Samaritan sacrilege. The assumption that there was a specific act of provocation on this occasion, however, is pure speculation.

measures to protect the sanctity of the Temple. There is no precedent for assuming that the Romans had taken responsibility for the administration of the Temple, nor that Jewish non-priests alone directed Temple affairs.[1]

This incident has an important bearing on our understanding of who performed actions in early first-century AD Judaea. In a matter involving sub-sections of the local community Jewish priests appear to have been active. What the priests instituted regarding the Temple was put into effect: they were able to bar entry to certain groups. Furthermore, the actions of the priests appear to have been sufficient to maintain peace and order. Finally, the incident appears to be an example of the Romans remaining separate from a dispute which involved the local inhabitants. In turn, it is evident that trouble in Judaea did not stem only from conflict between the Romans and the Jews.

2. *Two Protests under Pilate's Prefectship*

a. *The Effigies*
War 2.169, Pilate places effigies of Caesar in Jerusalem at night, 170, next day city and country Jews protest, 171, travel to Caesarea to see Pilate, 172, surrounded by troops, 173, Pilate threatens the Jews, 174, Pilate removes the effigies.

Ant. 18.55, troops quartered in Jerusalem for winter, effigies of Caesar on standards, 56, introduced at night, 57, populace go to Caesarea to protest, 58, troops surround the Jews, Pilate threatens them, 59, Pilate decides to remove the effigies.

Leg. Gai. 299, shields with gold, name of inscriber and of the dedicatee placed in Herod's palace, 300, four sons of Herod, other descendants and 'the leading' (οἱ ἐν τέλει) Jews appeal to Pilate, 303, 'the leading men' write to Tiberius, 305, he orders Pilate to take the shields to Caesarea.

---

1. Smallwood (*Jews under Roman Rule*, p. 158) suggests that the lack of any form of protest was due to Coponius's careful handling of the situation. She does not attempt to explain, however, why no reference is made to his supposed diplomatic triumph. Feldman (*Josephus*, IX [Loeb], p. 26) includes priests in his version. See also Smallwood, *Jews under Roman Rule*, p. 157 n. 53. Note P. Segal, 'The Penalty of the Warning Inscription from the Temple of Jerusalem', *IEJ* 39 (1989), pp. 79-84. He argues that it was priestly authorities that were responsible for the inscription (p. 79) and for the summary execution of all offenders (pp. 83-84).

b. *The Aqueduct.*
War 2.175, temple treasury money used by Pilate to build an aqueduct,
populace angered, protest when Pilate visits Jerusalem, 176, troops
disguised in the crowd, 177, they kill many Jews, protest ends.

Ant. 18.60, Pilate uses money from sacred treasury to build an aqueduct,
thousands of Jews protest, 61, troops disguised among the crowd, 62,
many Jews killed, protest ends.

Two incidents during Pilate's term of office as prefect of Judaea form
the next case. They are the introduction of standards, early in his term
of office, and later, the construction of an aqueduct. Both incidents
relate directly to affairs in Jerusalem and involve a Jewish protest that
concluded in different ways. Each incident will be examined
separately and the observations drawn together in terms of the early
first-century AD administration.

a. *The Effigies*
After the initial discontent over the census in AD 6, this is the first
incident recorded by Josephus and Philo where the Roman administrator comes into direct conflict with the Jews.[1] It is probable that

1. The majority of scholars who refer to Philo favour the idea that he was
narrating a different incident. See A. Doyle, 'Pilate's Career and the Date of the
Crucifixion', *JTS* 42 (1941), p. 190; P.S. Davies, 'The Meaning of Philo's Text
about the Gilded Shields', *JTS* ns 37 (1986), p. 109; H. Hoehner, *Herod Antipas*
(Cambridge: Cambridge University Press, 1972), p. 176; P. Maier, 'The Episode of
the Golden Roman Shields at Jerusalem', *HTR* 62 (1969), p. 111; M. Stern, 'The
Herodian Dynasty and the Province of Judaea at the End of the Period of the Second
Temple', in Avi-Yonah (ed.), *The Herodian Period*, p. 130; Zeitlin, *Rise and Fall*,
II, p. 142; Rajak, *Josephus*, p. 67; Bilde, *Flavius Josephus*, p. 33; Schürer,
History, I, p. 382; R.A. Horsley, *Jesus and the Spiral of Violence. Popular Jewish
Resistance in Roman Palestine* (San Francisco: Harper & Row, 1987), pp. 108-10;
Millar, *Emperor*, p. 377; and Smallwood, *Jews under Roman Rule*, p. 166, and
Philonis Alexandrini Legatio ad Gaium: Text and Commentary (Leiden: Brill, 2nd
edn, 1970), p. 302. Goodman (*Ruling Class*, p. 45 n. 27) claims it is unlikely that
the accounts of Philo and Josephus should be equated. Many acknowledge the
existence of ostensible similarities but point, in general, to two factors that argue
against a link. First, the date of the incidents; for example, see Doyle, 'Pilate's
Career', p. 192; G. Fuks, 'Again on the Episode of the Gilded Roman Shields at
Jerusalem', *HTR* 75 (1982), p. 503; and Maier, 'Episode', p. 113. Secondly, and
more significantly, Philo is clear that there was no image on the shields; for example,
see Smallwood, *Philonis*, p. 302, and Maier, 'Episode', p. 111. A few scholars
have argued that Philo and Josephus report the same incident, but from different
traditions. See, for example, F. Colson, *Philo* (Loeb), p. xviii, and D. Schwartz,

this incident took place in the first winter of Pilate's prefectship.[1]

Four points stand out from Josephus's narrative which are echoed in Philo's *Legatio ad Gaium*. First, Pilate was the instigator and main protagonist. According to *Antiquities of the Jews*, previous Roman prefects did not enter Jerusalem with ornamental standards. It is implied that Pilate knew his action would be unpopular. This idea is reinforced by the decision to introduce the standards at night. Furthermore, the rough tactics displayed by Pilate suggest that the action was intended to make his presence known to the local inhabitants.[2] Whatever his initial intention, Pilate did not desire greater

'Josephus and Philo on Pontius Pilate', *Jerusalem Cathedra* 3 (1983), pp. 26-45. Although the argument favoured by Colson that Eusebius supports a link has been successfully refuted by Smallwood (*Philonis*, pp. 37-43), a correlation should be favoured. It is not possible to explain all the discrepancies as particular oversights. This observation, however, does not warrant the drastic solution of claiming two separate incidents involving such similar circumstances. As argued by Schwartz, ('Josephus and Philo') a number of the differences between Philo and Josephus can be related to particular interests held by the authors, especially Philo. Support for this idea can be found in an admission by Maier ('Episode', p. 119) that 'any critical investigation of this incident must pick its way through the lush foliage of Philo's rhetoric in trying to find the truth'. It is apparent that Philo had some connection with Agrippa I for the narration of this incident and the one in which it is enclosed, the statue of Gaius. Furthermore, his interests were centred on the moral and theological lessons to be gleaned from these situations. It is, therefore, plausible to look for explanations of differences other than simply stating that Philo and Josephus narrate separate incidents. A further point to note is that no explanation is offered for why Pilate would make a second attempt to introduce standards into Jerusalem. Subsidiary to this is the failure of scholars to indicate why Josephus and Philo were ignorant of the 'other' incident. Where Philo and Josephus differ it will be indicated why one version is preferred over the other, if such a preference is warranted. There will always be a certain degree of doubt but there is no reason to believe that Philo and Josephus relate separate incidents. As such, arguments regarding why the gilded shields were an offence are of little value. For example, see Hoehner, *Herod*, p. 178; Maier, 'Episode', p. 111; Doyle, 'Pilate's Career', p. 191; Fuks, 'Episode', p. 507; Davies, 'Meaning', pp. 113-14; and Smallwood, *Jews under Roman Rule*, p. 166 and *Philonis*, p. 304.

1. As suggested by Doyle, 'Pilate's Career', p. 150, and Hoehner, *Herod*, p. 173. It is implied by Philo *(Leg. Gai.* 302) that the incident took place late in Pilate's term of office; cf. Doyle, 'Pilate's Career', p. 190, and Fuks, 'Episode', p. 505. This inference is the result of Philo's criticism of Pilate for his hatred of the Jews. As such, it is part of a moralistic point, and is not necessarily based on any concern for chronological accuracy.

2. C. Kraeling ('The Episode of the Roman Standards at Jerusalem', *HTR* 35 [1942], p. 265) and Stern ('Herodian Dynasty', p. 129) claim that Pilate did not

violence and was flexible enough to reverse his decision.[1]

The second point is connected to the reaction at the appearance of the standards. Josephus is determined to show that the Jews presented a united front. In *The Jewish War* the city dwellers and country inhabitants joined together to express their anger. For the populace to cease their daily labours their employers must have been involved in some manner, as the protest lasted six days. There is no indication of who, if anyone, organized the protest. Pilate did not attempt to exact reprisals on particular Jews. This may be due more to the fact that the protest remained passive rather than to the idea that no one led the Jews. By presenting the Jews as a united anonymous group it is possible that Josephus's intention was to highlight the passive nature of the protest, not to comment on the participants' identity.[2]

Josephus portrays Pilate as being overwhelmed by the willingness of the Jews to sacrifice their lives for the sake of their laws. Here Philo's

necessarily intend to destroy Jewish ancestral customs. Smallwood (*Jews under Roman Rule*, p. 161, and *Philonis*, p. 301) and Brandon (*Fall of Jerusalem*, p. 155), however, appear to be correct in stating that Pilate knew what he was doing. There is some debate regarding the exact nature of the protest. Kraeling ('Episode', pp. 277-79) and Mantel (*Studies*, p. 278) argue that it was the religious significance and location of the object that offended the Jews. Note also Horsley (*Jesus*, pp. 102-103, 114), who argues that the central issue was a challenge to the sovereignty of the Jewish deity.

1. This reversal should not be interpreted as a sign of weakness, as argued by D. Flusser, 'A Literary Approach to the Trial of Jesus', *Judaism* 20 (1971), p. 35. Nor is there any basis to Stern's claim ('Herodian Dynasty', p. 129) that Pilate over-reached his capabilities and was forced to retreat. Presumably Pilate was entrusted with the same powers as those given to the first prefect, Coponius (*War* 2.117; *Ant.* 18.2). Of more credence is the concept of Pilate being inexperienced, suggested by Doyle ('Pilate's Career', p. 190). Note the situation under Cumanus. Like Pilate, Cumanus chose to use violence to resolve one dispute (*War* 2.223-37; *Ant.* 20.105-12) while in another he upheld the Jewish protests (*War* 2.228-31; *Ant.* 20.113-17).

2. See Bilde, *Flavius Josephus*, pp. 184, 187, regarding the possible religious motives in the recording of this incident. Smallwood ('High Priests', p. 22) and, especially, Horsley ('High Priests', pp. 36-37) argue that the lack of reference to the high priest or aristocracy indicates that they sided with Pilate. Goodman (*Ruling Class*, pp. 46, 150, 174) also accepts that the ruling class did not participate in this incident. The problem with these interpretations is that they accept Josephus's notion of the masses dropping everything for six days without there being any reaction from or involvement by other sections of Jewish society. Note other references in Josephus to Jewish protests against images, all of which indicate a broad base of outright rejection of any image of a living creature (*War* 1.648-55; *Ant.* 15.278; 17.149-67; 18.121-22; and *Life* 64–66).

version of the incident adds valuable information. Although there is reason to doubt the report that Herod's sons were central to the issue, reference is clearly made to the Jews being represented in negotiations with Pilate by particular people. We cannot conclusively substantiate the amalgamation of the narratives on this point. However, the other features of the account suggest that there was a special element in this incident that ensured the success of the Jewish cause.[1]

The final point regarding this incident concerns the status of Jerusalem and Caesarea. Pilate displays a preference for Caesarea as the suitable place from which to administer the province. Moreover, it appears that the population of Caesarea accepted the return of the standards to their city. Jerusalem was recognized as being more sacred than other areas in Palestine (*Ant.* 12.146). Outside Jerusalem, however, an anti-Gentile bias was less discernible in such cities as Caesarea.

b. *The Aqueduct*

We are reliant on the complementary accounts in *The Jewish War* and *Antiquities of the Jews.* As in the standards incident Pilate is the chief instigator and the protest involves the Jewish multitude, not a specific group within the population. Furthermore, Pilate's proposed method of dealing with the protest was similar, the only difference being that the Roman troops were disguised. These obvious parallels aside, there is one major difference between the incidents. The protest over the standards was peaceful throughout, while the aqueduct incident ended in violence.[2]

---

1. Obviously Agrippa I was keen to highlight any role played by his relatives. The failure of Josephus to refer to the presence of members of Agrippa I's family makes it uncertain whether we should accept Philo's version as being historically accurate. See Smallwood, *Jews under Roman Rule*, p. 166; Hoehner, *Herod*, p. 178; Maier, 'Episode', p. 116; and Doyle, 'Pilate's Career', p. 191, on the identity of these four sons. Furthermore, it is apparent that the leading men were the main feature. Smallwood (*Jews under Roman Rule*, p. 165 and *Philonis*, p. 304) claims that 'the leading men' should be equated with the sanhedrin, based on a belief that there was permanent governing body of the Jews. Note that Horsley ('High Priests', p. 37) explains the reference to these men as an exception to the normal practice. The request made by 'the first men' (οἱ πρῶτοι) of the Jewish community to Vitellius that he would not march through with military standards (*Ant.* 18.121-22) may support the notion that such a situation occurred when Pilate introduced the standards.

2. Within the account of the aqueduct incident in *War* and *Ant.* the only difference

The cause of the protest over the aqueduct was Pilate's use of money from the sacred treasury to help fund the project. Josephus does not mention that Pilate entered the Temple precinct to collect the money.[1] Although I cannot argue any definite case from the silence of Josephus on this point there are two plausible interpretations. First, the relevant influential Jewish priests agreed to hand over the money to Pilate. The aqueduct was intended to benefit the residents of Jerusalem. It is even possible that it helped supplement the needs of the Temple. Secondly, Pilate may have told the Jews that he was going to get the money one way or another and the relevant Jews decided to concede. Both interpretations hold important connotations regarding the incident. I will be better able to elaborate upon which of these suggestions is believable when all aspects of the incident have been examined.[2]

Another feature of this incident is the timing of the protest. Josephus states that it was on a visit to Jerusalem by Pilate that trouble began. The aqueduct was already under construction, if not completed. Pilate's journey to Jerusalem may have been connected with the aqueduct but the Jews who protested did not act spontaneously against the taking of money from the treasury. Furthermore, the complaints were lodged only when Pilate appeared in Jerusalem. The protesters did not take their case to Caesarea, as in the standards incident. The impression is that not all Jews believed immediate action was required, or that any sort of protest was necessary. Josephus appears to imply that not all Jerusalem Jews were involved (*Ant.* 18.62).

Some Jews, therefore, appear to have accepted the use of Temple

---

is in the length of the aqueduct. For a discussion of the length and location see Schürer, *History*, I, p. 385 n. 136; cf. Smallwood, *Jews under Roman Rule*, p. 162 n. 63.

1. Note Zeitlin, *Rise and Fall*, II, p. 143, and Smallwood, *Jews under Roman Rule*, p. 162 n. 65 on the origin of this money. If Smallwood is correct then it enhances the second interpretation.

2. Smallwood (*Jews under Roman Rule*, p. 162) proposes that violence or intimidation was necessary. There is, however, no suggestion in Josephus that Pilate forced his way into the Temple. Horsley (*Jesus*, p. 107) accepts that the Temple officials co-operated with Pilate. Note that incursions into the Temple were referred to by Josephus in terms of a major denigration of the Jewish faith. For example, see *War* 1.32; *Ant.* 12.248-50 regarding Antiochus Epiphanes IV; *War* 1.148-53; *Ant.* 14.71-73, regarding Pompey; *War* 1.354; *Ant.* 14.482-83 regarding Herod; and *War* 2.293-94 regarding Florus.

money for the aqueduct. This could, in turn, provide a partial explanation for the silence about how the money was acquired. Some may
have decided to acquiesce to Pilate's plan, causing a split that resulted
in a lack of support for the protest.[1] Pilate's willingness to use force
on this occasion may have been based on a belief that he was not faced
with a serious problem and could thus quickly stamp out the protest.[2]
Such a view was vindicated by the absence of any further protest.

Josephus appears to have a purpose in relating these two incidents
which is in addition to the simple presentation of the facts. To
Josephus, a passive united protest to protect the law would succeed.
Although his main concern may have been to highlight this principle,
it is possible to propose that another perspective of affairs in Judaea
may be discerned within these two incidents. The success or failure of
the protest depended as much on the identity of the participants as on
any other factor. It is possible in the incident concerning the standards
that Pilate was persuaded by the arguments of particular Jewish
representatives as much as by the willingness of the crowd to die.[3]
With the aqueduct, however, Pilate may have had the passive support
of a number of Jews.

In these circumstances it is understandable that Pilate believed
different solutions were appropriate. Furthermore, the acceptance of
Roman involvement in Jewish affairs was a complicated matter. On
certain occasions their assistance met with some approval, yet at other
times interference with particular customs was positively rejected.

---

1. Horsley ('High Priests', p. 36) suggests that the silence of Josephus regarding
the role of the Temple officials and aristocracy indicates their support for Pilate.
Whether their motivation was entirely self-interested or mixed with concern for the
good of Jerusalem is not possible to establish. Horsley (*Jesus*, p. 117) also claims
that the protest was organized entirely by 'ordinary people'.

2. Smallwood (*Philonis*, p. 304) and Stern ('Province of Judaea', p. 351)
believe that Pilate's attitude toward the Jews had hardened. Smallwood (*Jews under
Roman Rule*, p. 162) also notes that in Roman terms the use of religious money
would have been considered sacrilegious. Doyle ('Pilate's Career', p. 190) and
Kraeling ('Episode', pp. 296-97) claim that Lk. 13.1 should be linked with at least
one of these incidents; cf. Hoehner, *Herod*, p. 176, and Loftus, 'Anti-Roman
Revolts', p. 90 n. 50, who reject such a link.

3. Note Philo, *Leg. Gai.* 302-305. The reference to Tiberius appears to be the key
reason for Philo to mention the entire incident. In comparison with Gaius, Tiberius
was fair and humane.

3. *The Trial of Jesus.*

Mk 14.10, Jesus betrayed to 'the chief priests' (οἱ ἀρχιερεῖς), 43, high priest, 'the scribes' (οἱ γραμματεῖς) and 'the elders' (οἱ πρεσβύτεροι) send men to capture Jesus, 53, at house of the high priest, all 'chief priests', 'elders' and 'scribes' gather, 55, 'chief priests' and all the *synedrion* want Jesus condemned, 60-61, high priest questions Jesus, 64, high priest and others condemn Jesus, 15.1, morning, gathering of all 'chief priests', 'elders', 'scribes' and all the *synedrion* take Jesus to Pilate, 2, he questions Jesus, 3, 'chief priests' accuse Jesus before Pilate, 6, tradition of releasing a prisoner at festival, 11, 'chief priests' rouse crowd against Jesus, 26, inscription on cross, king of the Jews, 43, Joseph of Arimathaea, a member of the *boule*, requests Jesus' body.

Mt. 26.3, 'the chief priests' and 'the elders' of the people gather in Caiaphas's house, 4, to plot against Jesus, 14, Judas goes to 'chief priests', 47, high priest, 'the elders' of the people send men to arrest Jesus, 57, he is taken to the house of Caiphas, 'scribes' and 'elders' gather, 59, 'chief priests' and all the *synedrion* want Jesus condemned, 62-63, high priest questions Jesus, 27.1, morning, all 'chief priests', 'elders' of the people, 2, take Jesus to Pilate, 11, he questions Jesus, 12, 'chief priests' and 'elders' question Jesus, 15, custom of releasing a prisoner at festival, 20, 'chief priests' and 'elders' rouse crowd against Jesus, 37, inscription on the cross, king of the Jews, 57, Joseph of Arimathaea requests Jesus' body.

Lk. 22.4, Judas goes to 'the chief priests' and commanders, 52, Jesus addresses 'the chief priests', captain of the Temple and 'the elders' who came to arrest him, 54, Jesus taken to the high priest's house, 66, morning, all 'the elders of the people', 'chief priests' and 'the scribes' take Jesus to their *synedrion*, 70, high priest questions Jesus, 23.1, Jesus taken to Pilate, 2, he questions Jesus, 4, Pilate tells 'chief priests' that he finds no crime, 7, he sends Jesus to Herod, 10, 'chief priests' and 'scribes' accuse Jesus before Herod, 11, who returns Jesus to Pilate, 13, he calls together 'the chief priests', 'the rulers/magistrates' (οἱ ἄρχοντες), 38, inscription on cross, king of the Jews, 50, Joseph of Arimathaea, a member of the *boule* , 52, requests Jesus' body.

Jn 18.3, Judas, men from 'the chief priests' and Pharisees search for Jesus, 13, Jesus taken to house of Ananus by soldiers, 19, Ananus, the high priest questions Jesus, 24, Ananus sends Jesus to Caiaphas, 31, Pilate tells Jews to judge the case, they say they cannot put a man to death, 33, Pilate questions Jesus, 38, Pilate finds no crime, 19.6, 'chief priests' and soldiers ask Pilate to execute Jesus, 19, inscription on the cross, king of the Jews, 38, Joseph of Arimathaea, a disciple of Jesus, requests Jesus' body.

The arrest, trial and death of Jesus has evoked much interest and debate for a variety of historical, polemical and theological reasons. The incident took place in the middle period of Pilate's term as prefect of Judaea. The primary concern here remains consistent with the other incidents being assessed, namely an examination of the administration of affairs in Palestine. We are dependent on the Gospel narratives for accounts of the incident.[1] There are several differences in the four Passion narratives, varying in their significance for the confines of this study.[2] It is evident that Matthew and Mark present the most elaborate accounts while John is the most succinct. My intention here is not to engage in a detailed exposition of the various arguments advanced to proclaim the priority of one or another particular version of the incident.[3] It is probable that the Gospels drew on a common

1. J. Blinzler (*The Trial of Jesus* [Maryland: The Newman Press, 1959], pp. 22-32) states that Josephus and *b. Sanh.* 43a are not historically relevant for an examination of the trial of Jesus; cf. F.W. Beare, *The Gospel according to Matthew* (Oxford: Basil Blackwell, 1981), pp. 520-21. See also Robinson (*Priority*, p. 275), who uses *m. Sanh.* 4.1 and *b. Sanh.* 43a to support the argument that John is probably the most accurate account of the Passion.

2. For example, the night trial, the morning meeting of the *synedrion*, the hearing before Herod Antipas and the reference to Caiaphas and Ananus. Apart from these ostensible differences there appear to be important authorial distinctions. See Fitzmyer, *Luke*, pp. 1362-1365; G.S. Sloyan, 'The Last Days of Jesus', *Judaism* 20 (1971), p. 68; and S. Sandmel, 'The Trial of Jesus: Reservations', *Judaism* 20 (1971), p. 71. See also A.E. Harvey (*Jesus on Trial. A Study in the Fourth Gospel* [London: SPCK, 1976], p. 17), who argues that John's entire Gospel is, in part, an extended trial. Fitzmyer (*Luke*, p. 1455) warns that we should not regard the Gospel accounts as actual case records. Similarly, B.D. Ehrman ('Jesus' Trial before Pilate: John 18.28–19.16', *BTB* 13 [1983], pp. 124-31) suggests that John's account is recorded not for what happened but for what it signified or was perceived as signifying.

3. Much debate has taken place regarding the source(s) behind the extant versions of the trial. Some argue for a common source among the Synoptic Gospels. For example, see Flusser, 'Literary Approach', p. 32. Some argue for a link between the evangelists, proclaiming the primacy of Mark in which the other evangelists made several alterations as appropriate. See C.S. Mann, *Mark* (AB, 27; New York: Doubleday, 1986), p. 611; G. Schneider, 'The Political Charge Against Jesus (Luke 23.2)', in Bammel and Moule (eds.), *Jesus*, p. 414; S.G.F. Brandon, *The Trial of Jesus of Nazareth* (London: Batsford, 1968), p. 128; H. Conzelmann, *The Theology of St Luke* (trans. G. Buswell; London: Faber & Faber, 1960), p. 84; and Efron, *Studies*, p. 324. Other scholars argue that changes may have been due to the use of different sources. See Catchpole, 'Historicity', pp. 54, 65; R.E. Brown, *The Gospel according to John (XIII–XXI)* (AB, 29a; New York: Doubleday, 1970),

understanding of how Jesus met his death. Although it is possible that more than one original account of the events associated with Jesus' death existed, and that the extant versions underwent several layers of amplification or adaptation to the specific requirements of their scribes, all the material is based on one particular event.

Two important observations guide the manner in which the record of Jesus' arrest and trial should be assessed. First, it is not possible to establish any one particular account of the incident as definitely being the earliest. Secondly, the accounts do not agree on all aspects of what happened during this incident. I have not attempted, therefore, to establish that a particular account of the incident presents the historical 'truth' more accurately than the others. Instead, the trial of Jesus has been examined in exactly the same manner as that used with the other incidents incorporated in this study. The four accounts of this incident are compared with one another. The aim is to establish the common elements in the accounts and to question what specific details are relevant to the historical event. On this basis three aspects of the narrative are assessed in detail: the identity of the participants; establishing who performed what action; and the possible motive(s) behind these actions. I will then comment on the proceedings taken against Jesus and its relevance to the administration of Palestine.

I commence by outlining the participants.[1] The information can be

---

p. 128; and R.T. Fortna, 'Jesus and Peter at the High Priest's House: A Test Case for the Question of the Relation Between Mark's and John's Gospels', *NTS* 24 (1978), p. 379. There is also some argument regarding whether there was one original tradition that was drawn upon. See M.A. Beavis, 'The Trial before the Sanhedrin (Mark 14.53-65): Reader Response and Greco-Roman Readers', *CBQ* 49 (1987), p. 583; Fortna,'Jesus and Peter', pp. 382-83; Beare, *Matthew*, p. 500; K. Schubert, 'Biblical Criticism Criticized: with Reference to the Markan Report of Jesus' Examination before the Sanhedrin', in Bammel and Moule (eds.), *Jesus*, p. 401; and M.J. Cook, *Mark's Treatment of the Jewish Leaders* (NovTSup, 51; Leiden: Brill, 1978), pp. 78-79. While accepting that the extant records reflect a variety of influences and interests (see Beare, *Matthew*, p. 523, and D. Hill, 'Jesus Before the Sanhedrin–On What Charge?', *IBS* 7 [1985], pp. 174-76) and may be the result of more than one version of the incident, there is no reason to doubt that they all relate to a historical event. The intention here is not to claim the historical reliability of any one particular version. Any such findings will be a subsidiary consequence of seeking to highlight the significance of the incident in terms of the administration of affairs in Palestine.

1. The following outline will focus our attention on whom the evangelists wanted their readers to notice as being involved. A conclusion regarding the participants,

divided into three sub-divisions: those people of whose involvement we can be certain; those we can consider as probable participants; and those about whom we remain uncertain. Prominent among the first sub-division are 'the chief priests'. These men feature in each account. Furthermore, the serving high priest, Caiaphas, was associated with this group.[1]

The evangelists are certain about the identity of two other participants. The first of these is Pilate, the prefect of Judaea. Pilate's presence in Jerusalem may have been connected with a concern to oversee the Passover festival. The Gospels also agree that Joseph of Arimathaea participated. There is some divergence regarding his status. Matthew remains silent while John describes him as a disciple. Luke and Mark, however, claim that he was a member of the *boule*. It appears that the evangelists are referring to a civic institution which they believed existed, the membership of which was not limited to residents of Jerusalem.[2]

The main group in the second sub-division, the people who probably participated, might best be described as associates of the chief priests. The exact identity of these people is uncertain. In the Synoptic Gospels these men are called 'elders', 'rulers' and 'scribes'.[3] John alone mentions Pharisees, and this reference is only made once. This divergence between John and the Synoptic Gospels and the variety of terms used by Matthew, Mark and Luke is difficult to account for. In part the sources used may be responsible. Similarly,

however, will not be possible until we have considered the identity of who is actually said to do something.

1. S. Westerholm (*Jews and Scribal Authority* [Lund: Gleerup, 1978], p. 45) uses Mk 14.55-56 to argue that the high priest was head of the sanhedrin.

2. Efron (*Studies*, p. 325) believes that Joseph was a member of the Jerusalem city council; he should not be linked with 'the sanhedrin' of the Gospels that allegedly tried Jesus. Tcherikover ('Was Jerusalem a Polis?', p. 69) also accepts that Joseph was a member of the city council. It must be acknowledged that we cannot entirely dismiss the possibility that the reference was to a *boule* in Arimathaea.

3. Matthew and Luke use 'elders' (οἱ πρεσβύτεροι)/'elders' of the people. It appears that the same group of people are referred to in both texts, that is, influential laymen. They were, however, separate from 'the scribes'. See Cook, *Mark's Treatment*, pp. 78-79. Westerholm, (*Scribal Authority*, p. 43) claims that 'the elders' and 'chief priests' of Mt. 26.3 should be equated with members of the sanhedrin. Such a claim is without substantiation. L. Morris (*The Gospel according to St Luke* [Leicester: Inter-Varsity Press, 1974], p. 314) states that the elders were lay members of the sanhedrin.

the use of authorial licence by the Synoptic writers to apportion the blame for Jesus' death among prominent Jews and, conversely, John's concentration of the blame, may be pertinent. It is even possible that the evangelists did not fully comprehend the situation in mid-first century AD Jerusalem. Irrespective of the explanation, these men were distinguishable from 'the chief priests', achieving prominence as non-priests. What distinction should be made between 'the scribes' and the other prominent lay participants is unclear. Furthermore, how the Pharisees related to the members of the laity mentioned in the Synoptic Gospels is uncertain.[1] Further clarification regarding these lay participants may be possible when we consider the role played by various people in the incident.

Two individuals belong to this second sub-division. The captain of the Temple and the high priest's father-in-law are each mentioned by name in only one account, the former by Luke and the latter by John. There is no reason to doubt that the captain was involved, at least in the arrest of Jesus. Similarly, it is plausible that Caiaphas's father-in-law was among those Jews seeking to find a means to remove Jesus.

The final sub-division incorporates the people and institutions whose participation remains uncertain. Herod Antipas is mentioned only in Luke's version. Nothing in his account indicates that Herod did not participate. Uncertainty also remains regarding the references to the *synedrion*. John does not include the *synedrion* in the proceedings. Matthew combines the *synedrion* with the 'chief priests' and draws a distinction between the two. Mark separates the *synedrion* from the 'chief priests', 'elders', and 'scribes'. Luke, on the other hand, refers to *their synedrion*, suggesting that *synedrion* did not denote one specific institution.[2] Matthew and Mark appear to believe there was a

---

1. Whether 'the scribes' should be equated with the Pharisees is uncertain. See E.P. Sanders, *Jesus*, p. 318; J.A. Ziesler, 'Luke and the Pharisees', *NTS* 25 (1978/9), pp. 146-57; and Cook, 'Mark's Treatment', p. 96. Smallwood (*Jews under Roman Rule*, p. 163) assumes that the Pharisees were involved in the trial. The Herodians may have been another group who opposed Jesus (Mk 3.6). The exact relationship of these references to the historical situation are questioned by the argument of J.D. Kingsbury, 'The Religious Authorities of Mark', *NTS* 36 (1990), pp. 54-56. He indicates that Mark structures his account to unify and intensify the conflict between Jesus and the 'authorities'.

2. Note the Lukan usage of *synedrion* as a reference to a place. See Chapter 3, section 5. There is also debate regarding the number of meetings. See J. Blinzler, 'The Trial of Jesus in the Light of History', *Judaism* 20 (1971), p. 54, who argues

formal Jewish trial against Jesus, which they describe with the term *synedrion*. This, however, is despite the separation of the *synedrion* from the other participants. Luke and John move away from such a stance, although the former probably believes there was a formal gathering.[1]

The other uncertain element in the narrative is the relevance of the Jewish populace. The story associated with Barabbas is not one that can be supported or refuted. Its value to the Passion narrative in theological terms is apparent, but we are not able to comment on its historicity.[2] Crowds probably did gather, but clarification of their involvement, and that of Herod and the *synedrion*, would depend on establishing who was responsible for performing what action.

'The chief priests' are portrayed as being central to all Jewish initiatives.[3] It was 'the chief priests', including the serving high priest,

for one Jewish and one Roman hearing. Morris (*Luke*, p. 317) and R.A. Cole (*The Gospel according to Mark* [Leicester: Inter-Varsity Press, 1961], p. 272) are examples of those who accept the notion of an evening and morning meeting.

1. Catchpole ('Historicity', p. 54) believes that the divergences do not threaten the historicity of the trial before the sanhedrin.

2. There has been much discussion of the Privilegium Paschale, without any clear conclusion arising. Few scholars dispute the theological significance of the Barabbas pericope. For example, see R.L. Merritt, 'Jesus, Barabbas and the Paschal Pardon', *JBL* 104 (1985), p. 68; Beare, *Matthew*, p. 529; and S.G.F. Brandon, 'The Trial of Jesus', *Judaism*, 20 (1971), p. 48. For those who accept the tradition as historical, see E. Bammel, 'The Trial Before Pilate', in Bammel and Moule (eds.), *Jesus*, p. 427; F.F. Bruce, *New Testament History* (London: Oliphants, rev. edn, 1971), p. 193; Flusser, 'Literary Approach', p. 35; Merritt, 'Jesus, Barabbas', p. 59; and Cole, *Mark*, pp. 234-35. For those who doubt the tradition, see P. Winter, *On the Trial of Jesus* (Berlin: de Gruyter, 1961), p. 99; W.F. Albright and C.S. Mann, *Matthew* (AB, 26; New York: Doubleday, 1971), p. 344; S. Zeitlin, *Who Crucified Jesus?* (New York: Harper & Brothers, 2nd edn, 1947), p. 156; H. Cohn, 'Reflections on the Trial of Jesus', *Judaism* 20 (1971), p. 14; Beare, *Matthew*, p. 529; F. Watson, 'Why Was Jesus Crucified?, *Theology* 88 (1985), p. 106; and R. Gordis, 'The Trial of Jesus in the Light of History', *Judaism* 20 (1971), p. 7.

3. Goodman (*Ruling Class*, p. 115) takes this approach. See also E.P. Sanders, *Jesus*, pp. 310-11, 318, on the prominence of 'the chief priests'. R.J. Cassidy (*Society and Politics in the Acts of the Apostles* [New York: Orbis Books, 1987], pp. 69-70) argues for the enmity between 'the chief priests' and Jesus. Note also the people listed as being involved in earlier attempts to oppose Jesus and the forewarnings of what was to happen to him. In Mt. 20.18 'the chief priests' and 'scribes' are mentioned and in Mt. 16.21, Mk 8.31, Lk. 9.22 reference is made to 'chief priests', 'elders', and 'scribes'. Of the people who are recorded as opposing

who organized Jesus' arrest. These men proceeded to question Jesus under the leadership of the serving high priest and possibly his father-in-law. These two individuals, may have acted as the leading spokesmen among the Jewish protagonists. Having questioned Jesus and prepared their strategy, 'the chief priests' take Jesus to Pilate and then negotiate with him to ensure that Jesus is executed.

In their efforts 'the chief priests' appear to have been supported by other like-minded men. Thus, it was the captain of the Temple, mentioned by Luke, who headed the party that arrested Jesus.[1] Where some doubt must remain is the role played by other Jews. I have noted John's silence as opposed to the numerous references to 'elders', 'rulers' and 'scribes' in the Synoptic accounts. These people, primarily acting as the influential among the laity, probably joined in the actions against Jesus. At no stage, however, do the Synoptic Gospels mention these people alone initiating action; they are always listed as being in league with 'the chief priests'.

The other participant who was central to the outcome of the incident was Pilate. He ordered the execution of Jesus.[2] For whatever reason, Pilate accepted the arguments put forward by 'the chief priests

Jesus earlier in his career it is notable that 'chief priests' were predominant. Pharisees and Herodians joined 'the chief priests' and 'the elders' and 'scribes' in challenging Jesus. See Mt. 21.15, 23, 45; 22.15, 16, 23; Mk 3.6; 11.18, 27; 12.13; Lk. 13.41; 19.47; 20.1, 19; 22.2; Jn 7.32; 8.3; 11.47; 12.57. Note that in John the Pharisees take a prominent role in the narrative regarding the early challenges to Jesus.

1. M.S. Enslin ('The Temple and the Cross', *Judaism* 20 [1971], p. 25) and Blinzler (*Trial*, p. 70) argue that it was Jews who arrested Jesus. Whether they were in the service of 'the highest native authority', the sanhedrin, as suggested by Blinzler is debatable. Zeitlin (*Who Crucified Jesus?*, p. 153) believes that John is correct in claiming that Jews and Romans arrested Jesus. He does not explain why Jews took charge of the incident if Romans were involved in the arrest. It is important that 'the chief priests' and their associates were able to gather a crowd to arrest Jesus. Having the support of the captain of the Temple appears to have enabled these Jews to engage in their quest.

2. See Fitzmyer, *Luke*, p. 1489; E.P. Sanders, *Jesus*, p. 318; and Efron, *Studies*, p. 323. Bilde (*Flavius Josephus*, p. 224) argues that Pilate in the New Testament is a 'crypto-Christian Nicodemus type'. Smallwood (*Jews under Roman Rule*, p. 169) and Morris (*Luke*, p. 322) argue that Pilate submitted to Jewish pressure; cf. C.H. Giblin, 'John's Narration of the Hearing Before Pilate (John 18.28–19.16a)', *Bib* 67 (1986), p. 238. P.E. Guillet ('Entrée en scène de Pilate', *CCER* 24 [1977], pp. 1-24) even claims that Pilate was an addition to the original tradition, while Efron (*Studies*, p. 321) believes that Matthew did much to relieve Pilate of the blame for Jesus' death.

and their associates'. Jesus was executed by the Romans as a criminal who allegedly disrupted the status quo of Roman Judaea.[1]

Although the exact details of how 'the chief priests', their associates and Pilate interacted are not possible to establish conclusively, the general pattern is discernible. Jews with a high public standing in the Jerusalem community combined to oppose Jesus. Most prominent were 'the chief priests', whose leading spokesman appears to have been the serving high priest. These people organized the arrest of Jesus. The subsequent questioning of Jesus was probably not intended to establish his guilt or innocence. What was at issue was either how these people were to proceed against Jesus, or simply their desire to confirm their original intentions.[2] These Jews then sought the assistance of Pilate to put an end to Jesus' activities. The incident was quickly completed; Jesus was apparently arrested on one day and executed on the next. It appears that the Jewish protagonists knew what they wanted to do and how to achieve their aim without too much difficulty.

It is possible to suppose that Herod was involved. Pilate may have decided to allow Herod to hear the case as it involved one of his own subjects. Such a scenario, however, is of little relevance in historical terms. The theological reasons for introducing the hearing before

---

1. On whether crucifixion was a form of Roman and/or Jewish punishment see Fitzmyer, 'Crucifixion in Ancient Palestine, Qumran Literature and the New Testament', *CBQ* 40 (1978), p. 498; cf. M. Hengel, *Crucifixion* (trans. J. Bowden; London: SCM Press, 1977), p. 85; J.G. Sobosan, 'The Trial of Jesus', *JES* 10 (1973), p. 84; E. Bammel, 'Crucifixion as a Punishment in Palestine', in Bammel (ed.), *Trial*, p. 164; and Winter, *Trial*, p. 66. A number of scholars have interpreted the incident in terms of who was responsible for Jesus' death in a moral sense. It is in this framework that Zeitlin (*Who Crucified Jesus?*, p. 154), Mantel (*Studies*, p. 288) and Rivkin (*What Crucified Jesus?*, pp. 74-75) argue. E. Bammel ('Trial Before Pilate', pp. 428, 435, 445) claims that it was the Jews who executed Jesus, while Pilate only decided whether it was expedient for Jesus to receive Roman punishment; cf. Conzelmann, *Theology*, p. 87, and E.P. Sanders, *Jesus*, p. 318. Cohn ('Reflections', p. 12) argues that the Jews played no part in the Roman trial. Enslin ('Temple', p. 29) notes that the Jews were not quislings; cf. Mann (*Mark*, p. 611), who states that there is no evidence of official Jewish condemnation.

2. A remark in Mt. 27.1 may add a further insight here. Although we cannot be certain of its historical relevance, he follows the idea that the initial action was undertaken by a section of 'the chief priests'. In other words, it is possible that not all 'chief priests' and their associates were originally involved, necessitating a gathering of them to act in unity.

Herod are apparent. Although we cannot dismiss the story outright, its inclusion is of little significance for the final outcome of the incident.[1] Similarly, possible theological interests make it difficult to confirm what role, if any, a crowd played in the incident. It appears that only a small section of the community was actively involved throughout the proceedings. Whether those people represented, and were supported by, the larger corpus of the Jewish community remains debatable.

Of more significance is the use of *synedrion* in the Synoptic Gospels. Whether or not a formal Jewish trial took place, all that transpired among the Jews was under the guidance of 'the chief priests'. We cannot dismiss the fact that Matthew and Mark believe there was a formal Jewish trial, nor that Luke recognizes the existence of a meeting of some description. It is, however, incorrect to confuse this with any arguments regarding the existence of one or two permanent councils in Jerusalem.[2]

1. H. Hoehner ('Why Did Pilate Hand Jesus over to Antipas?', in Bammel [ed.], *Trial*, p. 90), Morris (*Luke*, p. 320) and Blinzler (*Trial*, p. 203) accept the story as historically accurate; cf. Conzelmann, *Theology*, p. 86; M.L. Soards, 'Tradition, Composition, and Theology in Luke's Account of Jesus Before Herod Antipas', *Bib* 66 (1985), pp. 358, 363; and P.W. Walaskay, 'The Trial and Death of Jesus in the Gospel of Luke', *JBL* 94 (1975), pp. 88-89. Even Blinzler (*Trial*, p. 203) acknowledges that the story is of little relevance regarding the final outcome of the trial. Sherwin-White (*Roman Society*, pp. 22-23, 31) points out that Pilate was under no obligation to send Jesus to Herod.

2. See Mantel (*Studies*, pp. 268, 288), Zeitlin (*Who Crucified Jesus?*, p. 165) and Rivkin (*What Crucified Jesus?*, p. 64), who argue that it was the political *synedrion*, not the religious sanhedrin that tried Jesus. Similar to Rivkin is Winter (*Trial*, p. 14) on the role of the sanhedrin. Note that Mantel and Zeitlin are in dispute regarding whether the proceedings were legitimate. Blinzler (*Trial*, p. 290) concludes that the Jews followed Sadducean law. Brown (*John*, p. 797) is probably correct in arguing that we cannot comment on the proceedings in any detail. Similarly, Beare (*Matthew*, p. 519) states that the evangelists were not concerned with the legal proceedings of the case. Other interpretations have been presented regarding the intention of the sanhedrin's meeting. For example, see Cohn, 'Reflections', pp. 16-17; Cole, *Mark*, p. 225; and J.E. Allen, 'Why Pilate?', in Bammel (ed.), *Trial*, p. 82. For those who uphold the historicity of a formal sanhedrin trial see Catchpole, 'Historicity', pp. 58-59; J.C. O'Neill, 'The Charge of Blasphemy at Jesus' Trial before the Sanhedrin', in Bammel (ed.), *Trial*, p. 72; Hill, 'Sanhedrin', p. 178; Sobosan, 'Trial', p. 80; and Blinzler, *Trial*, p. 122. Fitzmyer (*Luke*, p. 1463) accepts that the sanhedrin had a role in the incident. Kennard ('Assembly', p. 50) believes that we should only speak in terms of a Jewish indictment , while Beare (*Matthew*, p. 519) concludes that it is difficult to determine whether Jesus appeared before the sanhedrin. Robinson (*Priority*, p. 254) argues

It is important to acknowledge that the execution of Jesus was instigated by a powerful, select group of Jews. The action was formal and legitimate because the Jewish protagonists were influential men of high public standing, able to manipulate the situation to their advantage, and obtaining Roman support. This sense of 'legality' appears to have been misconstrued by Matthew and Mark. A lack of understanding combined with an overriding theological concern to lay formal blame on the 'Jewish establishment' leave these Gospel accounts presenting the incident as dominated by a formal Jewish trial. The *synedrion* is a trial court in this instance.[1] There is no doubt that the principle of holding trials existed in Judaea and was put into practice whenever necessary. Knowledge of this principle may have been transformed by Matthew and Mark into the notion of a formal court case by Jews who held a permanent official position.[2] Moreover, the evangelists may have viewed Jesus as being in conflict with the same elements of Jewish society, resulting in the tendency to perceive those people as a permanent official fixture in the Jewish community.

The final aspect of the incident that requires some comment is the motivation behind the actions taken. Unfortunately, the reasoning behind what 'the chief priests', their associates and Pilate did is extremely difficult to ascertain.[3] In part this is because we are

that we should not follow Matthew and Mark regarding the notion of a Jewish trial. Throughout all this discussion there is no doubt expressed regarding the existence of a permanent formal institution referred to in Greek as *synedrion*. At issue for these scholars is which representative council it was. Note also Jn 11.47-53 where it was the chief priests and Pharisees who summoned together the *synedrion*.

1. Although Bosker claims that *synedrion* is used as a common noun he accepts the existence of the great sanhedrin. See Sobosan, 'Trial', p. 80, who refers to B.Z. Bosker, *Judaism and the Christian Predicament* (New York: Alfred A. Knoff, 1967), pp. 226-27. J.T. Sanders (*The Jews in Luke–Acts* [London: SCM Press, 1987], p. 221) argues that Luke generally uses *synedrion* in terms of a place.

2. Efron (*Studies*, p. 327) appears to be correct in placing the reference to the *synedrion* in Christian apologetic concerns. See also E.P. Sanders, *Jesus*, p. 317 n. 73, where he highlights the question of whether a trial was actually necessary. Note Flusser, 'Literary Approach', pp. 33-34, who views the gathering of the Jews against Jesus as a Temple committee. His basis for such a conclusion is questionable. The assumed link between Pharisees and the sanhedrin is unsubstantiated. Zeitlin (*Who Crucified Jesus?*, pp. 170-71) also argues along similar lines to refute the idea that Jesus was tried by the religious sanhedrin.

3. As suggested by E.P. Sanders, *Jesus*, p. 299. Many scholars believe it is possible to make conclusions about the timetable and components of the incident. Despite this belief it is apparent that consensus has yet to be reached. Central to much

dependent on particular Christian interpretations of what happened.[1] Despite this limitation it does appear that 'the chief priests' and their associates were responding to a perceived threat. The teachings and actions of Jesus, especially regarding the Temple, were probably viewed as a challenge to the established order.[2] This situation was treated seriously because prominent Jews believed their influence was under threat from Jesus and from the possible response of the Romans if order was not maintained by the Jews.[3]

Once it was decided that action was necessary, what remained was to determine how to deal with Jesus. The solution was to involve Pilate. How this was achieved probably lay in the presentation of Jesus as a troublemaker, allegedly gaining public support in the guise of the king of the Jews to usurp the established public order. 'The chief priests' and associates publicly rejected Jesus. Irrespective of any possible manipulation in terminology by the Jews, Pilate was willing

of the discussion regarding the charge against Jesus has been the assumption that it is correct to distinguish between political and religious affairs. There is no evidence to justify such a division. Note E.P. Sanders, *Jesus*, p. 296. See Winter, *Trial*, p. 109, on the use of the titulus as a basis for reaching a conclusion regarding the charge; cf. E. Bammel, 'The *titulus*', in Bammel and Moule (eds.), *Jesus*, pp. 363-64. Conzelmann (*Theology*, p. 86), O'Neill, ('Trial', p. 77) and Zeitlin (*Who Crucified Jesus?*, pp. 160-61) refer to Jesus as a religious messiah figure.

1. Against the general trend some scholars have pointed out that the evangelists should not be read at face value when describing the charge against Jesus. For example, J.T. Sanders (*The Jews*, p. 222) argues that Luke purposefully omitted reference to a blasphemy charge in an attempt to highlight the idea that Jesus died as the result of false political charges. Also see Schneider, 'Political Charge', pp. 408-409; P.W. Walaskay, *And So We Came to Rome* (Cambridge: Cambridge University Press, 1983), pp. 39, 42, 44-45, 87, 93; and Conzelmann, *Theology*, p. 85. Brandon (*Trial*, p. 140) argues that Mark introduced a version of the trial sympathetic to Gentile Christian needs. Note that the issues of earlier open disputes between Jesus and members of the Jewish community were matters of Jewish beliefs and their practical application.

2. See E.P. Sanders, *Jesus*, pp. 302-304.

3. A number of scholars highlight the alleged threat posed by Jesus. For example, see Enslin, 'Temple', p. 27; Morris, *Luke*, p. 319; and Watson, 'Crucifixion', p. 109. Winter (*Trial*, p. 135) also notes the possible effect of Jesus' popularity; cf. Mantel (*Studies*, p. 273), who sees no offence in what Jesus said or did regarding the Temple. It is possible that popular appeal arising from the story of the raising of Lazarus (Jn 11.38-45) caused the Jewish authorities to seek the removal of Jesus. See also Horsley, *Jesus*, pp. 324-25, who concludes that Jesus was a social revolutionary.

3. *Direct Roman Rule:* AD 6–41 99

to remove Jesus.[1] Rather than view Pilate as a 'puppet' in the hands of 'the chief priests', it is conceivable that he and 'the chief priests' acted in league.[2] The presence in Jerusalem of a man who openly opposed by words and deeds the established order of affairs and had gained some public sympathy was likely to anger those Jews who were interested in maintaining the balance of power.[3] Whether Jesus was concerned with spiritual and/or temporal matters, his message

1. Here we break from the rigid framework which has dominated much of the past scholarly debate. The question was not whether Jesus was blasphemous, nor whether this was presented in terms of a political offence, as suggested by Blinzler (*Trial*, p. 111), Bruce (*History*, p. 189), Smallwood (*Jews under Roman Rule*, p. 169), Hill ('Sanhedrin', p. 184), Harvey (*Jesus on Trial*, pp. 4-5), Morris (*Luke*, p. 319), B. Reicke ('Judaeo-Christianity and the Jewish Establishment, AD 33–66', in Bammel and Moule [eds.], *Jesus*, p. 145) and Kennard ('Assembly', p. 51). Note Sherwin-White, *Roman Society*, pp. 22-23, who has pointed out that the Roman prefect did not require a formal charge to execute a non-citizen. However, he proceeds to explain (pp. 45-47) that the sanhedrin condemned Jesus for blasphemy and then turned to Pilate on political grounds. A similar view is held by R.L. Overstreet ('Roman Law and the Trial of Christ', *Bibliotheca Sacra* 135 [1978], pp. 323-32). See E.P. Sanders, *Jesus*, p. 317 n. 73. What was important was that Pilate had to be given a reason for executing Jesus, not necessarily a formal charge. This reason may have been based on a fear of a loss of independence by the Jews, as presented by Winter (*Trial*, p. 43) and W. Grundmann ('The Decision of the Supreme Court to Put Jesus to Death (John 11.47-57) in its Context: Tradition and Redaction in the Gospel of John', in Bammel and Moule [eds.], *Jesus*, pp. 295-318. Horsley (*Jesus*, p. 161), as part of an attempt to reject notions of Jesus as a violent radical, notes that the civil nature of the charges was justified because Jesus had pronounced judgment on the existing social order. See also Rivkin (*What Crucified Jesus?*, pp. 64-65).

2. See Efron, *Studies*, p. 324. In these circumstances establishing whether Pilate believed Jesus was a political or religious criminal is not relevant. See Zeitlin, *Who Crucified Jesus?*, p. 166; Cohn, 'Reflections', p. 11; Bammel 'The Trial before Pilate?', p. 418, who suggests that Pilate did not investigate the charge; and Sherwin-White, *Roman Society*, p. 32.

3. See R.M. Grant, 'Trial of Jesus in the Light of History', *Judaism* 20 (1971), p. 38. There is no reason to doubt the evangelists in the sense that the Jews initiated the action against Jesus. Brown (*John*, p. 802) may be correct in claiming that the motivation for Jewish action combined genuine and selfish reasons. Note, however, that Brown (pp. 799-800) follows the notion of a clear division existing between religion and politics. There is no reason to follow Brandon (*Trial*, p. 140) that Jesus was actually the leader of a revolutionary party, despite the willingness of several scholars to claim the political nature of the charge as the reason for Jesus' death. See Winter, *Trial*, p. 50; Allen, 'Why Pilate?', p. 83; Kennard, 'Assembly', pp. 48-50; Smallwood, *Jews under Roman Rule*, p. 168; and Mantel, *Studies*, pp. 286-87, who is eager to remove Jesus' death from the realm of Jewish jurisdiction.

certainly roused the anger of the influential Jews.

One issue which it is not possible to resolve is why Pilate was involved. John appears to provide an overt clue, stating that the Jews were legally unable to execute Jesus. The historical relevance of John's statement is debatable.[1] Although the evangelists present the Jews as actively wanting to try and execute Jesus it is conceivable that the Jews did not hold any such plans. 'The chief priests' and their associates believed that Jesus should be removed, but they purpose-fully chose to call on Pilate. While it is possible that Jews could not decide in capital cases, it is also plausible that, in order to dispel overt criticism of them from any quarter, Jesus was presented to Pilate as a public troublemaker who opposed the status quo.[2] They were aware that in such circumstances Pilate would be guaranteed to act, reducing

---

1. In conjunction with other references to trials in the New Testament many scholars claim that the Jews were unable to try and execute people. See Stern, 'Province of Judaea', p. 337; R.M. Grant, 'Trial of Jesus', p. 39; and Efron, *Studies*, p. 324. Other scholars dilute this stance, accepting that Jews could try but could not execute in religious cases. For example, see Catchpole, 'Historicity', p. 59; Sherwin-White, *Roman Society*, p. 40; Brown, *John*, p. 850; Blinzler, 'The Trial', p. 53; Hill, 'Sanhedrin', p. 178; and Smallwood, *Jews under Roman Rule*, p. 150. As a result, it is necessary for these scholars to present Jesus' trial in religious and political terms. Another approach is that the Jews could try and execute in religious cases. See Winter, *Trial*, pp. 10, 88-89, who argues that Jn 18.31 is historically irrelevant. Similarly, E. Bickerman ('Utilitas Crucis', in *Studies in Jewish and Christian History*, Part 3 [ed. E. Bickerman; Leiden: Brill, 1986], pp. 122, 130-31) argues that Jn 18.31 was part of a theological explanation for how Jesus was executed by the Romans. See also Zeitlin, *Jesus and the Judaism of His Time* (Cambridge: Polity Press, 1988), p. 155, who claims that Jn 18.31 meant that Jesus' case was political; Robinson, *Priority*, pp. 255-57; and Cohn, 'Reflections', p. 10. Still further, see Allen, 'Why Pilate?', p. 78, who claims that the Jews could try Jesus but that Jn 18.31 indicates they were unable to find him guilty. Bruce (*History*, p. 190) points out that the question of capital jurisdiction was not of any particular relevance to this case. Note also that the Jews could not punish Jesus at this particular time of the year because of religious purity laws regarding festivals (*m. Sanh.* 4.1; 5.5). See St Augustine, *In Johannis Evangelium*, Tractatus CXXIV.4 (Corpus Christianorum, Series Latina, 36; Turnholti: Typograhi Brepols Editores, 1954) (cf. CXXIV.5). It is possible that the Jews made reference to this regulation in their negotiations with Pilate. J. Ramsay Michaels ('John 18.31 and the "Trial" of Jesus', *NTS* 36 [1990], p. 477) views Jn 18.31 within the broader context of John as a whole. He concludes that it is part of an underlying criticism of the Jews for attempting to remove Jesus throughout his public ministry.

2. This should not be viewed as support of Brandon's thesis that Jesus was a political rebel with a large popular following.

the official responsibility of 'the chief priests'.

To conclude, the outline that we are able to construct from the common elements of the accounts indicates that certain prominent Jews, especially 'the chief priests', enlisted the assistance of Pilate to remove a perceived threat to their status. The action was construed as being formal simply because the people involved had the ability to achieve their aim. Furthermore, the references to the *synedrion* are a Christian embellishment. The evangelists are not aware of the exact charge laid against Jesus, if there was one, and they do not seek to make a distinction between religion and politics. A public threat to certain people's status, based on doctrinal differences, was readily expressed in terms which suggested that the established temporal order was threatened.

Four observations regarding the administration can be derived from this incident. First, the prefect became involved in a Jewish dispute. Prominent members of the Jewish community wished to dispose of Jesus, an aim they achieved by convincing Pilate that Jesus was dangerous. Jesus' accusers probably acted to preserve the status quo of Jewish life under the veil of Roman supervision out of both genuine conviction and self-interest, if such a distinction is warranted.

Secondly, this incident does not clarify whether the Jews had the ability to try and execute people in the mid-first century AD. The gathering of men to question Jesus before he was taken to Pilate probably sought to confirm their approach in dealing with the matter. There is no reason to assume, however, that the Jews actually wanted to take responsibility for trying Jesus, despite the intentions of Matthew and Mark. It is, therefore, not appropriate to view the incident in terms of the extent of Jewish judicial independence.

Thirdly, 'the chief priests' and influential laymen were involved in this incident. They were united under the supervision of 'the chief priests'. Furthermore, within 'the chief priests' there existed an inner hierarchy. The serving high priest, possibly accompanied by a previous high priest, participated as the leading spokesman of Jesus' opponents.

Finally, the use of *synedrion* in the narrative of this incident is not of special historical significance. The term referred to a trial court. The evangelists, especially Matthew and Mark, may have believed that some type of formal Jewish trial occurred. Their narrative, however, suggests that there was no such formal trial before Jesus' execution.

4. *First Hearing against Peter and John*

Acts 4.1, priests, captain of the Temple and Sadducees, 3, arrest Peter
and John, 5, next day, 'the rulers/magistrates' (οἱ ἄρχοντες), 'the
elders' (οἱ πρεσβύτεροι) and 'the scribes' (οἱ γραμματεῖς) assemble, 6,
Ananus, Caiaphas, John and Alexander and others of 'the chief priests'
(οἱ ἀρχιερῖς)/high priest's family, 7, question the apostles, 8, Peter
addresses 'rulers/magistrates' of the people and 'elders' 15, Peter and
John leave the *synedrion*, 18, they are told not to speak about Jesus, 21,
and warned, 23, they then tell their associates of what 'the chief priests'
and 'elders' said to them.

On the basis that the hearing post-dated the death of Jesus and
preceded the death of Stephen this incident took place in the middle of
the AD 30s, while Pilate was prefect of Judaea and Caiaphas was high
priest. Detailed comment is necessary on the identity of the apostles'
opponents. In the two stages of the incident, the arrest and the
hearing, Luke mentions a variety of people.

Priests, Sadducees and the captain of the Temple are connected
with the arrest. Later, in the hearing, Luke refers to 'rulers',[1]
'elders', 'scribes' and 'chief priests'. Within this incident, therefore,
all bar one of the groups connected with the prosecution of Jesus are
named. There are several complications: first, the involvement of
certain people at one stage of the incident but not the other; secondly,
the lack of consistency in the reference to the people involved in the
hearing.

It is possible that the people associated with the arrest of the apostles
were in league with those who tried Peter and John. Whether 'the
chief priests', 'rulers', 'elders' and 'scribes' were all involved in the
hearing is debatable. The reference to 'rulers' and 'scribes' may be a
reflection of the historical situation. On the other hand, it may simply

---

1. 'Rulers/magistrates' and 'rulers/magistrates' of the people are probably
variations of the same group. Such variation may be due to a lack of understanding
regarding the exact identity of the participants, the sources used or simply authorial
licence. Within the context of this incident it appears that Luke uses the term to refer
to the more general 'rulers', describing influential laymen. Note I.H. Marshall, *The
Acts of the Apostles* (Leicester: Inter-Varsity Press, 1980), pp. 98-99, who suggests
that the Sadducees were lay people assisting the priests and that 'the rulers', 'elders'
and 'scribes' represented the three elements of the *synedrion*. J.T. Sanders (*The
Jews*, p. 238) argues that the original source intended to highlight the presence of
priests.

reflect the author's desire to indicate the overwhelming nature of the 'official' opposition to the apostles.[1]

It is 'the chief priests' who have the leading role in the prosecution of the case. They question the apostles and are linked with the warning that is given to Peter and John. Some of 'the chief priests' can be identified. The reference to Caiaphas and Ananus indicates that the term was applied to people directly associated with the high priesthood. The mention of Alexander and John, however, suggests that association with 'the chief priests' was possible through family connections.[2] These 'chief priests' were assisted by certain influential lay Jews, described as 'elders', possibly also 'rulers' and 'scribes'. These men took the necessary steps to counter the activities of the apostles.

The motivation for the hearing probably lies in the nature of the apostles' offence. The Sadducees are cited as being concerned by the growing popularity of the apostles because of their teachings on resurrection.[3] Although the contents of their teachings may have roused concern, it was primarily the popularity which perturbed 'the chief priests' and influential laity. Such fears were heightened by the popular reponse to the healing performed by Peter. The combination of the act performed in the name of Jesus and the public response worried Jews who sought to maintain the status quo.[4]

1. See J.T. Sanders, *The Jews*, pp. 23, 313-14, for a discussion of Luke's possible motives in portraying the trial as he did. Also see J. Neyrey, *The Passion according to Luke* (New York: Paulist Press, 1985), pp. 89-93, for the possible interests Luke held in terms of the trial of Jesus. Walaskay (*Rome*, p. 35) argues that Luke's concern was to criticize the Jewish leaders in whatever way was plausible. Note also Kingsbury, 'Authorities', p. 63, who observes how the opponents of Jesus are presented as a united front in Mark's Gospel.

2. J. Munck (*The Acts of the Apostles* [AB, 31; rev. W.F. Albright and C.S. Mann; New York: Doubleday, 1967], p. 34) suggests that John was the son of Ananus. Note that Ananus was not the officiating high priest at the time of the incident. Also see R.N. Longenecker, *The Acts of the Apostles* (The Expositor's Bible Commentary, 9; Grand Rapids: Zondervan, 1981), p. 302.

3. J.T. Sanders (*The Jews*, p. 238) supports this view; cf. Haenchen (*Acts*, p. 221), who notes the apparent inconsistency of the Sadducean policy. Munck (*Acts*, p. 31) follows Haenchen but does accept the notion that the Sadducees wanted to persecute the Christians (p. 49). Marshall (*Acts*, p. 98) also accepts the accuracy of the Sadducean complaint. If the prime concern was the doctrine of resurrection, however, then it would follow that the Sadducees also wanted to arrest all Pharisees for their views on resurrection.

4. Note J.T. Sanders, *The Jews*, p. 243, who argues that Luke intended to praise the non-Christian Pharisees, in opposition to Christian Pharisees and Sadducees.

The seriousness of the hearing should not be overestimated. It is unlikely that popular anger prevented the apostles from being punished. Rather, the hearing should be perceived as an attempt to determine the extent of the threat. The issuing of a warning suggests that the threat did not pose an imminent danger to the prominent Jews.[1]

The concern of this gathering of influential priests and lay Jews was the threat to the established order. Luke presents this as a major trial where the teachings of Jesus are challenged by the *synedrion*. Although clearly a trial, the gathering was not necessarily conducted by a permanent body. Rather, it appears the trial court was activated at the beckoning of particular influential Jews to establish the extent of a perceived threat. Furthermore, it is conceivable that Luke uses *synedrion* as a reference to a place.

I conclude with three comments that pertain to the administration of Palestine. First, the dispute was entirely Jewish. There is no reason to suggest that the Romans participated. Certain Jews were concerned by the increasing popularity of the apostles whose actions and teachings were perceived to be destabilizing the established order. In this instance, it is apparent that maintaining order was a task with which the Jewish community were concerned in an independent manner.

Ziesler ('Luke', p. 147) believes that Luke purposefully portrays the Pharisees and Christians as '"political" friends'. R.L. Brawley (*Luke–Acts and the Jews* [SBLMS, 33; Atlanta: Scholars Press, 1987], p. 111) claims Luke was attempting to be critical of the Sadducees and 'chief priests' while presenting the priests and Pharisees in a positive light. See also Haenchen, *Acts*, p. 221, who refutes the claim that the dispute was about the practice of black magic. Neyrey (*Passion*, p. 90) supports the notion of healing being important to Luke. Marshall (*Acts*, p. 97) notes that the healing gained Peter public approval but opposition from the Jewish leaders. A. Ehrhardt (*The Acts of the Apostles* [Manchester: Manchester University Press, 1969], p. 17) suggests that the sermon of Peter 'endangered the legal order in Jerusalem' as it was perceived by the Sadducees.

1. See Cassidy, *Society and Politics*, pp. 40-41. He assumes the existence of 'the sanhedrin' and that Acts 4.18 indicates the active role of this body. He also acknowledges that the apostles dispute the judgment, not the right of this body to judge. Note Marshall, *Acts*, p. 101. He regards Acts 4.15-17 as describing the council chambers, not the institution itself. Brawley (*Luke–Acts*, p. 111) believes that 'the rulers', 'scribes' and 'elders' constituted the council under the leadership of the high priest; cf. Ziesler, 'Luke', p. 147, who argues that Luke does not actually state that the formal council was involved in this case, thereby explaining the lack of reference to Pharisees. According to Ziesler, 'that there were Pharisees on the Council is certain' (p. 155).

Secondly, the case was decided by a sub-section of the Jewish community, the 'chief priests' and influential laity. The captain of the Temple led a *quasi* police force which brought the apostles before a gathering of 'the chief priests' and influential laity who sought to preserve the established order in Jerusalem. Peter and John did not question the status of these men. Furthermore, their adjudication of the case provided its legitimacy. Luke, however, perceived this gathering as a formal permanent institution. Whether this trial court was limited in the action it could take is not possible to establish.

The final comment pertains to the meaning of chief priests. Luke believes that it was possible to be associated with this group through family connections. Furthermore, the serving high priest and a previous incumbent were included among the 'chief priests'.

5. *Second Hearing against Peter and John*

Acts 5.17, high priest and Sadducees, 18, imprison Peter and John, 21, high priest and followers call together the *synedrion* and all 'the *gerousia* of the sons of Israel' (γερουσία τῶν υἱῶν 'Ισραήλ), 24, 'the chief priests' (οἱ ἀρχιερεῖς) and captain of the Temple perplexed at disappearance of apostles, 27, captain of the Temple and soldiers bring apostles into the *synedrion*, high priest questions them, 34, Gamaliel, a Pharisee, speaks in the *synedrion*, 36, refers to Theudas, 37, Judas the Galilaean, 40, apostles beaten and then released, 41, Peter and John leave the presence of the *synedrion*.

The second hearing against the apostles presumably took place in the mid-AD 30s.[1] Similar to the first hearing there are problems associated with the identity of the participants and the nature of the dispute.

A few brief comments are required on two details, the miraculous release from prison and the speech of Gamaliel. The escape episode is probably an addition to the incident based on the events recorded in Acts 12.1-11.[2] Its position within the text is of little relevance for the

---

1. Despite similarities, it is accepted that Acts 5.17-41 narrates a different incident to that in Acts 4.1-23. See Reicke, 'Judaeo-Christianity', p. 146; Cassidy, *Society and Politics*, p. 42; Longenecker, *Acts*, p. 222; Marshall, *Acts*, p. 97; Neyrey, *Passion*, p. 93; and Haenchen, *Acts*, p. 255. H. Conzelmann (*Acts of the Apostles* [trans. J. Limburg, A.T. Kraabel and D.H. Juel; Philadelphia: Fortress Press, 1987], p. 41) argues that 5.17-42 was drawn from several sources. Sherwin-White (*Roman Society*, p. 40) believes that they are two versions of the one event.

2. See Haenchen, *Acts*, p. 256, and Marshall, *Acts*, p. 118. The presence of this

outcome of the incident. More significant, however, is Gamaliel's speech. According to Luke, Gamaliel was able to persuade the *synedrion* that the apostles should not be harmed, having referred to the cases of Judas and Theudas.[1] The apostles, however, were beaten. Although Gamaliel may have spoken to the gathering, calling for moderation, it is unlikely that the present form of the speech is historically accurate.[2] The apostles were arrested, questioned, punished and released by Jews. Two queries remain: who acted against the apostles, and for what reason?

The high priest is the one person whose involvement throughout the incident can be accepted. He acted as accuser and judge. Where difficulty arises is in the identity of the high priest's associates in this incident. The nomination of Gamaliel as one of the men who assembled to hear the case against the apostles is the only one we have no reason to doubt. The reference to Sadducees suggests a degree of continuity between the first and the second hearings, implying that

story here implies that Luke did edit his work, presumably to enhance his particular interests.

1. See Conzelmann, *Acts*, p. 42; Munck, *Acts*, p. 49; and Longenecker, *Acts*, p. 228, who argue that Luke did not use Josephus regarding Theudas and Judas. Compare Munck, *Acts*, p. 48, and Longenecker, *Acts*, p. 228 regarding the correct explanation for the chronological problem. Haenchen (*Acts*, p. 250) and M. Dibelius (*Studies in the Acts of the Apostles* [trans. and ed. H. Greeven; London: SCM Press, 1956]) highlight Luke's lack of understanding. Marshall (*Acts*, p. 122) believes it is unlikely that Luke used Josephus for the Gamaliel speech, which spoke of an unknown Theudas. Note some of the arguments forwarded regarding the possible purpose of including the incident. For example, J.T. Sanders (*The Jews*, p. 23) views it as an opportunity to criticize the Jewish leaders, and Neyrey (*Passion*, p. 89) speaks of the account as Luke continuing the trial against Jesus. Zeitlin (*Who Crucified Jesus?*, p. 187) argues that the reference to Judas and Theudas indicates that Peter was a political offender. Ehrhardt (*Acts*, p. 28) believes that the speech was entirely secular and that Gamaliel was an 'onlooker', out of touch with Christianity.

2. See Haenchen, *Acts*, p. 258, who doubts the reliability of the account but recognizes that it is not possible to reject the idea that Gamaliel spoke. In comparison, Longenecker (*Acts*, p. 321) believes that the Pharisee's intervention saved the apostles from death. He also believes that the speech was the reason Luke included the incident. Munck (*Acts*, p. 49) accepts that a speech may have been made, while Brawley (*Luke–Acts*, pp. 113-15) never questions the authenticity of the speech, despite the fact that it forms the basis of his argument. Marshall (*Acts*, p. 117) states that we have no evidence that Gamaliel did not act this way, therefore it should be accepted.

they maintained their opposition to the apostles.[1] Whether the Sadducees actually participated in this hearing, however, is not possible to establish. Similarly, the reference to the captain of the Temple and 'chief priests' positioned as it is within the prison scene is difficult to accept. The later reference to the captain of the Temple, however, appearing within the account of the trial, is more probably an indication that he participated. Although Luke is aware that the high priest acted in league with other Jews he remains uncertain about their exact identity.

The uncertainty is further expressed in the reference to the *synedrion* and *gerousia* in this incident. The use of '*gerousia* of the sons of Israel' is unique to the New Testament. It appears that members of the *gerousia* were called upon to act as judges in association with the high priest and other men in the case against the apostles.[2] It is implied, therefore, that Luke believed the Jews had a formal institution of government. The term *synedrion* is used once as an institution, twice as a place and once where it could be either a place or an institution.[3] Furthermore, the use of the article appears to imply that the *synedrion* was a permanent institution. We are, however, unable to establish Luke's intended usage of *synedrion* other than its role as a place/institution for trials. This hearing was instigated and judged by a particular group of people. Its authority is not questioned by the apostles, nor is there any indication that its ability to inflict punishment is disputed. Furthermore, the source of its authority lay in the people who participated.[4]

---

1. See Munck, *Acts*, p. 31. Brawley (*Luke–Acts*, p. 111) claims that the high priestly party was closely allied with the Sadducees.

2. Note Conzelman (*Acts*, p. 41), who views the *synedrion* as a committee of the *gerousia* and Longenecker (*Acts*, p. 303), who equates *synedrion* with *gerousia*. The use of *gerousia*, according to Longenecker, indicates that it was a full meeting, including the Pharisees. Mantel (*Studies*, p. 298) argues that it was not the Great Sanhedrin of the Mishnah. Marshall (*Acts*, p. 117) states that Acts 5.17 indicates it was the high priest and the Sadducean element of the sanhedrin that acted and that the reference to *gerousia* is a 'hendiadys' (p. 118).

3. See J.T. Sanders, *The Jews*, pp. 4-5, regarding Luke's use of *synedrion*. He favours its use as a place/courtroom, although in Acts 5.21 it is a group within the plenary session (p. 241). Zeitlin (*Who Crucified Jesus?*) argues that this is a reference to the political *synedrion* because Luke implies that it was the meeting of a *synedrion* (p. 184) and because the high priest was arresting a rebel, acting out of fear of Roman criticism (p. 185).

4. Luke may have believed that this was a permanent institution. It is also possible

The other query pertains to the motivation of the high priest and associates in opposing the apostles. Whatever had been suggested to the apostles at the first hearing had not been heeded. The apostles' popular standing was maintained and their destabilizing influence had been intensified by their disobedience. Although we cannot be certain, there is no reason to argue that it was simply a religious doctrinal dispute devoid of temporal connections.[1] According to Luke's record of Gamaliel's speech both Theudas and Judas disturbed the existing order of affairs by their proclamations and deeds. The apostles are portrayed by Luke as engaged in similar activities. This suggests that Luke wished to present the dispute as centring on some Jews' need to maintain the status quo.

Two points emerge from this incident that are pertinent to the administration of affairs in Palestine. First, this was a Jewish matter which was resolved by Jews. Despite any possible authorial purpose for negating Roman involvement, there is no reason to suspect that such a distortion has taken place. The significance of this point lies in the fact that the dispute concerned the ramifications of the apostles' teachings and actions on the status quo. By implication it appears that the Jews were able to control certain matters connected with public influence and standing.[2]

The second point is that the incident was dictated by those Jews who held the greatest influence in Jerusalem. The high priest and his associates formed a trial court to consider the case of the apostles in order to protect the interests of the community as they understood them. The lack of any complaint regarding this practice, or of any

that Luke wanted to believe that these people were part of a permanent institution for other reasons. For example see P. Doble, 'The Son of Man Sayings in Stephen's Witnessing: Acts 6.8–8.2', *NTS* 31 (1985), p. 74, for the notion that Luke may have wanted to show that the apostles chose obedience to God over mankind, as represented by the *synedrion*.

1. Longenecker (*Acts*, p. 320) supports this idea when he claims that the Sadducees were not interested in the content of the teaching for its own sake but in their own self-interest.

2. The way in which the apostles' actions and words were interpreted does not support any notion that the apostles were political rebels. The type of punishment inflicted may indicate that the offence was perceived in terms of religious teaching and practice. Reicke ('Judaeo-Christianity', p. 146) views the offence as false teaching, not political rebellion. Zeitlin (*Who Crucified Jesus?*, p. 80) claims that the apostles were arrested on a political charge.

repercussions, suggests that this situation was an accepted common-place. The legality of the trial appears to have been based on the identity of the participants rather than on any concept of there being a permanent institution independently arbitrating. In the view of Luke it is possible that this gathering could only be regarded as legal if it was 'the' *synedrion*. Subsidiary to this point is the fact that we have no means of establishing what limitations, if any, existed on the type of punishment this gathering could inflict in this instance.[1]

6. *The Trial of Stephen*

Acts 6.9, synagogue of freedmen, from Cyrene, Alexandria, Cilicia and Asia, argue with Stephen, 12, they rouse the people, 'the elders' (οἱ πρεσβύτεροι) and 'the scribes' (οἱ γραμματεῖς), Stephen arrested and taken to the *synedrion*, 7.1, high priest questions Stephen, 58, he is taken out of the city and stoned.

Luke gives no information within the narrative of the incident to indicate its precise timing. In the context of the text of Acts the death of Stephen takes place after the hearings against Peter and John and before the reign of Agrippa I in Judaea, suggesting a date between the mid-to-late AD 30s.[2]

I commence with several general observations. Much debate exists regarding the content and purpose of the incident for the developing portrait of Christianity in Acts.[3] The incident was of much benefit to

---

1. Compare Cassidy, *Society and Politics*, pp. 40-42 and Longenecker, *Acts*, pp. 320-21 on what information this incident provides regarding the power of the sanhedrin, especially in terms of capital punishment. Sherwin-White (*Roman Society*, p. 40) states that the sanhedrin lacked executive power to inflict severe punishment, or that it only possessed such power in a restricted form regarding the temple precinct. Marshall (*Acts*, p. 124) argues that the beating was not a light punishment and (p. 121) that Luke did not know word for word what happened in the sanhedrin meeting. According to M. Hengel (*Acts and the History of Earliest Christianity* [trans. J. Bowden; London: SCM Press, 1979], p. 74) the apostles were flogged because the Jews could not inflict capital punishment.

2. Because of uncertainty regarding the dating, there are numerous variations regarding the identity of the prefect and high priest. They include Pilate (until AD 36), Marcellus (AD 36–37), Marullus (AD 37–41), Caiaphas (until AD 36), Jonathan, son of Ananus (AD 36–37) and Theophilus, son of Ananus (AD 37–?). As stated by Schürer (*History*, I, p. 383) it is possible that Marcellus and Marullus are the same person, Marcellus being a corruption of Marullus.

3. See, for example, Haenchen, *Acts*, p. 273-74; C.H.H. Scobie, 'The Use of

Luke in terms of emphasizing the relationship between Christianity and Judaism, highlighting their differences.[1] The death of Stephen was also important in Luke's understanding of the stages by which Christianity spread beyond Judaea.[2] Although it is necessary to question the accuracy of the details recorded by Luke, there is no reason to question the existence of a Christian called Stephen who was killed by Jews in Jerusalem. Whatever Luke or his source(s) may have included to develop the narrative, we do not have any reason to doubt Stephen's death as a historical event.[3]

Opposition to Stephen began within one section of the Jewish community living in Jerusalem, the Jews born outside Judaea but now residing there. These men were connected with particular synagogues in the city and they appear to have maintained an identity distinct from the Jews born in Judaea.[4] They sought the assistance of other

Source Material in the Speeches of Acts III and VII', *NTS* 25 (1978/79), p. 420; and Conzelmann, *Acts*, p. 61. Discussion of the source(s) used by Luke is especially relevant to the speech made by Stephen and the means by which he died. With regard to the speech see Scobie, 'Source Material', pp. 420-21; Marshall, *Acts*, p. 133; and Ziesler, 'Luke', p. 147. On the issue of how Stephen was killed, as the result of a formal trial or mob lynching, scholars argue that Luke intertwines two separate sources. For example, see D. Hare, *The Theme of Jewish Persecution in the Gospel according to St Matthew* (Cambridge: Cambridge University Press, 1967), p. 20; M. Hengel, *Between Jesus and Paul. Studies in the Earliest History of Christianity* (trans. J. Bowden; London: SCM Press, 1983), p. 20; and Sherwin-White, *Roman Society*, p. 40. Note Conzelmann, *Acts*, pp. 47-48, and Haenchen, *Acts*, p. 273, who argue that the confusion is more a reflection of Luke's varying interests than a reliance on any particular source. Note also Hengel, *Acts*, pp. 40-49, regarding the importance of Acts as a source of history.

1. See J.T. Sanders, *The Jews*, pp. 248-49. The issue of contrasting Christianity with Judaism is raised primarily in connection with Stephen's speech. For example, see Munck, *Acts*, p. 67, and Longenecker, *Acts*, p. 337.

2. There is some debate as to whether Luke intended to use this incident as a bridge between events in Jerusalem and the 'Gentile mission', or to the world in general. Note Conzelmann, *Acts*, p. 57, and Munck, *Acts*, pp. 65, 67. Both scholars accept that Luke perceived the incident as an opportunity to link different aspects of the development of Christianity. See also Hengel, *Acts*, pp. 71-80, on the significance of the incident for Luke's understanding of the history of Christianity.

3. In contrast, some scholars tend to accept the narrative as entirely authentic. For example, see the commentaries of Marshall and Longenecker. For a more critical approach see Haenchen.

4. As noted by F.F. Bruce (*The Acts of the Apostles* [London: Tyndale Press, 2nd edn, 1952], pp. 155-57), Longenecker (*Acts*, p. 335) and Marshall (*Acts*, p. 120), we are unable to establish the exact number of synagogues. On the

Jews living in Jerusalem in their attack on Stephen. It is implied that the new participants, Judaean Jews, were encouraged to take a leading role in the subsequent events. The reference to the populace of Jerusalem at large, the serving high priest, 'the elders' and 'scribes' may simply result from Luke or his source(s) wishing to portray Stephen as being opposed by those Jews who attacked Jesus.[1] It is also possible that these men did participate, with the high priest acting as a leading figure among Stephen's opponents.[2]

The non-Judaean Jews did not take action against Stephen. It is implied that support was sought from those Jews who held sufficient prominence in the community to take positive steps to remove Stephen without attracting much negative reaction from the Romans or the remainder of the Jewish population. Moreover, the involvement of respected Jews may have legitimized the removal of Stephen.

Against this outline it is necessary to note that Luke was not primarily concerned with narrating the legal proceedings. As a result, there is confusion regarding how Stephen met his death and the nature of the dispute. It is evident that Stephen's words and actions angered certain Jews. Although much debate remains regarding how much of the speech associated with Stephen originated with Luke, it is plausible to accept that Stephen did refer to the Temple and Mosaic law.[3]

reference to non-Judaean Jews instigating the whole affair compare Haenchen, *Acts*, p. 271, and J.T. Sanders, *The Jews*, p. 245.

1. The few scholars who comment on Stephen's opponents tend to highlight one particular aspect of the narrative. For example, although Cassidy (*Society and Politics*, p. 49) notes that 'the people' expressed their opposition, it was the leaders of the sanhedrin that stoned Stephen. Marshall (*Acts*, p. 130) expresses surprise that priests were not mentioned, because they were members of the sanhedrin, which he accepts as dealing with the matter. Zeitlin (*Who Crucified Jesus?*, p. 190) believes that the religious sanhedrin tried Stephen but because the stoning of Stephen contradicted the talmudic practice either the populace (p. 191) or zealots (p. 192) killed Stephen. Ehrhart (*Acts*, p. 32) simply notes that 'the mob' participated throughout the incident.

2. Saul is mentioned by Luke but it appears that this is not part of the historical situation. See Conzelmann *Acts*, p. 61, and Haenchen, *Acts*, p. 294 n.2; cf. Marshall, *Acts*, p. 150.

3. The long speech by Stephen justifiably receives detailed assessment by a number of scholars. J.T. Sanders (*The Jews*, p. 248) and Conzelmann (*Acts*, p. 57) note the fact that Luke made use of the speech. For the significance of the speech see Longenecker, *Acts*, p. 334, and Dibelius, *Studies*, p. 167. M. Simon (*St Stephen and the Hellenists in the Primitive Church* [The Haskell Lectures, 1956; London: Longman, Green, 1958], p. 31) indicates that the speech was not a word

Whatever the comments were that annoyed the non-Judaean Jews in their initial dispute with Stephen, any claims he made regarding the Temple and Moses were probably noted, and conceivably exaggerated by Luke, his source(s), or Stephen's opponents. In an attempt to distance themselves from Stephen, non-Judaean Jews protested against his teachings.[1] In turn, these people persuaded the Judaean Jews that something had to be done about Stephen.[2]

Doubt also remains as to the means by which Stephen met his death. The narrative oscillates between the notion of a formal trial and a mob lynching. The former concept is derived from the reference to the *synedrion* and high priest. Whether a formal institutional hearing took place is debatable. The connotation here is that of a trial court, not necessarily a permanent institution. It is possible that there was some sort of gathering of influential Jews to decide what should be done.[3] It is possible, however, that much of the narrative regarding

for word account of what Stephen said, while E. Richard ('The Polemical Character of the Joseph Episode in Acts 7', *JBL* 98 [1979], p. 265) seeks to establish 'the' historical core of what belongs to Stephen. Also see Haenchen, *Acts*, pp. 286-89, for a general assessment of the purpose of the speech. On the idea of a Samaritan influence compare E. Richards, 'Acts 7. An Investigation of the Samaritan Evidence', *CBQ* 39 (1977), p. 207, and Scobie, 'Source Material', p. 410-11.

1. Several options are favoured for the community in which Stephen lived and worked. For example, see Simon, *St Stephen*, p. 140-41; Longenecker, *Acts*, p. 334; and Richards, 'Polemical Character', pp. 255-67.

2. Discussion among scholars has primarily centred on the nature of the formal charge against Stephen. This approach, however, suffers from an assumption that the hearing was definitely formal and followed legal procedure. For example, see Bruce, *Acts*, p. 52, and Zeitlin, *Who Crucified Jesus?*, pp. 189-90, who interpret Stephen's offence in terms of blasphemy. Other scholars refer more generally to the 'offence' of Stephen without necessarily implying there was a formal hearing. For example, see Reicke, 'Judaeo-Christianity', p. 146, and Longenecker, *Acts*, p. 349. Brawley (*Luke–Acts*, p. 121), Hare (*Jewish Persecution*, p. 23) and D.D. Sylva ('The Meaning and Function of Acts 7.46-50', *JBL* 106 [1987], pp. 263-65) question whether Stephen was actually opposed to the Temple and thus blasphemous. See Simon, *St Stephen*, pp. 96-97. Note also Cassidy, *Society and Politics*, pp. 34-35, who emphasizes Stephen's criticism of the high priest and members of the sanhedrin for their actions and those of their forefathers.

3. Despite the numerous efforts to establish whether Stephen died as the result of a formal trial or a mob lynching, no clear solution has been obtained. Hare (*Jewish Persecution*, pp. 22-23) and Zeitlin (*Who Crucified Jesus?*, pp. 189-90) favour the death of Stephen being the result of a lynching, basing their argument on accepting *m. Sanh.* 6.6a as being historically accurate. Munck (*Acts*, p. 68) favours the idea of a lynching while Ehrhardt (*Acts*, p. 35) believes no formal judgment was passed

Stephen has been modelled on the account of Jesus' death by Luke. Consequently, references are made to the high priest, 'the elders' and the *synedrion* without clearly establishing their precise role in the incident.[1] Whatever the means, Stephen was removed without any apparent ramifications, implying that the deed met with a certain degree of public approval.

Despite the lack of uniformity, there are three observations pertinent to the administration of Palestine. First, this was a Jewish affair throughout. There is no evidence of Roman involvement: a matter relevant only to the Jewish community was in dispute.[2] The death of Stephen, therefore, may be an example of the Romans allowing the Jews to deal with an internal matter.

Secondly, a sense of propriety was obtained because of the involvement of influential members of the Jewish community in Jerusalem. These men prevented the event from being perceived as a rebellious, unruly action. The non-Judaean Jews continued to be involved, acting in league with Jews who held a high public standing, the high priest and 'elders'. It is even conceivable that the Jews informed the prefect of what was being done. Furthermore, this

---

against Stephen. Cassidy (*Society and Politics*, p. 49) asserts that the sanhedrin leaders were present at the execution. Marshall (*Acts*, p. 148) and Longenecker (*Acts*, p. 351) seek a compromise, with the latter accepting the notion of a trial that was unruly. Longenecker (p. 352) even claims that the lack of reference to Pharisees indicates that they were not willing to save Stephen. The sanhedrin, therefore, was allowed to do as it liked. More credence should probably be given to such approaches as those favoured by Haenchen (*Acts*, pp. 273-74), Hengel (*Jesus and Paul*, pp. 20-21) and Doble ('Stephen's Witnessing', p. 74), who view the material from this part of Luke's narrative more in terms of its relevance to his polemical purposes than as a strict record of historical events. Hengel (*Jesus and Paul*, p. 20) suggests that the *synedrion* reference was not to the sanhedrin of Jerusalem, it was a literary tool used by Luke to provide a framework for Stephen's speech. Hare (*Jewish Persecution*, p. 21) and Conzelmann (*Acts*, p. 61) appear to be correct in concluding that this incident is of little value in terms of Jewish legal independence.

1. Note that Luke makes no reference to 'chief priests', Sadducees or Pharisees. Zeisler ('Luke', p. 147) assumes that the Pharisees were among the council members who heard Stephen's speech.

2. We are not in a position to determine exactly who was serving as high priest when Stephen was killed. Josephus does not mention any person connected with the high priesthood during this period who lost his position because of an event which involved the Romans or a disturbance among the Jews. Note Hengel, *Jesus and Paul*, p. 20 n. 130, who argues that the case was decided by synagogue authorities and that there was no reason for the Romans to become involved.

incident was instigated by a sub-section of the Jews residing in Jerusalem who, although personally lacking public standing, were able to involve other Jews with sufficient influence and desire to protect the status quo.

Thirdly, the use of *synedrion* in this instance appears to mark a desire by Luke, or his source(s), to view the death of Stephen as the result of a formal trial in which Jewish refusal to accept Jesus as the messiah led to the hasty death of Stephen. Luke was aware of the legal connotations of the term *synedrion*. In effect, however, it appears that a gathering of influential Jews gave sanction to the desires of some non-Judaean Jews to have a 'trouble-maker' killed.

7. *The Statue of Gaius*

War 2.185, Petronius ordered to instal a statue of Gaius in Jerusalem, using force if necessary, 192, Jews protest on plain of Ptolemais; Petronius summons the people and 'the notable men' (οἱ γνώριμοι) to Tiberias, 199, private meetings with 'the powerful men' (οἱ δυνατοῖ), public meetings with the people, 200, Jews continue to protest, Petronius concerned regarding the sowing, delayed already by fifty·days, 201, he decides not to follow the order, 203, Gaius threatens Petronius but dies.

Ant. 18.261, Petronius ordered to instal a statue of Gaius in Jerusalem, using force if necessary, 263, many Jews petition Petronius in Ptolemais, 272, Jews continue to protest, fields unsown for forty days, 273, Aristobulus, Agrippa's brother, Helcias the elder and 'the first men' (οἱ πρῶτοι) appeal to Petronius, 276, they influence him 278-83, Petronius talks to the Jews at Tiberias, work the land, statue will not be erected, 284, Petronius requests 'the leading men' (οἱ ἐν τέλει) to restore agricultural production and conciliate the populace, 289-301, Agrippa's banquet for Gaius, 297, Agrippa requests that the order be rescinded, 301, Gaius agrees and writes to Petronius, 302, Gaius receives letter from Petronius, believes that Jews are rebellious, 304, he writes to Petronius, 308, news of Gaius's death arrives before the letter condemning him.

Leg. Gai. 207, Petronius ordered to place a statue of Gaius in Jerusalem, 213, Petronius is slow to act, 222, he sends for 'the leading men', priests and 'rulers/magistrates' (οἱ ἄρχοντες), tells them to pacify the Jews, 225, Jews go to Phoenicia to protest, 229, *gerousia* speaks to Petronius, 244, wheat and other cereal crops ripe, Petronius fears Jews might burn them, 254, *synedrion* approves Petronius's plan, Gaius is angered, 265, he tells Agrippa of the order, 276, Agrippa petitions Gaius to stop, 333, Gaius agrees to rescind the order.

There are detailed accounts of the protest over Gaius's order in Josephus's *Antiquities of the Jews* and *The Jewish War* and in Philo's *Legatio ad Gaium*. We also possess a summary statement made by Tacitus in his *Histories* 5.9. The incident occurred while Judaea was a Roman province, in approximately AD 40–41. A survey of the three major accounts highlights a number of common elements in their understanding of the incident. Petronius, the legate of Syria, was ordered by Gaius to erect a statue of the emperor in Jerusalem, using whatever force was necessary. The Jews protested, appealing directly to Petronius. At some point before the statue was to be erected Petronius postponed any further action and attempted to convince Gaius that it was expedient to revoke the order. This is the extent of agreement among the three accounts.[1]

Several aspects of the incident as it is narrated by Josephus and Philo are problematic. There is no obvious agreement as to Gaius's motivation, the attitude of Petronius, the place(s) of Jewish protest, the identity of the protesters, the timing of the incident, the reason Petronius postponed the order, and the final reason why the order was not put into effect. Although not all these aspects are of major importance, some comment on them is necessary. I shall compare the accounts, commencing with *Antiquities of the Jews* and *The Jewish War*, to clarify aspects of the incident and in order to provide an outline of what happened.[2]

Josephus presents extensive accounts of the incident, especially in *Antiquities of the Jews*. There are a number of differences of detail

---

1. A.R.C. Leaney (*The Jewish and Christian World 200 BC to AD 200* [Cambridge Commentaries on Writings of the Jewish and Christian World, 200 BC–AD 200, 7; Cambridge: Cambridge University Press, 1984], p. 112) notes that, despite differences in certain details, Josephus and Philo agree in terms of the main outline of the incident. Other scholars tend to favour one particular account, calling on the others to add extra information. For example, see Zeitlin, *Rise and Fall*, II, p. 180, who follows *Ant.*; Rhoads, *Revolution*, p. 63, who follows the *War* version of events; Smallwood, *Jews under Roman Rule*, p. 174, 'The Chronology of Gaius' Attempt to Desecrate the Temple', *Latomus* 16 (1957), p. 5, and *Philonis*, p. 32, who outlines her reasons for favouring Philo above Josephus; Jones, *Herods*, pp. 197-98; and Goodman, *Ruling Class*, p. 211, who favours Philo over Josephus's 'fantastic' elements.

2. The contemporary nature of Philo's writing has been repeatedly highlighted by Smallwood (*Philonis*, p. 23). This, however, does not necessarily mean that Philo was more accurate. Such comment will be reserved until I am in a position to compare all aspects of the accounts.

between his texts, as well as some elements of the narrative appearing exclusively in one or other text. Such differences as the number of days the fields lay unsown, the number of legions Petronius led and the precise meaning of Gaius's instructions regarding Petronius's punishment are not of significance for the overall outline of the incident. Why Josephus allowed these differences to remain is not apparent. It is possible that he used different sources for the two texts and was not concerned to ensure consistency between them. Numerical differences may simply be the result of carelessness. The inclusion of such information as the rainfall, however, and, more importantly, the reference to Agrippa I, may indicate that when Josephus wrote *Antiquities of the Jews* he had additional material to draw upon. The existence of such differences and additions indicates the need to query the reliability of Josephus's narrative. While the general outline may be accurate, specific statements may reflect the interests of the author and his source rather than the historical events.[1]

There are two significant differences between the accounts in *Antiquities of the Jews* and *The Jewish War*. The most prominent of these pertains to the identity of the Jewish protesters. Both accounts record that the Jewish populace protested in Ptolemais, and then followed the legate to Tiberias to continue their protest. In *The Jewish War,* Petronius takes the initiative by summoning the 'notable men' to Tiberias, where he holds private conferences with 'the powerful men'. In *Antiquities of the Jews*, however, Aristobulus, Helcias and 'the first men' appeal to Petronius. Later Josephus repeats the reference to the role played by Aristobulus and the others in influencing Petronius. The addition of specific named individuals in *Antiquities of the Jews* appears to provide valuable information. It is possible, though, that the specific reference to Aristobulus and Helcias may be a reflection of Josephus's own interests, or those of his source, to favour Agrippa's family and highlight their role rather than to narrate the actual situation.

The direct involvement of Agrippa I also reinforces the importance of his family in the version in *Antiquities of the Jews*. Whereas in *The Jewish War* the incident concludes because of Gaius's death, in

1. Smallwood (*Jews under Roman Rule*, p. 174 and 'Chronology', p. 4 fn. 3) has correctly pointed out several legendary elements and the inaccuracy of describing Ptolemais as part of Galilee. Regarding the timing of the Alexandrian mission, see P.J. Sijpesteijn, 'The Legationes ad Gaium', *JJS* 15 (1964), pp. 87-96.

Antiquities of the Jews Josephus had a long account of how Agrippa managed to persuade Gaius to change his mind. Elements of the pro-Herodian account in *Antiquities of the Jews*, like the presence of Agrippa I in Rome, are quite plausible. Furthermore, the fact that Petronius entered Agrippa's territory makes it reasonable to believe that he participated in the incident.[1] It was to Agrippa's advantage, therefore, that the dispute be settled. It is possible that the banquet story and the reference to Agrippa's relatives derived from a source that presented a pro-Herodian version of events. The extent to which Agrippa's personal intervention aided the Jewish cause, however, remains uncertain.[2] Although Josephus singled out members of Agrippa's family, they were part of a larger corpus of representatives. The sanctity of Jerusalem, especially the Temple, was an issue that concerned Jews whether from Judaea, Galilee or the diaspora.[3]

In *The Jewish War* this group of Jews consists of 'the notable men' and 'the powerful men'. In *Antiquities of the Jews* Josephus refers to 'the first men' accompanying Aristobulus and Helcias. These terms are equated in meaning, referring to the people with whom Petronius held meetings. The term 'the leading men' is used in *Antiquities of the Jews* to describe the Jews whom Petronius requested to conciliate the populace and ensure that the fields were tended. These 'leading men' are probably 'the first men'/'powerful men'/'notable men' mentioned earlier in the incident. They were the men that Petronius believed were capable of influencing the populace.

1. Philo's reference to Gaius's believing that Petronius had been bribed may contain an element of truth. See P. Bilde, 'The Roman Emperor Gaius (Caligula)'s Attempt to Erect his Statue in the Temple of Jerusalem', *Studia Theologica* 32 (1978), p. 86. This notion is dependent on Agrippa being aware of the order before he left Judaea. For the timing of Agrippa's trip to Rome see Schürer, *History*, I, p. 394 and J.P.V.D. Balsdon, 'Notes Concerning the Principate of Gaius', *JRS* 24 (1934), p. 19. If Agrippa was ignorant of the order no explanation is provided for his decision to travel to Rome. See Schürer, *History*, I, p. 394 n. 176.

2. One problem that cannot be resolved is the meaning of Agrippa's absence from the *War* account. The silence of *War* does not necessarily indicate that the references to Agrippa in *Ant.* were an invention; they were probably drawn from a different source. It is possible that comparison with Philo may help clarify which account of Josephus is more historically accurate.

3. See Freyne, *Galilee*, pp. 259-304 and *Galilee, Jesus and the Gospels. Literary Approaches and Historical Investigations* (Dublin: Gill and MacMillan, 1988), pp. 182-90, regarding Galilaean attachment to the Temple. Philo is an example of Jews from the diaspora being concerned regarding what happened to the Temple.

The other, less significant difference between the two accounts concerns the portrayal of Petronius. In *The Jewish War* Josephus presents Petronius without prejudice. Petronius follows the orders of Gaius, opting for persuasion before the use of force. He informs the Jews of the consequence of their protest. Before long, however, he decided that it was no longer advantageous to pursue the order. In *Antiquities of the Jews* Josephus introduces comments about Petronius's state of mind, culminating with outright praise of the legate. It is implied that Petronius positively sought to help the Jews. Such a development may have been the result of a different source, or an idealization of Petronius as the archetypal administrator.

The Jewish War and *Antiquities of the Jews* each offer a cohesive narrative. Gaius ordered Petronius to erect a statue of the emperor in Jerusalem. Petronius set about his task, ready to fulfil the instructions. News of the order provoked an immediate response from the Jews. When Petronius arrived in Ptolemais he was met by a large number of Jews, presumably from the province of Judaea and the surrounding territories of Agrippa I. Failing to persuade the Jews to accept the order, Petronius decided to continue the talks. It is possible that he was made aware that the Jews were willing to rebel rather than accept the statue. The choice of Tiberias indicates that the issue concerned Jews outside Jerusalem. Petronius spoke to the general populace and with certain influential Jews, including members of Agrippa I's family. Weighing up the situation, he decided to risk his career by postponing the order. In the meantime, Agrippa probably appealed directly to Gaius. Although angered at the obvious disobedience displayed by Petronius, Gaius appears to have abandoned the plan.

I turn now to the account contained in Philo's *Legatio ad Gaium*, the most extensive of the three versions. Viewed in comparison to Josephus's account there are a number of differences, some significant, others less so. Philo presents the incident within an allegorical framework, depicting Gaius as an evil man. As a result, it is understandable that the other main individuals mentioned, Petronius and Agrippa, are depicted as men who recognized the foolishness of the order. Gaius is obsessed with conquering the Jews by making them recognize him as a god. Agrippa is horrified by the plan because of its religious implications for the Jews. Petronius, on the other hand, as the experienced Roman administrator, recognizes the unnecessary trouble and friction the order would cause.[1] Intermixed with these somewhat obvious characterizations, Philo presents several details of what he understood to have happened which require clarification in comparison with Josephus.

The first difference is that Philo offers a specific motive for the order, thus adding clarity to his account. The disruption of Gentile practices by Jews in Jamnia meant a breakdown in the established order.[2] It was appropriate, therefore, to take some action. The absence of the Jamnia incident from Josephus does not lessen the probability that it acted as the immediate cause for issuing the order.

The second and third differences relate to the timing of the incident and the place of protest. Philo refers to particular Jews being summoned by Petronius without indicating whether the legate had left Antioch. When the Jews of Jerusalem and the country appear before the legate Philo claims that they travelled to Phoenicia. It is apparent that Philo lacks detailed information. The details provided by Josephus can be added to Philo's account without too much explanation. There are two possibilities. 1) The two gatherings of Jews mentioned by Philo should be equated with Josephus's reference to Jews going to Ptolemais. In this case Philo remains ignorant of the protest being continued at Tiberias. 2) The first gathering of Philo is to be equated with Josephus's Ptolemais protest and the reference to Jews travelling to Phoenicia should be linked with the meeting at Tiberias. Of these interpretations the second appears to be the more plausible. It is unlikely that Petronius would order Jews to travel to Antioch to be told of an order to be introduced by him in Judaea. That certain Jews were summoned to appear before Petronius at his first port of call in the region is plausible, as is the notion that news

1. Bilde ('Roman Emperor', p. 71), in particular, notes the overriding interests of Philo in his depiction of Gaius. While examining the letter of Agrippa, Zeitlin ('Did Agrippa Write a Letter to Gaius Caligula?', *JQR* 56 [1965–66], p. 29) acknowledges Philo's 'theological overtones'; cf. Smallwood, 'Chronology', p. 5, who argues in favour of Philo's version where the two authors are in conflict.

2. Most scholars refer to the Jamnia incident, rejecting Josephus's broad claim that Gaius wanted to destroy Judaism. See Zeitlin, 'Did Agrippa Write?', p. 22; Stern, 'Province of Judaea', p. 355; Smallwood, *Jews under Roman Rule*, p. 177 and 'Chronology', p. 4; and Bilde 'Roman Emperor', pp. 73-74, who clearly outlines the significance of the protest at Jamnia. Note Bilde's ('Roman Emperor', p. 74) important comment that the incident at Jamnia does not provide an explanation for the way Gaius reacted, merely the necessity of some action.

of the order resulted in many Jews travelling to Ptolemais.[1]

Josephus and Philo disagree on two aspects of timing: the season when the protest occurred, and when Gaius wrote to Petronius. The reference to the grain harvest in Philo and the season of seeding in Josephus has generated much debate. There is no obvious explanation for this contradiction. Either Josephus or Philo, or their source, appears to be incorrect.[2] Such an error, however, is not significant in terms of the immediate context of the incident. The time of year is mentioned because Petronius was concerned with the breakdown of economic order. Whether it was because the harvest was unpicked or because the fields were fallow, therefore affecting the following year's harvest, Petronius had to make a decision to prevent the loss of a year's produce. The dates of spring or autumn are of similar long-term economic significance.

Philo states that Petronius received two letters from Gaius, while Josephus only refers to one such letter. It is chronologically possible that Petronius wrote to Gaius and then received a reply reaffirming

1. Smallwood (*Philonis*, pp. 33, 273 and 'Chronology', p. 4 n. 3), contrary to her general approach, expresses doubt over Philo's version here. Several scholars assume that Josephus is accurate on the location of the protest. For example, see Jones, *Herods*, p. 197, and Stern, 'Province of Judaea', p. 357. Zeitlin ('Did Agrippa Write?', p. 24) expresses doubt as to whether the Jews were ordered to appear before Petronius.

2. With the exception of Bilde, Horsley (*Jesus*) and Zeitlin, all scholarly discussion of the incident centres on the timing of the events. See especially Balsdon, 'Principate', pp. 13-24; Smallwood, 'Chronology', pp. 3-16; and Schürer, *History*, I, pp. 394-96. For a comparison on the suggested timing see Schürer, *History*, I, p. 396 n. 180; Smallwood, *Jews under Roman Rule*, p. 117 n. 115; and Balsdon, 'Principate', p. 19. A number of points regarding this discussion are worthy of note. Smallwood (*Jews under Roman Rule*, p. 177 n. 115 and *Philonis*, pp. 33, 267) appears to be correct in claiming that Philo was referring to the spring harvest (cf. Balsdon, 'Principate', p. 23; Stern, 'Province of Judaea', pp. 356-57; and Bilde, 'The Roman Emperor', p. 91), therefore requiring us to make a choice between Philo and Josephus. There is, however, no reason to choose one above the other. Goodman (*Ruling Class*, p. 60) notes that the lack of crops necessitated action by Petronius. It also appears that the incident took place within the space of one year, not two, that being AD 40. See Balsdon, 'Principate', p. 24; Smallwood, 'Chronology', p. 5; and Schürer, *History*, I, p. 396 n. 180; cf. Leaney, *World*, p. 111, who proposes AD 41. Smallwood ('Chronology', p. 9) and Stern ('Province of Judaea', p. 357) are probably correct in arguing that the events in Ptolemais and Tiberias were chronologically closely connected; cf. Jones, *Herods*, pp. 197-98 and Schürer, *History*, I, p. 395). Note that Smallwood ('Chronology', p. 17) acknowledges the problem of favouring one particular approach.

his original orders. Whether such an addition is historically warranted is debatable. By quoting a reply to Petronius's request, Philo effectively isolates Agrippa I as the only person who was able to influence Gaius. His narrative immediately moves to Rome and Agrippa's intervention. It appears to be more likely that Petronius only received one letter, the original order.[1]

A further difference is the portrayal of Petronius. Originally presented in a neutral manner in *The Jewish War*, Petronius was praised for his moral decency in *Antiquities of the Jews*. Philo goes further than Josephus, claiming that Petronius was opposed to the order from the outset. Philo's portrayal of Petronius is related to the characterization of Gaius, partly to highlight the failings of the latter. Why Petronius did not begin by attempting to persuade Gaius is not considered.[2] Petronius's willingness to take heed of the circumstances once he arrived in Galilee appears to have been expanded by Philo into total opposition of the order. Philo, therefore, elevates Petronius to a status beyond that of Josephus's *Antiquities of the Jews*.[3]

The other difference that requires comment is the identity of the prominent protesters. Among the influential men which he describes as the 'notable men'/'powerful men'/'first men'/'leading men', Josephus refers to Aristobulus and Helcias. Philo provides greater detail. The 'leading men' appeared before Petronius. These men were

---

1. To accommodate two letters from Gaius it is necessary to argue a chronological break between the meetings in Ptolemais and Tiberias. Such a break is extremely difficult to substantiate from the narrative. Jones (*Herods*, p. 198), Zeitlin ('Did Agrippa Write?', p. 25) and Schürer (*History*, I, p. 396) favour there being two letters; cf. Smallwood, *Jews under Roman Rule*, p. 177 fn. 114, 'Chronology', p. 9, and *Philonis*, pp. 33, 281.

2. It is in this context that Philo referred to Tiberius and the incident under Pilate's prefectship as a comparison to the attitude of Gaius. Philo creates a problem for himself. If Petronius did not want to follow the order he apparently was powerful enough to refuse, but he did not. See *Leg. Gai.* 259.

3. Bilde ('Roman Emperor', pp. 77-78) makes this point. Note the number of scholars who accept Philo's portrayal of Petronius without question. For example, see Smallwood, *Philonis*, pp. 33, 269; Stern, 'Province of Judaea', p. 357; Zeitlin, 'Did Agrippa Write?', p. 23 and *Rise and Fall*, II, p. 180, who claims Petronius went to Tiberias to seek the advice of Agrippa's family; and Jones, *Herods*, p. 198. Smallwood's acceptance of Philo on this point brings into question her argument that Philo is the more historically reliable of the two authors. See also Rajak, *Josephus*, pp. 68-69.

priests and 'rulers'. [1] Together they were perceived by Petronius as being able to influence the course of events in Judaea and Galilee. The prominent Jews in this instance, therefore, included both priests and non-priests.

The reference to the *gerousia*, presumably a formal institution that represented the Jews, causes several problems within the narrative of Philo, primarily in terms of its connection to the influential Jews. There is no evidence to indicate whether the men who originally appeared before Petronius were members of this *gerousia*. Although it is possible that some of the *gerousia* were among 'the leading men', there is nothing to suggest that we should equate the two groups. According to Philo the involvement of the *gerousia* appears to have been necessitated by the popular protest. The select group of Jews who initially appealed to Petronius, possibly as a response to notification of the order, apparently represented the 'Jewish cause' and not a specific institution. While it is possible that the *gerousia* participated at Tiberias, its inclusion in the narrative may have been primarily a reflection of the seriousness of Jewish protest.

Josephus makes no reference to the involvement of an institution. There is no obvious solution to this difference. It is possible to explain both the inclusion and absence of the *gerousia*. Philo or his source may have assumed an institution was involved in such an important event.[2] He may also be narrating a detail of which Josephus was ignorant. Conversely, Josephus or his source(s) did not believe any institution played a significant enough role in the incident to warrant inclusion in the narrative.[3]

---

1. The general 'rulers' is favoured here above the more specific 'magistrates'. Philo appears to be referring to a large corpus of important people that were distinguishable as two separate parts, priestly and non-priestly. Smallwood (*Philonis*, p. 274) believes 'the leading men' can be equated with members of the sanhedrin. There is, however, no evidence for such a claim.

2. Philo may have drawn on personal experience in his reference to *gerousia*. See *Flaccus*, 74. It is probable that *gerousia* was used by Philo because it was the term with which he was familiar. It is also possible that Philo incorporated the notion of an official body participating in the incident on the basis of his knowledge of affairs in Alexandria and a general belief as to how matters should be resolved.

3. Note the attitude of Josephus and Philo toward Agrippa I's involvement. Philo makes Agrippa the hero of the Jews. Although Josephus praises Agrippa and gives him some credit for bringing a peaceful end to the incident in *Ant.*, he distributes the glory among members of Agrippa's family. It appears, therefore, that these authors or their sources changed the emphasis on who among the Herodian family helped

It is now possible to elaborate upon the common elements mentioned at the beginning of this case. Josephus and Philo generally
differ only in detail. In a few instances it is impossible to distinguish
which version is more historically accurate. On these occasions, however, our understanding of the incident is not hampered. It is not
appropriate, therefore, to proclaim preference for one or other text.[1]

Gaius instituted the order as a response to the action of Jews at
Jamnia. The Jewish disruption of the Roman custom of tolerance and
non-interference sparked the necessity for punishment. Gaius ordered
Petronius to use whatever force was required to fulfil his plans and
Petronius set about his task with every intention of following the
order, although his later actions suggest a preference to achieve his
aim without resorting to the use of violence. Word was probably sent
ahead to inform the Jews, either inviting or ordering certain Jews to
appear before him when he reached Ptolemais. Petronius assumed that
the support of prominent Jews would reduce the likelihood of trouble.
Josephus and Philo, especially the former, describe these people in
general terms, possibly because of a lack of detailed information.
They were the 'powerful men'/'notable men'/'first men' and,
according to both Philo and Josephus, the 'leading men'. Philo gives
some hint regarding their identity, referring to priests and 'rulers'.[2]

Aside from these influential protesters, Petronius was confronted by
a large section of the Jewish populace at Ptolemais and Tiberias. The
change in location indicates that the legate did not wish to exert undue
military pressure on the Jews. Although he may have intended to fulfil
the order, he was not willing to do so at all costs. In Tiberias the
influential Jews continued in their efforts. Possibly now included
among these representatives were members of the *gerousia* and of

conclude the incident without any violence.

1. Smallwood's ('Chronology', p. 5) preference for Philo is questioned when
she uses Josephus to clarify Philo on points where they are in dispute. The stated
preference is probably based on a desire to follow the chronology of Philo above that
of Josephus.

2. There is no evidence to support Horsley's claim ('High Priests', p. 39 and
Jesus, p. 113) that the protest did not involve influential Jews from the outset. It is
conceivable that Jonathan and Theophilus were among the influential Jews, as
claimed by Smallwood ('High Priests', p. 23) and Horsley ('High Priests', p. 38),
although we cannot be certain. The failure to mention them by name is not
necessarily indicative of anything in particular in this instance. It is clear that the
source material favours Agrippa and his family.

Agrippa I's family. The mention of the *gerousia* suggests that Philo, or his source, believed that a Jewish council participated in the negotiations regarding a matter pertaining to Jerusalem and Jewish customs. The role played by Agrippa's family points to a factor that we cannot fully explain, the decision to hold the talks in Tiberias. It is understandable that Petronius did not travel directly to Jerusalem, but the choice of a city in the domain of Agrippa, who had no direct legal authority in Judaea, is interesting. The agricultural strike appears to have affected both Galilee and Judaea: Jews in general protested about the order. It was, therefore, to Agrippa's advantage that his family worked to solve the problem.[1]

Throughout the incident the Jewish protest appears to have remained passive. Petronius did not need to quell any disturbance. The intensity of the protest and the persistence of the Jews probably made Petronius aware of the serious military implications if the order was carried out. Although militarily stronger, Petronius may have believed that victory would only be achieved at great cost.[2] Furthermore, the immediate situation was not without tension. Regardless of the number of days and whatever the time of year, the Jewish strike threatened to cause the loss of a year's produce. This could have resulted in a breakdown of social order. In these circumstances, and as a result of the machinations of the influential Jews, Petronius decided to postpone the order and attempt to persuade Gaius to revoke his instructions.[3]

Although Petronius only had limited success, two other factors

1. Agrippa was probably also genuinely concerned about the implications of the order for Jewish religion. Stern ('Province of Judaea', p. 358, and 'The Herodian Dynasty', p. 138) notes that the protest was not the action of an extremist group, a point Petronius became aware of at Tiberias, thus his letter. Bilde ('Roman Emperor', p. 82) notes the use of Galilee for the negotiations.

2. Tacitus claims that the Jews went to war. Smallwood (*Philonis*, p. 275) and Bilde ('Roman Emperor', p. 82) clearly point out that there is no evidence for such a claim. Petronius may have been aware that a revolt would take place. See Smallwood, *Jews under Roman Rule*, p. 176, and Rhoads, *Revolution*, p. 63. Bilde ('Roman Emperor', p. 82) also highlights the point that as Tiberias was the scene of the agricultural protest there is no reason to assume that it was a political protest against Rome, as the Jews were protesting in Jewish territory. See also Goodman, *Ruling Class*, p. 2, who notes the threat posed by the order to the ancestral customs of the Jews.

3. Petronius's request to 'the leading men' mentioned by Josephus emphasizes the point that certain Jews were perceived as able to influence the populace.

combined to ensure that the order was never carried out, the intervention of Agrippa and the death of Gaius. We cannot be certain of the extent of Agrippa's involvement. There is no reason to doubt that he did protest but we cannot establish whether the greater credit should be attributed to Petronius or Agrippa. Finally, irrespective of the rumours recorded by Philo, the death of Gaius ensured that no further attempt was made, for the moment, to erect a statue of the emperor in Jerusalem.[1]

Several points pertaining to the administration can be derived from the combined accounts. First, it was the Syrian legate who was chosen by Gaius to fulfil the task of erecting the statue. There is no evidence to suggest that the Judaean prefect took any part in the affair. It is conceivable that he was one of Petronius's attendants, but it was the Syrian legate who represented Gaius. The appearance of Petronius in Judaean affairs is not surprising in this instance. Gaius considered the task important. He chose to call on someone he trusted and considered to have the military capacity to fulfil the project. Although the prefect was expected to maintain Roman control of the territory, major changes were delegated to the leading military commander in the region, the Syrian legate.[2] This was an incident that arose because of a specific Roman order. The Jews were given the opportunity to accept the statue peacefully. That they were able to debate the matter appears to have been due to the approach chosen by

1. Most scholars agree that Agrippa participated but do not agree on how important his contribution proved to be; cf. Bilde, 'Roman Emperor', pp. 88, 92; Zeitlin, 'Did Agrippa Write?', p. 31; and Smallwood, *Philonis*, p. 292 and *Jews under Roman Rule*, pp. 178-79. Zeitlin ('Did Agrippa Write?', p. 31) correctly notes that Philo and Josephus construct their account of Agrippa's appeal. Stern ('Province of Judaea', p. 358) believes that Gaius was willing to wait until the end of the agricultural season.

2. Smallwood (*Philonis*, p. 267) notes the prominence of Petronius. For the possible timing of his appointment as legate and the identity of the Judaean prefect see Smallwood, *Philonis*, p. 267 and 'Chronology', p. 8. Note that there are several other incidents where the legate intervenes in Palestinian affairs. For example, see *Ant.* 18.1-3, 18, where Quirinius was ordered to carry out a census of the territory and settle Herod's will. As part of this task he removed the high priest, Joazar. See also *Ant.* 18.88, where the *boule* of the Samaritans is described as appealing to Vitellius to intervene and punish Pilate. During his tour of the region, Vitellius gave the Jews control of the high priests' vestments (*Ant.* 18.90) and then replaced the high priest (*Ant.* 18.95, 123). These actions were undertaken while there was no prefect in office.

Petronius, not necessarily to any order that he had received.

The second point is that the Jews in the region protested as a united front. The proposed measure violated the existing Jewish religious code. The protest was widespread and there is no reason to suggest that it was instigated by any particular group of Jews.[1] Implicit here is the notion that there were some issues which Jews believed were so important that they would defend them with their lives. In such circumstances it appears that the majority of Jews in the region held a notion of independence under direct Roman rule through their common identity. Thus, Galilaeans risked their lives and Agrippa and his family expressed concern because of the possible implications in Galilee and to Judaism.

Thirdly, Petronius spoke with a small select number of Jews. These 'powerful men'/'notable men'/'first men'/'leading men' were a specific section of the Jewish community who Petronius believed held influence amongst the general populace. Included among this group were priests and non-priests and members of Agrippa's family. Petronius's request that 'the leading men' restore order in the countryside implies a certain degree of effective influence. A Jewish institution which Philo describes by the term *gerousia* may have been involved in a minor capacity. Its presence may reflect the need to make a formal appeal to Petronius as he approached Jewish territory. The influential Jews retained an identity separate from the *gerousia*.

The final point is derived from Philo's account. The term *synedrion* is used twice to describe the process by which a decision was reached by Romans. The term does not appear in reference to a specific formal institution. Instead, *synedrion* describes Petronius's conference with his associates and his personal assessment of the situation.[2]

---

1. It is, therefore, incorrect for Horsley ('High Priests', p. 39) to attempt to place responsibility for protest in the hands of the populace. Although it is plausible that the intensity of protest by the influential Jews increased with the agricultural strike, their involvement cannot be simply restricted to being a response to the foreseeable disruption to the economy.

2. Smallwood (*Philonis*, p. 279) acknowledges that Philo uses *synedrion* here in the sense of *consilium*.

Chapter 4

THE RETURN OF DIRECT ROMAN RULE: AD 44–65

1. *Petition over the High Priests' Robes*

Ant. 20.6. Fadus tells 'the chief priests' (οἱ ἀρχιερεῖς) and 'the first men' (οἱ πρῶτοι) of Jerusalem to place the robes under Roman control in the Antonia, 7, they petition Fadus and Longinus, who allow Jews to petition Rome, children left as hostages, 9, Agrippa speaks for the Jews, 11, Claudius favours the Jews, 14, envoys named, Cornelius, son of Ceron, Tryphon, son of Theudion, Dorotheus, son of Nathanael and John, son of John.

After the death of Agrippa I in AD 44 his kingdom was placed under direct Roman rule. The first of the new Roman procurators, Fadus, ordered the Jews to return the high priests' vestments to his control. The absence of the account from *The Jewish War* does not necessarily indicate that we should question its authenticity. It is probable that Josephus was aware of the proceedings but did not believe that it was directly relevant to his primary concerns in *The Jewish War*.[1]

The account is self-explanatory, with one exception, the appearance of Longinus in Jerusalem. Josephus does not indicate why the Syrian legate was in Jerusalem at the time of the dispute.[2] It is possible that he appeared as a result of a request from Fadus or the Jews. Alternatively, Longinus may have decided to intervene when he was informed of Fadus's intentions, possibly by Fadus himself. Once in Jerusalem, Longinus took an active part in the proceedings, working in league

1. It is possible that Josephus derived much of his information regarding the incident from Agrippa II, after he wrote *War*. On this point, however, we can only speculate.

2. Compare with *Ant.* 15.406-07. Why Josephus should contradict himself is puzzling. Although not conclusive, Smallwood (*Jews under Roman Rule*, p. 260 n. 16), appears to be correct in accepting that Longinus was not involved with the initial order. Note that it is in the summary statement where Josephus has probably been inaccurate or careless.

with Fadus. Although we cannot be certain, there is no reason to argue that the legate responded primarily to any physical violence that resulted from the order. Rather, it appears that his involvement was that of a concerned superior.[1]

The incident provides a number of important observations regarding Jewish–Roman relations in the mid-first century AD. The first point to note is that certain Jews believed that they had the right to dispute particular Roman instructions. Both Fadus and the Jews perceived the responsibility for storing the high priests' vestments as an important issue, possibly in symbolic and practical terms.[2] Furthermore, Fadus assumed that it was within his right to order the Jews to hand over control of the vestments to him.[3]

Secondly, Fadus and Longinus display a willingness to negotiate the matter. Whatever private comments were passed between these men, they are portrayed as being in public agreement.[4] Josephus's lack of surprise at Longinus's presence suggests that the Syrian legate was often involved in an issue that would result in a change to the status quo. Although the Jews did not hand over the robes, the obvious military presence, and subsequent use of hostages, suggest the Roman

---

1. This is implied by Josephus (*Ant.* 20.7). Most scholars who comment on this incident argue that Longinus became involved to maintain order. See Stern, 'Province of Judaea', p. 360 and 'Herodian Dynasty', p. 150, and Zeitlin, *Rise and Fall*, II, p. 208. Smallwood (*Jews under Roman Rule*, p. 260) assumes Longinus arrived after the negotiations between Fadus and the Jews reached a 'stalemate'. Whether Longinus timed his arrival to co-ordinate with a major festival, such as Pentecost or Passover (Smallwood, *Jews under Roman Rule*, p. 260), is a matter of conjecture.

2. The significance and possible symbolic undercurrents of the Jewish protest have been noted by several scholars. Stern ('Herodian Dynasty', p. 150) and Jeremias (*Jerusalem*, p. 149) view the incident as a matter of preserving the religious integrity of the Jews. To distinguish the incident as clearly religious is to ignore the strong temporal connotations of the order. Goodman (*Ruling Class*, p. 112) presents a slightly different emphasis, highlighting the protest in terms of Jewish subjection to 'secular authorities'.

3. Smallwood (*Jews under Roman Rule*, p. 260) suggests that Fadus wanted to reinstitute the original Augustan practice. She appears to be correct in claiming that Fadus did not act on orders from the emperor (p. 260 n. 16). The final outcome and Claudius's subsequent decision to meet Herod of Chalcis' request suggests that he remained neutral regarding who should control the Temple. Note the earlier decision by Vitellius to allow the priests to keep control of the vestments (*Ant.* 18.90).

4. See Smallwood, *Jews under Roman Rule*, p. 260. She suggests that Longinus persuaded Fadus to allow a deputation to be sent to Rome.

intention to ensure that the situation was kept under control. Implicit in these actions is an acknowledgment of the seriousness of the Jewish protest. Furthermore, the use of hostages indicates a belief that holding the children of a certain section of the Jewish community would actively increase the chances of preventing the outbreak of trouble.[1]

Thirdly, and possibly most significantly, the Romans interact with a particular group of Jews. A combination of the 'first men of Jerusalem' and 'the chief priests' represent the Jewish cause, presumably throughout the incident. Several of the envoys are named. They were Cornelius, Tryphon, Dorotheus and John, possibly counted among 'the first men'[2] Fadus and Longinus, as well as the Jews, accepted these men as delegates. Furthermore, Fadus considered 'the first men' and 'chief priests' to be influential within the Jewish community, and able to fulfil his demand. There is no evidence within the narrative to suggest that these men were involved because of membership in any particular Jewish administrative institution or that Fadus and Longinus negotiated with any formal institution. The events that followed Fadus's initial demand justify his assessment in one sense. These 'first men' and 'chief priests' were the appropriate people to speak to: they did not refer the matter to any other group within the community. The problem for Fadus was that these men were unwilling to comply with his instructions.[3] Despite this setback Fadus did not exert excessive military pressure. Instead the request for the matter to be resolved in Rome by Claudius was granted.

The fourth observation relates to the letter of Claudius. At question is the accuracy of the introduction referring to the 'rulers/magistrates' (οἱ ἄρχοντες),[4] *boule*, people of Jerusalem and the nation. If the

---

1. Goodman (*Ruling Class*, p. 175) relates this action specifically to the 'ruling class'. There is no doubt that it directly affected a particular section of the community. The action was also probably intended to have an effect on the attitude of the Jewish community at large.

2. Goodman (*Ruling Class*, p. 141) suggests that Cornelius may have been a Roman citizen and notes that the envoys are not said to have come from high priestly families. His claim that the high priestly families were not represented in the deputation because of a 'lack of local prestige' is difficult to substantiate.

3. It is interesting that Horsley ('High Priests'), arguing that 'the chief priests' and wealthy aristocrats were collaborators with the Romans and motivated by thoughts of personal gain, fails to make any reference to this incident.

4. We cannot establish whether this term is used in its broad or specific meaning

introductory form of this letter is accurate, the lack of any reference to the *boule* in the account of Fadus's dealings may indicate the minor role played by such an institution in matters pertaining to the administration. There is no doubt that Claudius was responding to a particular issue. From this incident alone, however, we are unable to establish if it accurately reflects the situation in Jerusalem.[1] Clearly, the Romans assumed that Jerusalem had a *boule* and 'rulers/ magistrates'. There is no reason to suggest that Claudius or his secretary was ignorant about Jerusalem, especially as his knowledge of the envoys' names indicates that he was aware of certain aspects of what happened. It is, therefore, plausible that the *boule* was the formal administrative institution of Jerusalem.[2] Among other implications, this suggests that the *boule* was notified of the decision by Claudius because it was an official matter of correspondence. The role of negotiating the Jewish cause, however, was fulfilled by 'the first men' and 'chief priests', and consequently the *boule* is not mentioned in the earlier narrative of the incident.

in this instance.

1. Note that Josephus cites a number of letters in *Ant.* from the period of Julius Caesar with similar introductions. For example, see *Ant.* 14.190, 213, 235, 244.

2. Only a small number of scholars have specifically commented on this letter and its possible significance in terms of the administrative structure of Palestine. Of these only Tcherikover ('Was Jerusalem a Polis?', pp. 61-78) discusses the text in any detail. Within the context of his general argument that Jerusalem was not a polis, Tcherikover (p. 72) claims that *boule* was a new name for the traditional Jewish administrative body, and that the Greek terminology was employed because Josephus wrote *Ant.* in Greek. In fact, he believes (p. 76) the introductory sentence to the letter was simply a 'rhetorical embellishment' and the real force behind the protest was the Jewish nation (p. 75). Despite this claim he does accept that there was a municipal council in Jerusalem. Efron (*Studies*, p. 315) correctly points out that although the use of *boule* may not have necessarily meant that Jerusalem was a polis as such, there is no reason to equate *boule* with *synedrion*. Like Tcherikover, Hoenig (*Great Sanhedrin*, p. 155) believes *boule* and *synedrion* are synonymous while the 'rulers/magistrates' were 'magistrates'. He also states that the *boule* of the letter was probably an administrative body that controlled the Temple and possibly the city under the command of Agrippa II. Hoenig, however, ignores the fact that Agrippa II had no legal connection with affairs in Jerusalem at this point in time. On a more general level, Goodman (*Ruling Class*, p. 44) suggests that Claudius addressed the letter as he did on the assumption that Jerusalem had 'a natural aristocracy as in a normal Greek city'. However, more knowledge than this can be postulated because someone within Claudius's administration presumably heard the case presented by the Jewish envoys, knew their names and whom they claimed to be representing.

Finally, the people who secured the success of the Jewish request were not those sent from Jerusalem. Despite any standing held by the envoys within Judaea, it was Agrippa II who managed to persuade Claudius to uphold Jewish control of the vestments. This may indicate that in matters pertaining to the high priesthood and Temple customs, the Jews were united, irrespective of the geographical region in which they resided. It is also possible that Agrippa supported the envoys for reasons of personal and family gain.[1] The foundation of the success, however, was the action of influential Jews in Judaea, 'the first men of Jerusalem' and 'the chief priests'. It should also be noted that Claudius displayed a belief that to have direct physical control over the vestments was not essential to maintaining control of the Temple. Claudius was willing to share responsibility for the administration with certain Jews.[2]

2. *Dispute between Galilaeans and Samaritans*

War 2.232, Samaritans kill a Galilaean, 233, many Galilaeans gather to attack Samaritans, 'the notable men' (οἱ γνώριμοι) of Galilee see Cumanus, 234, Jerusalem Jews march to Samaria, ignoring pleas of 'the rulers/magistrates' (οἱ ἄρχοντες), 235, they are led by Eleazar and Alexander, 236, Cumanus attacks the Jews, 237, 'rulers/magistrates' of Jerusalem, 238, persuade Jews to disperse, 239, 'the powerful men' (οἱ δυνατοί) of the Samaritans go to Quadratus, 240, 'the notable' Jews , including Jonathan, protest, 242, Quadratus executes eighteen Jews, 243, he sends 'the high priests/chief priests' (οἱ ἀρχιερεῖς) Jonathan and Ananus and Ananias, two other of 'the most powerful men' (οἱ δυνατώτατοι) and 'the notable' Jews and 'the most eminent /distinguished' (οἱ ἐπιφανεστάτοι) Samaritans, 244, and Celer and Cumanus to Rome, 245, Agrippa speaks for the Jews, 'the powerful' Romans support Cumanus, Caesar executes three of 'the most powerful Samaritans', banishes Cumanus, 246, and sends Celer to Jerusalem for execution.

Ant. 20.118, Samaritans kill Galilaeans en route to Jerusalem, 119, 'the

---

1. Zeitlin (*Rise and Fall*, II, p. 208) notes that the envoys received the support of Agrippa II. Smallwood (*Jews under Roman Rule*, p. 260 n. 18) and Rajak (*Josephus*, p. 66 n. 1) place more responsibility for the decision with Claudius and his policy in dealing with the Jews.
2. This willingness appears to be supported by the subsequent decision to pass direct control of the Temple into the hands of Herod of Chalcis and then Agrippa II. See *Ant.* 20.15, 104.

first men' (οἱ πρῶτοι) of Galilee go to Cumanus, 121, 'the leading men' (οἱ ἐν τέλει) offer to negotiate, masses ask Eleazar to lead attack on Samaritans, 122, Cumanus attacks the Jews, 123, 'the first men' of Jerusalem plead with the Jews, 124, who disperse, 125, 'the first men' of the Samaritans go to Quadratus, 129, he executes Jews and Samaritans, 131, and later Doetus and four others, he sends Ananias, the high priest, and Ananus, the captain, and their followers in chains to Rome, 132, 'the first men' of the Samaritans and Jews, Cumanus and Celer go to Rome, 135, Agrippa speaks to Agrippina, 136, Claudius finds in favour of the Jews, executes Samaritans, banishes Cumanus and returns Celer to Jerusalem.

Annals, 12.54, Cumanus commands Galilee while Felix commands Samaria, they are rivals, Quadratus favours Felix, Cumanus is condemned.

During the term of the third procurator who controlled the province of Judaea after the death of Agrippa I, a major incident is recorded in some detail by Josephus, in *The Jewish War* and *Antiquities of the Jews*. A dispute between Galilaean Jews and Samaritans developed into a general Jewish–Samaritan conflict in which the Roman procurator, Cumanus, and the legate of Syria, Quadratus, became embroiled. Tacitus also alludes to the incident but his main interest is in the Roman machinations and he gives no details of a dispute between Galilaeans and Samaritans. My examination of this incident is based on an assessment of *The Jewish War* and *Antiquities of the Jews*, drawing upon Tacitus's account where it is appropriate.

A comparison of Josephus's two narratives indicates general agreement on the chronology of the incident. There are, however, two aspects of Josephus's accounts that require detailed assessment. They are: specific points of detail where *The Jewish War* and *Antiquities of the Jews* differ, or lack clarity; and the varying descriptions of the Jewish and Samaritan participants.

The first of the four elements of the two narratives that disagree and/or display a lack of clarity pertains to the cause of the dispute. In the version in *The Jewish War* the Samaritans killed one Galilaean, while in *Antiquities of the Jews* the Samaritans attacked and killed many Galilaeans. In both texts it is a group of Galilaeans that were attacked, increasing the likelihood that more than one man was killed.[1]

1. M. Aberbach ('The Conflicting Accounts of Josephus and Tacitus Concerning Cumanus' and Felix' Terms of Office', *JQR* 40 [1949], p. 1 n. 1) claims that the

The number killed is not, in its itself, significant. What was more important according to Josephus was that the Samaritans made an unprovoked attack on Jews who were in the process of fulfilling an act of religious homage.

The two narratives are also in slight disagreement regarding the events immediately after the initial Samaritan attack. The version in *Antiquities of the Jews* states that the Jewish populace was exhorted to take up arms by the Galilaeans after Cumanus had been approached to intervene. In *The Jewish War* the attempt to gain aid from Cumanus was preceded by the Galilaeans gathering to attack the Samaritans. Again, this difference is not significant. It is plausible that some Jews gathered in preparation to seek action. Josephus does not suggest in *The Jewish War* that anything was actually done before Cumanus was asked to intervene. Moreover, the request may have been partly motivated by a concern that the Jewish populace in Galilee and Judaea was ready to take action.

It is also not entirely clear which Jews were actually attacked by Cumanus. In *The Jewish War* Josephus distinguishes between the brigands and the masses, suggesting that Cumanus directed his attack against Alexander and Eleazar. The Jerusalem populace, however, had been persuaded to disperse, some carrying out minor robberies as they departed. Alternatively in *Antiquities of the Jews* Cumanus attacks the Jews as a general group. After the battle both the populace and the rebels departed to their respective homes. It appears that the version in *The Jewish War* was structured in an attempt to distinguish between a rebellious aggressive element and a peaceful majority among the Jews. In both accounts, however, Eleazar had been encouraged to participate by the populace. Although Cumanus may have been keen to capture Eleazar, it is unlikely that he would have ignored the involvement of the populace.[1]

difference can be explained by the fact that in *War* Josephus used the official Roman report while in *Ant.* an anti-Jewish source was used. Even if it is accepted that Josephus did alter his sources, it is the *Ant.* account that tends to favour the Jews. Note also Cohen, *Josephus in Galilee*, p. 149, who argues that the account in *War* of the incident is neutral while in *Ant.* Josephus is anti-Samaritan. It is possible that Cohen lays too much emphasis on this division as an explanation for all the differences in detail that exist between *Ant.* and *War*. Smallwood (*Jews under Roman Rule*, p. 265 n. 29) and Loftus ('Anti-Roman Revolts', p. 91 n. 56) give priority to the version in *Ant.* on this point in the light of the events that followed.

1. Goodman (*Ruling Class*, p. 63) points out that Eleazar was a well-known

Comment is also necessary on the involvement of Quadratus. Both texts state that Quadratus was requested to intervene by the Samaritans. This is slightly puzzling because Josephus states that Cumanus favoured the Samaritans and that he was taking action to stop the Jews.[1] This inconsistency is recognized in *The Jewish War* where Josephus suggests that Cumanus was incapable of effectively dealing with the matter to the liking of the Samaritans. Although it is conceivable that Cumanus told the Samaritans to seek Quadratus's assistance, it is more likely that Josephus is partly correct: Cumanus did not resolve the matter in a manner that satisfied the Samaritans, so they turned to his superior. Support for this notion comes from the reference to Quadratus executing the Jews and Samaritans arrested by Cumanus. It appears that Cumanus, rather than being pro-Samaritan as Josephus implies, held both Jews and Samaritans responsible for the dispute.[2]

The negotiations involving Samaritans, Jews and Romans after Cumanus's military intervention constitute the major part of the narrative and require detailed assessment. In particular, the terminology used to describe the participants will be examined.

The identity of the Romans, who all became involved because of the actions of other people, is clear. The Galilaeans approached Cumanus, and Celer, a military tribune, probably acted as Cumanus's subordinate in the battle with the Jews.[3] Quadratus displayed no qualms about taking action after the Samaritans sought his arbitration and there is no evidence to suggest that his jurisdiction was limited. It is possible that he considered the matter to be too provocative to be resolved in

bandit. See also R.A. Horsley and J.S. Hanson, *Bandits, Prophets, and Messiahs. Popular Movements in the Time of Jesus* (Minneapolis, MN: Winston Press, 1985), pp. 67-68. Aberbach ('Conflicting Accounts', p. 7) may be correct in stating that the Jews who attacked the Samaritans were Judaeans and Galilaeans who were in Jerusalem for the festival.

1. Josephus claims that Cumanus accepted money from the Samaritans (*Ant.* 20.127); cf. Tacitus, *Annals*, 12.54. See Goodman, *Ruling Class*, p. 149.

2. Smallwood (*Jews under Roman Rule*, p. 266) simply notes that it is unclear from Josephus's narrative as to why the Samaritans appealed to Quadratus. Note also Aberbach, 'Conflicting Accounts', p. 8, who attempts to explain the appeal as the result of the Jews being militarily stronger than the Samaritans, and as having the support of Felix.

3. Aberbach ('Conflicting Accounts', p. 12) suggests that Celer was the soldier who had previously committed a public act of indecency. See also Smallwood, *Jews under Roman Rule*, p. 268 n. 36.

the region.[1] Whatever the case, Quadratus involved Claudius, sending Jews, Cumanus, Celer and Samaritans to present their case before the emperor, where the dispute was finally resolved.[2]

Mention of Tacitus's account is relevant here. According to Josephus, when Cumanus went to Rome the province had no procurator. Tacitus, however, presents an entirely different administrative structure. Cumanus and Felix served as procurator at the same time, one having been procurator of Samaria and Judaea, the other of Galilee. Furthermore, Tacitus states that Quadratus and Felix decided Cumanus's case. There is no precedent for the division of Palestine claimed by Tacitus, and it therefore appears that his understanding of the structure was in error.[3] It is possible, however, that Quadratus assigned men, including Felix, to maintain order in Judaea and Galilee until the matter was resolved.[4]

The identity of the Samaritans is also straightforward. Although

1. There is a general agreement among scholars who comment on this incident that Quadratus did not need to take any major military action to calm the situation. For example, see Goodman, *Ruling Class*, p. 174, and Smallwood, *Jews under Roman Rule*, p. 267. Smallwood points out that Quadratus only took immediate action against the Jews he considered had directly defied Roman authority, while the original dispute was sent to Rome for adjudication.

2. Freyne (*Galilee*, p. 74) notes that this incident indicates that Cumanus came under the direct jurisdiction of the Syrian legate in practical terms.

3. Most of the scholarly discussion pertaining to this incident has been in terms of the obvious discrepancies that exist between Josephus and Tacitus regarding the administrative structure of Palestine. Aberbach ('Conflicting Accounts', p. 1) seeks to reconcile the accounts rather than claim priority for one or other of the sources. As a result he alters what Tacitus actually said, but accepts the basic principle that Palestine was divided under the control of Cumanus and Felix. Freyne (*Galilee*, p. 76) also concludes that Cumanus controlled Samaria and Judaea while Felix controlled Galilee. The use of *War* 2.247 as evidence that Palestine had been divided before Felix became procurator of the whole province is incorrect. There is no overt statement in Josephus to support the notion that Palestine was officially sub-divided during this period. Schürer (*History*, I, p. 459 n. 15) is probably correct in stating that it is not possible to resolve the differences between Josephus and Tacitus in a way that accommodates both versions. Felix may have been assigned the task of maintaining law and order while the matter was under investigation. See Smallwood, *Jews under Roman Rule*, p. 266 and 'Some Comments on Tacitus, Annals, XII, 54', *Latomus* 18 (1959), pp. 560-67 for a detailed assessment of this question. See also Stern, 'Province of Judaea', pp. 374-75.

4. Note that in this instance Josephus refers to Jerusalem being orderly and quiet. At other points in the narrative Josephus is quick to claim that religious festivals were an occasion of disorder. See *War* 2.10-12; *Ant.* 13.213; 17.254; 20.106.

different terminology is used in *The Jewish War* and *Antiquities of the Jews*, they refer to the same people. Apart from the initial reference to the inhabitants of Gema/Ginae, all other Samaritans mentioned are the men who represented their community in discussions with the Romans. In *Antiquities of the Jews* Josephus consistently refers to the Samaritan representatives as 'the first men'. In *The Jewish War* they are 'the powerful'/'the notable' and 'the most powerful'. The use of 'the most powerful' to describe the three men executed by Claudius suggests that there was an inner elite among 'the powerful'/'notable' Samaritans who represented their community. Josephus uses these terms to refer to a group of influential people within the Samaritan community. They are not noted as being representatives of any institution.

Of the Jews involved I have already noted the Galilaean pilgrims, Eleazar and the Jewish populace, which included Galilaeans and Judaeans. Their participation was crucial to the incident but most of the action after the initial dispute involved only a small section of the Jewish population.[1]

There is no evidence to suggest that the Jews who participated in the negotiations were part of any formal institution.[2] These spokesmen participated in discussions with the Romans and in attempts to influence the Jewish populace to follow a particular course of action. Apart from two instances where *The Jewish War* and *Antiquities of the Jews*

---

1. Horsley ('High Priests', pp. 40-41) views this incident as an occasion where the priestly aristocracy became involved primarily because the populace was keen to take drastic action. The formal involvement of this priestly aristocracy was due to the appeal made by the influential Samaritans. If the priestly aristocracy remained as pro-Roman as Horsley suggests and the populace were the main spur of action, some explanation is necessary for the silence of the populace throughout most of the incident and the willingness of the priestly aristocracy to present the Jewish case to the extent that they did. Note the description of the dispute between the Philadelphians and the Peraeans under the procuratorship of Fadus (*Ant.* 20.2-4). Fadus takes his revenge on 'the first men' of Peraea, despite the claim by Josephus that they were not in favour of fighting the Philadelphians. Fadus believed that these men could be held responsible for what happened, possibly on the basis that they were actually involved in what took place (*Ant.* 20.4).

2. Several scholars assume that these Jews were representatives of a formal institution. For example, see Smallwood, *Jews under Roman Rule*, p. 265, who refers to the sanhedrin; and G. Alon, 'The Burning of the Temple', in *Jews, Judaism and the Classical World*, pp. 261-62, who mentions the sanhedrin and the leading priests; cf. Rajak, *Josephus*, p. 70.

differ in content, the references to the Jews vary only in the terminology used.

In *Antiquities of the Jews* Josephus consistently refers to the influential Jews as 'the first men'. On only one occasion he uses 'the leading men' Two comments are required on the variety of terms used in *The Jewish War*. The first relates to the use of 'rulers/magistrates'. These men were linked with Jerusalem and sought to persuade the populace to remain peaceful. We cannot determine for certain that they were officials. If Josephus meant 'magistrates' then some explanation for their involvement in this part of the incident alone is necessary.[1] The parallel reference in *Antiquities of the Jews* to 'the leading men' suggests that the men who made the first appeal to the populace were different from the other Jews involved. It is, however, also plausible that 'rulers/magistrates' and 'the leading men' should be equated with 'the notable'/'first men'.

Secondly, Josephus identifies those Jews involved in negotiations with the Romans as 'the notable'/'first men'. Included in this group is Jonathan. Later, however, Jonathan and several others are grouped separately from 'the notable'/'first men' Furthermore, this distinction is expressed by the term 'the most powerful' Jews. This apparent contradiction can be explained. Josephus understood there to be a group of 'the notable'/'first men', within which there was a sub-section of prominent men.

Several points of clarification can be made regarding the identity of the Jewish participants. First, Josephus equates 'the notable' with 'the first men'. They are the people who argue the Jewish case. These 'notable'/'first' men were recognized by Cumanus and Quadratus, despite their failure to obtain Cumanus's support. Furthermore, Josephus affirms the existence of an elite in this group, referring to them as 'the most powerful'. Thirdly, Josephus uses high priest to describe a previous incumbent, namely, Jonathan. The fourth point relates to the involvement of Jonathan. In *The Jewish War* he has a high profile, but is not included in *Antiquities of the Jews*, where only Ananias and Ananus are named. There are several possible explanations for the change. Different sources may have been used,

---

1. Efron (*Studies*, p. 315) assumes that the references in this incident indicate that there were 'magistrates' in Jerusalem. See also Aberbach, 'Conflicting Accounts', p. 8.

Josephus may have made a mistake, or chosen to ignore Jonathan in *Antiquities of the Jews* in order to place greater emphasis on Ananus and Ananias. Either account may narrate the historical situation. There is, however, no apparent reason to suggest why Josephus would specifically add Jonathan to *The Jewish War* and then remove him from *Antiquities of the Jews*.[1] As in *The Jewish War*, the text in *Antiquities of the Jews* draws a distinction between Ananus and Ananias and the other 'notable'/'first men', adding that they and their followers were sent to Rome in chains. What is significant is that the individuals who stood out among the Jews were all connected with the high priesthood.

Finally, both accounts agree that Agrippa II intervened on behalf of the Jews in Rome. Not only did Agrippa consider himself an appropriate spokesman, he was acknowledged as such by Claudius, or at least by Agrippina and the Jewish envoys.[2] Furthermore, Agrippa acts on behalf of the Jews in the province of Judaea, even though he was under no legal obligation to do so.

Particular Samaritans and Jews represented their respective communities before the Romans in this dispute. These men are described as 'the powerful'/'notable'/'first men' and possibly 'rulers'/'magistrates'/ 'leading men'. Within this group of influential Jews and Samaritans Josephus recognizes an inner circle, 'the most powerful'. Some of the Jews in this group are named. They include Ananus and Ananias, and probably Jonathan, each of whom had some link with the high priesthood. Quadratus held these Jews above all others as responsible for the actions of their community.[3]

---

1. Most scholars who comment on this incident are in agreement that Jonathan did participate. See, for example, Horsley, 'High Priests', p. 41; Smallwood, 'High Priests', pp. 24-25; and Goodman, *Ruling Class*, p. 49.

2. On the events in Rome, see Smallwood, *Jews under Roman Rule*, p. 268. Note that Josephus refers to 'the powerful' Romans supporting Cumanus. Implicit here is the notion that 'the powerful' as a descriptive term of certain people was applicable to more than one ethnic group within the narrative of the same incident.

3. Doetus and four other Jews who were executed by Quadratus appear to have been active in the physical violence that broke out. It is possible that these men did play a part in what happened as much as they were men chosen at random because the Jews had to have some leaders, as indicated by Goodman, *Ruling Class*, p. 175 n. 28. Although Goodman appears to be correct in suggesting that some of the fighting was without obvious leadership, it must be remembered that the Jewish cause was represented by several influential Jews.

Four general observations regarding this incident are pertinent to our understanding of the administration of Palestine. First, this was an ethnic dispute. The incident took place within the geographic confines of the Roman province of Judaea but arose between Galilaeans and Samaritans. Although Roman involvement was requested by the Jews, it it was not until fighting broke out that Cumanus decided to act.[1]

A second, related observation is that the Romans Cumanus and Quadratus were requested to arbitrate. The subsequent events, however, indicate that some Jews were willing to take matters into their own hands if the relevant Roman authority failed to act in a favourable manner. In turn, such vigilante action brought a quick response from the Romans.

Thirdly, the Jews and Samaritans were represented by a sub-section of their respective communities. These men were part of an informal hierarchy. Furthermore, in both communities, Josephus accepted the existence of an elite within the influential group. There is no reason to suggest that any of these men were part of a formal institution.

Finally, the most prominent Jews in this dispute were linked with the high priesthood, either personally or through a close relative. Although the incident had its origins in Galilee men connected with the Temple became the central Jewish spokesmen.

3. The Trial of Paul

Acts 21.30, people of Jerusalem seize Paul, 32, tribune intervenes, 22.24, he orders Paul to be beaten, 25, Paul states that he is a Roman citizen, 30, next day tribune orders 'the chief priests' (οἱ ἀρχιερεῖς) and all the *synedrion* to gather, 23.2, high priest questions Paul, 10, Paul taken to Roman barracks, 14, plot to kill Paul by some Jews, 24, he is sent to Felix, covering letter from tribune, 24.1, Ananias, Tertullus the orator and 'the elders' (οἱ πρεσβύτεροι), 5, accuse Paul, 27, Paul in prison two years, 25.2, 'the chief priests' and 'the first men' (οἱ πρῶτοι) of the Jews ask Festus to bring Paul to Jerusalem, 5, Festus says 'the

---

1. The decision by the Romans to improve the road network in the region implies a recognition of Palestine as a possible place of tension, between racial groups if not between the inhabitants and the Romans. See Goodman, *Ruling Class*, p. 174, referring to R.G. Goodchild, 'The Coast Road of Phoenicia and its Roman Milestones', *Berytus* 9 (1948), pp. 91-127. See also Rhoads, *Revolution*, pp. 72-73, on the possible significance of this incident for Jewish–Roman relations.

powerful men' (οἱ δυνατοί) should come to Caesarea, 11, Paul appeals
to Claudius, 23, Paul before Festus, Agrippa and Bernice.

The final New Testament incident is the arrest and trial of Paul.
Approximately one quarter of Acts is devoted to this incident, which
took place during the terms of two of the procurators, Felix and
Festus. Paul is credited with making three lengthy speeches: to the
Jews, to the *synedrion*, and to Festus and Agrippa.

Despite the obvious significance attached to the arrest and trial of
Paul by Luke, he does not necessarily display an understanding of the
actual details of the incident's development. Luke's primary concern
was probably not to outline exactly the legal proceedings. Rather,
several themes are apparent which appear to have affected Luke's
narration: he emphasizes the 'Jewish' nature of the dispute, implicitly
declares Paul's innocence under Roman law and overtly criticizes
certain Jews. Luke's concern to draw out these, and other, themes
makes it difficult to establish the historical reliability of such scenes as
the speech by Paul after his arrest, and Agrippa's involvement.[1]
Consistent with my approach to all other incidents assessed, the prime
concern is to present a general outline of what happened, drawing
upon specific details where they appear to be historically plausible.

Two aspects of Luke's account require detailed assessment: the identity of the participants, and the nature of Paul's offence. Regarding the

---

1. Discussion of possible underlying themes is the focus of attention for much of
the scholarly assessment of this section of Acts. For example, see Brawley, *Luke–
Acts*, pp. 115-16, who argues that Luke uses the arrest and trial of Paul to portray
Christianity as the true 'hope of Judaism', and Marshall, *Acts*, p. 350, who views
the incident as a trial of Christianity in which Paul correctly understands that Judaism
reaches its fulfilment in Jesus. See also Longenecker, *Acts*, p. 523, who views the
narrative as an expression of Christianity's non-political nature. It is notable that
these scholars accept the existence of certain important themes, yet tend to uphold the
majority of the narrative as historically accurate. See especially Marshall, *Acts*,
p. 360, responding to the approach of Haenchen. Another approach, very critical of
Luke's manipulation of the historical situation to present a narrative that reflected his
interests, is held by such scholars as Efron (*Studies*, p. 328) and Winter (*Trial*,
p. 112). Haenchen (*Studies*, pp. 629, 693) believes that much of the narrative is the
result of Luke's concern to address the issue of how Christianity could exist within
the Roman world. The idea that Luke manipulated what information he had available
to him is also implied by Walaskay (*Rome*, p. 53) when he suggests that Luke
wanted to contrast the legal order of the Romans and Jews. Few scholars doubt that
the speeches are the words of Luke and that the details of what happened were not a
major concern for him. See, for example, Dibelius, *Studies*, p. 133.

participants, it is important to establish why people became involved and in what capacity they did so.

Three Romans are actively involved, Claudius Lysias, Felix and Festus. It is implied that Caesar would become involved once Paul reached Rome. As a tribune stationed in Jerusalem, Claudius Lysias was the first representative of the Roman administration involved in the incident. He responded to a disturbance in which Jews were attacking a man he assumed was wanted by the Romans. Although this case of mistaken identity was used in the dialogue between the tribune and Paul to highlight Paul's inherent acceptability within the Roman social system, it is conceivable that the tribune did believe Paul was a man wanted under Roman law.[1] The tribune, therefore, was intervening as a representative of law and order.[2] Furthermore, once he had intervened, the tribune controlled events until the matter was handed over to the procurator. The tribune gave protection to the accused man after it was established that he was a Roman citizen. He also took measures to determine the nature of the dispute, allowing the Jews opposing Paul to present their case and providing Paul with the opportunity to defend himself.[3]

The tribune was directly responsible for involving his superior, Felix. He held a hearing where both sides of the case were presented. Despite any pressure on the part of the Jews, however, nothing was done before Felix ended his term as procurator. Felix's inactivity, therefore, resulted in his successor, Festus, also becoming involved in the role of arbitrator. The opponents of Paul appeared before the new procurator and pressed for the case to be resolved. In these circumstances Luke states that Paul made an appeal to be tried in Rome

1. Haenchen (*Acts*, p. 622) notes that the confusion of Paul with the Egyptian enabled Luke to acquit Christianity of civil upheaval. That Paul inherited his citizenship also implied that Christians could be respectable people.

2. See Cassidy, *Society and Politics*, p. 97, and Walaskay, *Rome*, p. 5, who state that Claudius Lysias intervened to maintain order in Jerusalem.

3. Marshall (*Acts*, p. 361) intimates that the tribune decided who would be involved, although he does accept that it was a meeting of the sanhedrin. Other scholars give precedence to the sanhedrin, implying that the tribune was partly under the influence of its intentions. For example, see Munck, *Acts*, p. 222; Longenecker, *Acts*, p. 530; and Smallwood, *Jews under Roman Rule*, p. 276. Sherwin-White (*Roman Society*, p. 54) accepts that the tribune initiated the meeting but assumes it was a request rather than an order. It is not possible to establish the limits of the tribune's power in this instance.

before Caesar. Here the details of the legal proceedings are not clear. It appears most likely that Festus chose to refer the case to Caesar, not that he was obliged to do so. Withdrawing from the case, Festus was no longer in a position where he risked offending the inhabitants of his new province.[1]

Numerous Jews are linked with the incident. Initially the people opposed to Paul appear to have been Jews born outside Judaea, some of whom may have been visiting Jerusalem. These men obtained support from Jews who resided in the city.[2] After the tribune intervened, these Jews only appear as the audience for Paul's first speech.

Specific sections of the community or individual Jews occupy the remainder of Luke's narrative. The 'chief priests' and 'elders' were the prominent groups. The serving high priest appears as a leading Jewish spokesman. A second spokesman, the orator Tertullus, is referred to in negotiations with the Romans.

Luke uses two further terms to identify groups of Jews: 'the first men' and 'the powerful men'. Both of these appear to be equivalent to

1. The events before Felix, and especially Festus, as narrated by Luke have been the subject of much debate. A number of scholars have concentrated their discussion within the framework of the Lukan narrative without paying much attention to the Roman legal context. For example, see Haenchen, *Acts*, p. 669, and Bruce, *Acts*, p. 432. Others do not appear to have fully understood the circumstances. For example, see Munck, *Acts*, p. 238, and Winter, *Trial*, p. 125. For the debate concerning the right of appeal and ability of procurators to try Roman citizens note A.H.M. Jones, *The Criminal Courts of the Roman Republic and Principate* (ed. J.A. Crook; Oxford: Basil Blackwell, 1972); P. Garnsey, *Social Status and Legal Privilege in the Roman Empire* (Oxford: Clarendon Press, 1970), pp. 75-76; *idem*, 'The Criminal Jurisdiction of Governors', *JRS* 58 (1968), pp. 51-59; *idem*, 'The Lex Iulia and Appeal under the Empire', *JRS* 56 (1966), pp. 167-89; and Sherwin-White, *Roman Society*, pp. 57-62. These men accurately perceive that the incident must be viewed within the Roman legal context but differ in their interpretation. It appears that Garnsey ('The *Lex Iulia*', pp. 184-85) is correct in viewing Paul's request as one for a Roman trial and that Festus decided at what level the case would be heard. Cf. Jones, *Criminal Courts*, p. 102, and Sherwin-White, *Roman Society*, pp. 57-59, who uphold that it was an exceptional case of appeal before trial. See also F. Millar, 'The Emperor, the Senate and the Provinces', *JRS* 56 (1966), pp. 156-66, who highlights that a strict distinction was not upheld between the administration of imperial and senatorial provinces in the early principate. By analogy, it is possible that what happened in the case of Paul was not necessarily a response to a particular legal theory.

2. Brawley (*Luke–Acts*, pp. 80-81) appears to be correct in linking the events in Miletus with what happened in Jerusalem. See also Marshall, *Acts*, p. 347.

other terms used by Luke. The 'first men', referred to when the Jews approach Festus, should probably be equated with 'elders'. The reference to 'the powerful men' in the statement attributed to Festus appears to be a description of the men who were to present the case against Paul. In this instance 'the powerful men' were probably the 'chief priests' and 'elders'/'first men'.[1]

The other Jewish participant to whom Luke refers is Agrippa II. The public proclamation of Paul's innocence attributed to Agrippa was an obvious incentive for his inclusion. Luke, however, is careful not to claim that Agrippa had any official authority in the case. There is no reason to suggest that Agrippa was not an interested onlooker.[2]

Luke also refers to the involvement of *the synedrion*. The use of the definite article conveys the notion that it was a permanent institution.[3] Furthermore, it is implied that this *synedrion* was able to try Paul for his offence against the Jews. The notion of permanence may be the result of Luke, or his source's, understanding of the situation in Jerusalem. It is also possible, however, that it derives from Luke's perception that all recognizable Jewish authorities opposed Paul, including any appropriate legal apparatus that could be used.

There is some confusion over the membership of this *synedrion*, which is especially evident if it is assumed that Luke was referring to a permanent Jewish institution.[4] Luke draws a distinction between the

1. Note the suggestion of Smallwood (*Jews under Roman Rule*, p. 276) that the forty or more men were sicarii. The reference to 'the rulers/magistrates' (οἱ ἄρχοντες) should be understood in the general sense of the word, as suggested by its usage in Acts 21.18. Bruce (*Acts*, p. 413) believes that 'the chief priests' and 'elders' should be equated in meaning.

2. The consensus of opinion favours Agrippa's involvement being that of an advisor. See, for example, Longenecker, *Acts*, p. 548; Munck, *Acts*, p. 238; and Sherwin-White, *Roman Society*, p. 51. Whether the Roman authorities were as imperceptive to the subtleties of the arguments being put forward as is implied by some scholars is debatable. The possible parallel with the role of Herod in the trial of Jesus has been noted by Longenecker (*Acts*, p. 548).

3. See Acts 22.30; 23.1, 15, 20; 24.20, which appear to indicate that Luke was referring to an institution. In Acts 22.6, however, the *synedrion* appears to be used to describe a place. Note also Acts 23.28, where Luke depicts the tribune using *synedrion*, apparently on the basis that the term referred to a trial court that was not necessarily associated with one particular community.

4. Mantel (*Studies*, pp. 290-92) assumes that Luke was referring to a formal institution but attempts to point out that the Great Sanhedrin played no part in the trial of Paul. Cf. Marshall, *Acts*, p. 302, who assumes that Luke meant the sanhedrin but

synedrion and 'the chief priests' and 'elders', suggesting that these groups of people were not counted among the members (Acts 22.30). Although it is stated that Pharisaic and Sadducean opinions were held by some of the members, it does not clarify the identity of the members. Furthermore, Luke's presentation of the divergence of opinion between the Sadducees and Pharisees may have been the result of a concern to highlight the Jewish nature of the dispute and the apparent uncertainty regarding the offence, rather than interest in depicting the actual situation. It appears that the one person whom Luke definitely associated with the *synedrion* in this instance was the high priest.

The other aspect of the narrative that requires comment is the offence of Paul. The attempt to kill Paul had its origin outside Jerusalem. In the city, trouble began when it was claimed that he invited a non-Jew into the Temple. As this was the main charge it is puzzling that the case was not resolved sooner.[1] Luke proposes that the real issue was a doctrinal dispute between Jews. Although he may overemphasize this aspect of the case, it may explain in part the decision by the tribune and the procurator to refer the matter to a higher authority. Certainly, Paul was not guilty of any obvious offence against the Roman empire.[2]

What began as a dispute between Paul and non-Judaean Jews developed into a politically sensitive case which resulted in Paul being sent to Rome. The leading Roman representative in Jerusalem intervened, presumably in the belief that the Jews had found a man also sought by the Romans. The discovery that Paul was a Roman citizen

may not have been recording what actually happened, possibly because he wanted to present a parallel between the cases of Paul and Jesus. Bruce (*Acts*, p. 429) claims 'the first men' and 'chief priests' should be equated with sanhedrin. Efron (*Studies*, p. 332) points out the manipulation of the sanhedrin members by Luke, suggesting that he invented the narrative. Note also the discussion connected with Paul's response to the high priest and the variety of explanations offered. See, for example Longenecker, *Acts*, p. 531, and J.T. Sanders, *The Jews*, p. 289.

1. See E. Bickerman, 'The Warning Inscriptions of Herod's Temple', in *Studies in Jewish and Christian History*, Part 2 (ed. E. Bickerman; Leiden: Brill, 1980), pp. 210-24, regarding the ability of Jews to execute those who profaned the Temple.

2. On the original complaint see Sherwin-White, *Roman Society*, p. 49, and Mantel, *Studies*, p. 299. For the political connotations of the Jewish complaint registered with the Romans see Mantel, *Studies*, p. 300; Sherwin-White, *Roman Society*, pp. 50-51; Cassidy, *Society and Politics*, p. 104; and Walaskay, *Rome*, p. 54.

and the nature of the dispute prevented the case from being quickly settled. The Jews attempted to obtain control of the case, and failing that, sought conviction under Roman law. The Roman officials appear to have found little evidence to suggest that Paul was guilty of disturbing civil order but remained sensitive to Jewish feelings. This tension was resolved by a referral of the case to the jurisdiction of Caesar. Whether Paul ever actually faced a formal trial in Judaea is a matter of debate. His case was assessed on at least three occasions but was not necessarily the subject of a trial.[1]

Five general comments can be made regarding this incident. First, this was a Jewish dispute. Jews visiting Jerusalem pursued their protest against Paul, questioning his allegiance to Judaism. Secondly, the Roman involvement was intended to maintain order. Thirdly, it came under Roman jurisdiction once Paul's Roman citizenship became public knowledge and the dispute was no longer associated with the possible defilement of the Temple. There was no Jewish trial, despite the fact that the Jews attempted to have Paul placed in their control. Furthermore, it is apparent that the Jews conformed to the circumstances, presenting their case in such a way as to appeal to Roman interests. Fourthly, in this instance, select groups of Jews conversed with the Romans: 'chief priests', 'elders'/'first men' and the serving high priest. Finally, Luke's use of *synedrion* is not entirely clear. Although he accepts that the Jews had a permanent institution that could judge criminal cases, Luke is not sure about the nature of the relationship between the *synedrion* and the priestly and lay leadership.

4. *Petition regarding the Temple Wall*

Ant. 20.191, 'the respected men' (οἱ προύχοντες) of Jerusalem build a high wall to obscure Agrippa's view, 194, Jews allowed to send an embassy to Rome, Ishmael, Helcias, the treasurer, and ten of 'the first

---

1. Mantel (*Studies*, pp. 29, 290-91) assumes that Paul was tried. Similarly, see Sherwin-White, *Roman Society*, pp. 50-51. Winter (*Trial*, p. 116) and Garnsey ('The *Lex Iulia*', p. 184) argue against there being a trial. Winter's conclusion (p. 124) that the example of Paul's case indicates that the sanhedrin could try capital cases is not necessarily accurate. Rather than determining whether Paul was to be tried by Roman or Jewish law it is possible that Felix and Festus were attempting to establish whether or not there was a case for Paul to answer under Roman law and, if so, where the trial would take place.

men' (οἱ πρῶτοι) go, 195, Nero favours the Jews, Ishmael and Helcias detained in Rome.

During the procuratorship of Festus, AD 60–62, a dispute developed over the Temple wall. Josephus's narrative is without complication. In response to Agrippa II's construction certain Jews commenced building a wall to block the king's view of the Temple. This action was in direct opposition to Agrippa's wishes. Furthermore, it apparently impaired the view of the Romans. Whether the Jews were angered simply because of Agrippa's ability to view events in the Temple is uncertain.[1] Whatever arguments were used, they were enough for the procurator to refer the matter to Rome. It is possible that Festus himself did not want to force the Jews to demolish the new wall. It is, however, also conceivable that he was not greatly per turbed by the action, despite the fact that it blocked the view into the Temple precinct.[2]

The first point to note regarding this incident relates to control of

---

1. Smallwood ('High Priests', p. 25) suggests that Ishmael led the Jews in a protest against Agrippa II in an effort to defend Jewish law. A different approach is taken by Goodman (*Ruling Class*, p. 142), who implies that it was essentially a personal battle between Ishmael and Agrippa, with Ishmael being 'deliberately and provocatively' opposed to Agrippa. He does acknowledge the possibility of a religious element, referring to Schwartz. A major problem with this line of argument is that Agrippa was the first to act, not Ishmael. A further approach is that of Stern and, more specifically, Schwartz. Stern ('The Herodian Dynasty', p. 156) notes that it was a dispute between Agrippa and the priests of Jerusalem. D. Schwartz ('Viewing the Holy Utensils [P. Ox. V. 840])', *NTS* 32 [1986], p. 154) suggests that priests connected with the Temple jealously guarded access to cultic holiness, thus their outrage. The incident, therefore, is a combination of religious practice manifested in terms of worldly power and influence in the community. Horsley ('High Priests', p. 44) dismisses the incident as a matter involving the prerogatives of the high priesthood, not a dispute where these Jews represented the entire community before the Romans. There may have been some friction between Agrippa and Ishmael but it is not possible to view the matter as a minor incident, because, as noted by Schwartz, a wall was built and men went to Rome to defend their cause.

2. What remains unexplained is why Agrippa II and Festus did not prevent the wall from being built. It is possible that Festus believed it was essentially a dispute over ritual practice and, more importantly, not within the bounds of his jurisdiction. It may be that the success of the Jews in Rome was partly due to their presence and eagerness. We have no evidence to suggest that Agrippa or Festus believed the matter warranted their personal involvement. As a result, Rhoads (*Revolution*, p. 89) may be exaggerating when claiming that Festus was angered by the building of the wall because it was an act of independence.

the Temple. Despite Agrippa's official position as custodian of the Temple, it is implied in the account that he was not omnipotent in terms of what happened there. The construction work on the Temple was undertaken in direct defiance of him. Furthermore, when pressed, the Jews refused to remove the wall. It is also apparent that Jews connected with the Temple did not perceive Agrippa as its overlord. His permission was not considered necessary to engage in structural alterations.[1]

The second point pertains to the identity of the men involved in the protest. The Jews who opposed Agrippa, and subsequently to a lesser extent Festus, are described by Josephus as 'the respected men'. In this instance he appears to be referring to a general group of people, who, it is presumed, included members of the priesthood. We are given a clearer indication of their identity later in the narrative. The deputation sent to Rome included Ishmael and Helcias and ten of 'the first men'. Ishmael and Helcias attended in their official capacity as high priest and treasurer respectively. Their high profile, however, may not have been due to the office they held any more than it was to their general standing within the Jewish community.[2] That both men were detained in Rome indicates that Nero recognized them as the leading spokesmen of the group.[3] These prominent priests and laity

1. Agrippa II inherited Herod of Chalcis' status as custodian of the Temple (*Ant.* 20.104). Note that Agrippa II followed Herod in the practice of replacing the high priest as he saw fit (*Ant.* 20.16, 179, 197, 203, 213, 223). Other actions that Agrippa II performed in relation to the Temple were the completion of certain repairs, *Ant.* 5.36, 152; 7.97, and hearing the request of the Levites, *Ant.* 20.216-18. Note also that Agrippa II was requested to provide further work for the Jews who had been involved in the restoration of the Temple (see *Ant.* 20.219-22).

2. Stern ('Province of Judaea', p. 345) believes these ten men were a sign of Greek assimilation that went beyond terminology. They were, in the Greek tradition, a financial committee of the municipal council. No evidence, however, is provided to support this interpretation. In comparison, Rajak (*Josephus*, p. 40) suggests these men were the eminent of Jerusalem, similar to the ten first men of Greek cities but were not a particular committee and did not deal with financial matters. Also see Tcherikover ('Was Jerusalem a Polis?', p. 67 n. 13). The reference to Helcias, the treasurer, on this specific occasion may indicate that holding an office did not automatically mean public influence.

3. Without any clear evidence, Smallwood (*Jews under Roman Rule*, p. 278) states that it was the sanhedrin who opposed Agrippa. Goodman (*Ruling Class*, p. 143) appears to be correct in noting that Ishmael had influential supporters because Agrippa did not depose him when trouble broke out. Whether ex-high priests and Joseph, Ishmael's replacement, were opposed to Ishmael because of his

represented the elements of the Jewish community concerned with protecting the sanctity of the Temple against Agrippa's intervention.

Finally, some reference should be made to the proceedings in Rome. It is surprising that Nero upheld the action of the respected men. They had acted without the permission of Agrippa II, and, according to Festus, impaired his ability to oversee affairs in Jerusalem. Although Poppaea may have influenced Nero it is significant that the emperor chose to defy the interests of the Roman appointee. In other words, Nero did not follow a set pattern of supporting the appointee above the interests of the local inhabitants. The unusual nature of the decision is partly acknowledged by the concession granted to Agrippa.[1] Although defeated on this occasion, he was provided with a ready-made opportunity to appoint a new and more compatible high priest.

5. *The Trial of James and Several Other Men*

Ant. 20.200, Ananus convenes a '*synedrion* of judges' (συνέδριον κριτῶν) to try James and others, they are stoned, 201, those 'strict in observance of the law' (περὶ τοὺς νόμους ἀκριβεῖς) inform Agrippa II that Ananus was wrong in the first step he took, 202, they also complain to Albinus, 203, who threatens to punish Ananus, Agrippa deposes Ananus from the high priesthood.

While the new procurator, Albinus, was in transit to Judaea after the death of Festus, James and other unnamed men are executed at the instigation of Ananus, the serving high priest.[2] Unfortunately the

high profile is debatable. Presumably supporters of Ishmael ensured that day-to-day affairs in the Temple area were maintained. It is possible that the conflict between priests under Ishmael that Josephus records in *Ant.* 20.180 may have been reflected in the support offered to Agrippa and Ishmael.

1. Stern ('The Herodian Dynasty', p. 156 and 'Province of Judaea', p. 369) and Smallwood (*Jews under Roman Rule*, p. 279) note that keeping Ishmael and Helcias in Rome was a deliberate attempt to appease Agrippa. Smallwood (*Jews under Roman Rule*, p. 278 n. 79) is probably correct in stating that Poppaea was interested in religion in general, not that she had any special interest in Judaism above other religions. Note also that travelling to Rome to argue a case was not necessarily uncommon. See *Life* 13–16 on Josephus's mission to Rome.

2. Eusebius, in *Historia Ecclesiastica*, records the death of James from Josephus (II.23.20-24), Hegesippus (II.23.4-19), and Clement of Alexandria (II.1.3-5). Several scholars have suggested that the information provided by Hegesippus adds to our knowledge of the historical event. For example, see Brandon, *Trial*, p. 56, who

account is complicated.[1] Josephus uses the incident to voice his criticism of Sadducees, epitomized by Ananus.[2] Furthermore, Josephus is uncertain about the events that followed the execution, especially in terms of Ananus's offence and its severity. I shall, therefore, clarify what happened in Jerusalem before considering the events that followed the execution.

The details of what happened in Jerusalem are relatively easy to

is followed by R.P. Martin, 'The Life-Setting of the Epistle of James in the Light of Jewish History', in G.A. Tuttle (ed.), *Biblical and Near East Studies. Essays in Honor of William Sanford La Sor* (Grand Rapids: Eerdmans, 1978), p. 101 n. 8. F.F. Bruce (*Men and Movements in the Primitive Church* [Exeter: The Paternoster Press, 1979], pp. 114-16) notes the problem of distinguishing genuine tradition from legend, but does use Hegesippus in explaining the setting of the Epistle of James. This line of argument is difficult to support. Eusebius claims that Hegesippus was more accurate than Josephus, yet in *Demonstratio Evangelica*, III.5.116, Eusebius follows the version of Josephus. For further discussion of Eusebius's understanding of first-century AD events, especially regarding the death of James, see J. McLaren, 'Jerusalem to Pella', pp. 46-47. Note that J. Blinzler ('The Jewish Punishment of Stoning in the New Testament Period', in Bammel [ed.], *Trial*, pp. 157-60), Hare (*Jewish Persecution*, p. 33) and R.M. Grant ('Eusebius, Josephus and the Fate of the Jews', in P.J. Achtemeier (ed.), *SBL Seminar Papers, 1979*, II [Missoula, MT: Scholars Press, 1979], pp. 75-77) establish the priority of Josephus above all other accounts of James's death.

1. There is much debate regarding the *Ant.* 20.200 reference to Jesus. For example, see Schürer, *History*, Excursus II, pp. 428-41, who accepts that the text was subject to Christian editing but that Josephus probably did make some reference to Jesus. A similar approach is taken by Smallwood ('High Priests', p. 26 n. 2 and *Jews under Roman Rule*, p. 279 n. 82). A different approach is taken by Brandon (*Trial*, p. 55), who argues that there was Christian censorship of James's link with the lower order of priests. Such a claim is based on silence and is fraught with problems. Not one of the above approaches suggests that doubt should be cast on the narrative of the entire incident. Efron (*Studies*, p. 336) concludes that the number of vague elements in the account combined with the garbled reference to Christ implies that the whole episode was invented by a Christian editor. This approach, however, does not take into account the lack of any noticeable changes in linguistic style between this incident and the remainder of *Ant.* Also see Rajak, *Josephus*, p. 131 n. 73.

2. Note the contrast in the depiction of Ananus between *War* and *Ant.* For explanations of this difference see Smallwood, 'High Priests', p. 26, who argues that it reflects a change in attitude on the part of Ananus, and Efron, *Studies*, pp. 335-36, who includes it as one of the signs of Christian authorship of the whole incident. A more plausible approach is expressed by Goodman (*Ruling Class*, p. 145 n. 8) and Cohen (*Josephus in Galilee*, pp. 150-51), who point out that the change is most likely the result of differing interests on the part of Josephus in the two texts.

establish. The serving high priest wanted to remove some opponents, although his motivation is not possible to determine.[1] Although it is unlikely that Ananus acted alone, he was the prime mover in the entire affair.[2] Furthermore, Josephus implies that the death of the accused men was inevitable. Ananus, therefore, is presented as being very influential in Jerusalem.

Ananus achieved his aim by calling together a '*synedrion* of judges'. Here Josephus describes a trial court that was assembled to assess a specific case.[3] The members of the court are selected by the high

---

1. Catchpole ('Historicity', p. 60) argues that the method of execution, combined with the proceedings in the sanhedrin, indicates that James was put to death for a religious crime. Catchpole does not elaborate on what is meant by the sanhedrin proceedings. On a more general level, several scholars propose explanations for Ananus's motivation. S.G.F. Brandon ('The Death of James the Just: A New Interpretation', in E.E. Urbach, R.J. Zuri Werblowsky and C. Wirozubshi (eds.), *Studies in Mysticism and Religion, Presented to G.G. Scholem* [Jerusalem: Magnes Press, 1967], p. 67) and Martin ('Life-Setting', p. 99) view the incident as a conflict between the lower order of priests and the traditional priestly establishment, with James siding with the former in this struggle; cf. Bruce, *Men and Movements*, p. 112. This approach fails to make any concession to the fact that Ananus was deposed by one of the men allegedly favouring the traditional priestly establishment, Agrippa II. Other approaches view the action in terms of Jewish–Roman relations. See Smallwood, *Jews under Roman Rule*, p. 26, who concludes that it was a gesture of defiance against Rome, expressing independence. Horsley ('High Priests', p. 44) counters this claim. Although the action may not have been intended as a direct snub against Roman overlordship it appears that it was an indirect result of Ananus's actions. Hare (*Jewish Persecution*, p. 34) is probably correct when he states that Ananus acted out of personal animosity toward James. Implicit here is the idea that James was recognizable in some public context. There is no reason, as Hare (pp. 33-34) notes, to suggest that the death of James was part of any Jewish persecution of the Christians, nor that it was a cause for Christians to flee Jerusalem. For further discussion of this point see McLaren, 'Jerusalem to Pella', pp. 16, 21-89.

2. For discussion of Ananus's possible allies, see Goodman, *Ruling Class*, pp. 144-45. Note E.P. Sanders, *Jesus*, p. 316, who points out that irrespective of the views of people opposed to Ananus he was able to achieve his aim. See also Chapter 5, section 4.

3. There is no reason to support Feldman's translation 'judges of the sanhedrin'. Several scholars favour the rendering *synedrion* of judges. For example, see Zeitlin, *Rise and Fall*, II, p. 226; Rivkin, 'Beth Din, Boulé, Sanhedrin', p. 103; and Efron, *Studies*, p. 334; cf. Bruce, *Men and Movements*, p. 111, who translates the passage as 'judicial sanhedrin'. Mantel appears to have changed his opinion (cf. 'The High Priesthood and the Sanhedrin in the Second Temple Period', in Avi-Yonah [ed.], *The Herodian Period*, p. 276, and *Studies*, p. 65).

priest. The reference to the 'judges' may refer to a specially designated group from which Ananus selected the men appropriate to his
needs. It is equally possible that 'judges' is Josephus's means of
describing the people chosen by Ananus and that they only held the
status in this case.[1] In summary, the serving high priest instigates a
trial of his opponents, assisted by people sympathetic to his interests,
which Josephus describes by the term *synedrion*.[2]

The exact details of what happened after the execution are unclear.
Certain Jews critical of Ananus's deed complained vigorously to
Agrippa II and Albinus until action was taken against Ananus.
Josephus's sympathy lies with these men. They were 'strict in
observance of the law'. Although Josephus remains silent about their
exact identity, their actions provide some clues.[3]

1. Zeitlin (*Rise and Fall*, II, p. 226) concludes that Josephus was not referring to
the sanhedrin. See also Hoenig, *Great Sanhedrin*, p. 7, and Zeitlin, *Who Crucified
Jesus?*, p. 72. It was not the Great Sanhedrin but a general term simply indicating
council. In a similar vein, Rivkin ('Beth Din, Boulé, Sanhedrin', p. 103) views this
gathering as a political group, operating as an instrument of Roman imperial power.
It was not a religious gathering. Mantel (*Studies*, p. 65) also concludes that this was
not the sanhedrin, but a Sadducean court. Sherwin-White (*Roman Society*, p. 39)
assumes that it was a meeting of the sanhedrin.

2. This should not necessarily be taken as evidence that only the high priest could
instigate a trial of this type. As it is possible that this was an exceptional situation,
other examples of trials need to be considered. Furthermore, if Ananus was important in his own right then it is debatable whether the trial resulted primarily from the
high priest performing his job, or from Ananus's personal high public profile.

3. The use of 'strict in observance of the law' has been argued to indicate that
Josephus intended the reader to understand that these men were Pharisees. See
A.I. Baumgarten, 'The Name of the Pharisees', *JBL* 102 (1983), pp. 411-28.
Although it is probable that 'strict in observance of the law' could imply Pharisees, it
is not correct to assume that Josephus necessarily only meant Pharisees or that he especially intended *Ant*. 20.200 to mean Pharisees. Baumgarten ('Name', p. 413 n. 9)
acknowledges that Josephus is far from explicit. His claim, however, that
Josephus's intentions were clear is debatable. There is no reason to assume that
appealing to Agrippa II or Albinus regarding the high priest's actions was perceived
as being 'disloyal'. Furthermore, according to Baumgarten it was patently clear what
Josephus meant, in which case it is difficult to understand how this actually
diminished the 'embarrassment' of Ananus's opponents. While accepting that
Pharisees may have been among the protesters, we cannot be certain of this, nor
should we limit the opponents to one specific group because of the use of 'strict in
observance of the law'. It is important to note that Josephus uses this incident to
highlight a general dislike of Sadducees. We should not assume that references to the
Sadducees meant that the Pharisees were also mentioned. Saldarini (*Pharisees*,

The response to Ananus's action was the approach made to Agrippa and Albinus. These choices were significant. No attempt was made to oppose Ananus directly. Instead, Ananus's immediate superior, Agrippa II, and Albinus, who held overall authority in the province, were petitioned. In other words, the people angered by Ananus's action involved officials superior to him.

Of similar significance is the way the protest was couched. Josephus is ambiguous about the details of the complaint lodged with Agrippa.[1] There is no doubt, however, regarding the content of the protest as expressed to Albinus: Ananus had been obliged to consult with Albinus before he initiated the trial and had officially overstepped his authority.[2] At no stage is any reference made to James's execution as illegal.[3] Significantly, the opponents of Ananus did not believe that emphasizing the execution would help them win the support of Albinus. This may imply that the Jews could execute people if permission was obtained. Because they wanted some action taken, however, we must presume that they presented their case in a manner that would ensure a reaction. This, in turn, suggests that we should not

p. 105 n. 69) also expresses doubt that Josephus was necessarily referring to Pharisees.

1. Catchpole ('Historicity', p. 61) argues that it is possible to deduce the content of the complaint expressed to Agrippa: the Jews accused Ananus of instigating what amounted to an unjust trial.

2. The majority of scholars comment on the offence of Ananus in terms of his relationship with the procurator. Although this may in part be the result of the fact that Josephus provides information regarding the protest addressed to Albinus it may also be implied from Josephus's approach that Albinus was recognized as the person whose support was crucial. Ananus's offence is understood to be exceeding his official authority. See, for example, Smallwood, 'High Priests', p. 26, and Horsley, 'High Priests', p. 44. Rhoads (*Revolution*, p. 89), E.P. Sanders (*Jesus*, p. 284) and Catchpole ('Historicity', p. 61) argue that the crucial element was Ananus's convening of a trial regarding a capital case without the procurator's permission. Implicit in this approach is the notion that only the procurator was able to inflict the death penalty. Note also Bruce, *Men and Movements*, p. 111, who argues that the actual execution was the most important aspect of the violation. Only Rivkin ('Beth Din, Boulé, Sanhedrin', p. 184) notes that Ananus's direct superior in reference to the Temple was Agrippa.

3. Smallwood (*Jews under Roman Rule*, p. 280) is one of the few scholars who acknowledges the mildness of the punishment and the fact that the complaint was expressed purely in terms of the convening of the trial, not the execution. She concludes that this implies that the Jews could execute people but concedes that the procurator's permission may have been required.

overestimate the importance of the strict legality of the case at hand. The failure of Ananus to show respect for his official superiors, as much as his convening of a *synedrion* without permission, was the content of the protest.[1] It is conceivable that Ananus might have prevented any trouble by informing Albinus and/or Agrippa of his intentions.[2]

The central issue does not appear to have been that Ananus had broken the law. Rather, some of the people who were contending for prominence in Jerusalem may have been among Ananus's opponents.[3] Such men as Ananias or Jesus, son of Damnaeus, may have watched Ananus entangle himself in a legal matter. Joining in the protest against Ananus's illegal activities, his rivals may have championed the protest by petitioning Agrippa and Albinus. We may postulate, therefore, that this was an internal conflict within a small section of

---

1. E.P. Sanders (*Jesus*, p. 285) notes that the charge regarding Ananus's legal offence may have been 'trumped up'.

2. It is plausible that Ananus's failure to seek the support of the procurator was due to the nature of the dispute. If so, the conflict may have been personal, as suggested by Hare (*Jewish Persecution*, p. 33).

3. I have already noted the possible connection of 'strict in observance of the law' with the Pharisees. Many scholars assume that Josephus was referring to Pharisees without engaging in the process of examining the use of language. For example, see Efron, *Studies*, p. 335, and Horsley, 'High Priests', p. 44. Mantel (*Studies*, p. 275) even suggests that this is an example of the Pharisees keeping a close watch on the conduct of a Sadducean high priest. He does not, however, explain why these Pharisees did not stop Ananus from actually executing James. Zeitlin (*Rise and Fall*, II, p. 226) views the incident as an example of the Sadducees and Pharisees competing in the political arena. Smallwood ('High Priests', p. 26 and *Jews under Roman Rule*, p. 280) suggests that Pharisees and a philo-Roman party were opposed to Ananus; cf. Horsley, 'High Priests', p. 44. Sherwin-White (*Roman Society*, p. 39) is less specific, referring to the moderates of the sanhedrin who opposed the action of extreme members of the sanhedrin. These accounts neglect to consider the incident in terms of the contextual narrative of Josephus. According to Josephus, Ananias was soon able to wield influence over Albinus. See Chapter 4, section 6. It is possible that he was among the people involved in this incident, maybe bribing Albinus. Furthermore, there is no mention of the Jews active in Jerusalem who were seeking influence in the years leading up to the revolt (*Ant.* 20.180-81, 213-24). It is plausible that these people participated, either as supporters of Ananus or as opponents. Goodman (*Ruling Class*, pp. 144-45) outlines the possible composition of groups in Jerusalem vying for public status. It is as plausible to explain the identity of the opponents on the basis of the historical context contained in Josephus as much as it is from the bias he expressed against the Sadducees in this incident.

the Jewish community as much as it was a concern for questions of legal procedure.

Ananus was probably obliged to consult the procurator regarding a capital offence. The significant factor, however, was Ananus's failure to respect the authority of those above him while he had opponents in Jerusalem. These opponents took the opportunity to attack Ananus's status and his appropriateness to be high priest. The response of Agrippa and Albinus confirms the notion that the case was not a major legal battle but a dispute concerned more with public status. Although dispossessed of the high priesthood, Ananus suffered no further penalities. Albinus merely threatened him. Ananus had obviously held enough influence in Jerusalem while high priest to enable him to dispose of James and other people he wished to remove. At the same time, certain Jews in Jerusalem, the identity of whom we cannot categorically determine, did not approve of his status and took the opportunity to undermine his official standing as high priest when possible.[1]

Three observations regarding the administration of affairs in Palestine can be drawn from this incident. First, Josephus uses *synedrion* as a common noun. It describes a trial court, specifically brought together to assess a capital case at the instigation of the serving high priest. Whatever the significance of the term 'judges' is, their status in this trial was dependent on the high priest.

The second point relates to the nature of the dispute. Ananus's offence was presented as a failure to respect his superiors. It was a Jewish dispute in which the procurator was involved by the active petitioning of Jews vying for influence within the community. Maintaining official status required the support of compatriots and the recognition of superiors.[2]

Finally this incident does not greatly clarify the legal ability of the Jews to execute people. The focus of attention is placed on Ananus's actions in relation to the prestige of Albinus and Agrippa. No reference is made to James and the other men executed with him. If

1. I have already noted the argument of Brandon and Martin that James should be linked with the lower priests against the high priestly establishment. Although this approach notes the historical situation, it relies on an argument from silence.

2. Note that Agrippa's importance was due to his position as custodian of the Temple, in which he was able to change the high priest as he deemed necessary (*Ant.* 20.213, 223). As procurator, Albinus was able to inflict whatever punishment he believed was appropriate.

anything, we have no reason to believe that the Jews were unable to try and execute other Jews in practice, providing that the procurator had been informed of the situation.

6. *The Influence of Ananias*

Ant. 20.208, sicarii kidnap secretary of the captain, Eleazar, son of Ananias, 209, ransom is to persuade Albinus to release ten sicarii, 210, other members of Ananias's family are kidnapped.

In the early AD 60s the sicarii began kidnapping Jews, demanding the release of fellow sicarii in return for their hostages.[1] This initiative was probably a response to the success of Albinus's measures to quell the activities of the sicarii.[2] What is significant in terms of the administration is the extent to which this method of terrorism proved to be effective. The reason for this relates to the identity of the victims.

The sicarii acknowledged that the policing of the province was a Roman concern in which the procurator held power. Recognizing this

---

1. The identity of the sicarii and their possible relationship with the zealots has been the subject of much scholarly discussion. See C. Roth, 'The Zealots in the War of 66–73', *JSS* (1959), pp. 332-55; M. Stern, 'Sicarii and Zealots', in M. Avi-Yonah (ed.), *The World History of the Jewish People*, 1st series, VIII. *Society and Religion in the Second Temple Period* (Jerusalem: Massada Publishing House, 1977), pp. 263-301; cf. M. Smith, 'Zealots and Sicarii: Their Origins and Relation', *HTR* 64 (1971), pp. 1-19; S. Applebaum, 'The Zealots: The Case for Revaluation', *JRS* 61 (1971), pp. 155-70; R.A. Horsley, 'The Sicarii: Ancient Jewish Terrorists', *JR* 59 (1979), pp. 435-58, and 'Ancient Jewish Banditry and the Revolt against Rome, AD 66–70', *CBQ* 43 (1981), pp. 409-32. Smallwood's argument ('High Priests', p. 28) that they were anti-Roman rebels and Horsley's ('High Priests', p. 46) that they were opposed to the priestly aristocracy who collaborated with Rome are appraisals that reflect more on the indirect ramifications of the sicarii's actions than necessarily their prime motivation. They are shaped largely by the interests central to both scholars' arguments. Horsley ('The Sicarii', pp. 450-51) claims the sicarii activities branded the established 'ruling elite' as 'traitors'. Rhoads (*Revolution*, p. 79) is probably correct in interpreting the kidnappings as a sign that the sicarii were an organized group. Note also the involvement of the sicarii in the murder of Jonathan (*War* 2.256; *Ant.* 20.162). We are unable conclusively to reconcile the differences between these two texts regarding the idea that Felix and the sicarii were in league in an effort to remove Jonathan. The lack of a reference to any repercussions being taken because of Jonathan's death may indicate that the procurator was not angered by the action. For a discussion of the sicarii before the revolt see Horsley and Hanson, *Bandits*, pp. 200-11.

2. See *Ant.* 20.204.

situation, the sicarii chose to implement their aim by kidnapping people connected with particular Jewish individuals. This suggests that the sicarii believed that certain Jews were able to negotiate with the procurator in matters of Roman jurisdiction. Such a belief was vindicated by the choice of Ananias as the target: he was correctly viewed as being able to realize the demands of the sicarii.[1]

The choice of Ananias is important. He had no official jurisdiction yet he was able to influence the relevant authority, Albinus.[2] This was probably achieved by financial means.[3] To ensure that Ananias acted,

1. Connected with the perception of the sicarii is the understanding of their motivation to act as they did in this instance. We have evidence of the sicarii committing murder but this is the first reference to a policy of kidnapping. Smallwood ('High Priests', p. 28 and *Jews under Roman Rule*, p. 282) suggests that Ananias and the sicarii acted in league to further the anti-Roman cause in Judaea. Rhoads (*Revolution*, p. 89), although doubting whether Ananias purposefully acted against Roman interests, accepts the idea that the consequences of Ananias's actions were anti-Roman; cf. Horsley ('High Priests', pp. 46-47), who justifiably questions the plausibility of this approach. Stern ('Province of Judaea', p. 470) correctly comments that the sicarii exploited the state of affairs, using Ananias because he had influence over Albinus. Similarly, see Horsley, 'High Priests', p. 47. Goodman (*Ruling Class*, p. 215) proposes a different interpretation. The sicarii were 'the tools' of Ananias's opponents in a faction struggle in Jerusalem. It is possible that an indirect result of the sicarii's action was a redressing of the balance of power in Jerusalem but there is no evidence to suggest that the primary conflict was factional strife among particular Jews. The sicarii knew what they were doing, and they and Albinus were the only people to benefit directly from the action. Note *Ant.* 20.205, where Josephus openly refers to Ananias's high standing with Albinus.

2. Smallwood ('High Priests', p. 28) suggests that Albinus was a weak procurator, manipulated by Ananias. More credible is Stern ('The Herodian Dynasty', p. 157), commenting that Albinus recognized the obvious financial benefit for himself if he complied with the demands. It is possible that Albinus's willingness to release the sicarii implies a belief that these men were not a direct threat to Roman control in Judaea. Note the change between *War* and *Ant.* in the way that Josephus depicts Albinus. The critical view portrayed in *War* was probably dictated by Josephus's concern to explain the origin of the war. In *Ant.* Albinus is open to bribery but is also acknowledged for his positive actions. It appears that the presentation of Albinus in *War* is a distorted picture, highlighting particular characteristics rather than being the depiction of a different person. Note also that Josephus refers to Ananias as high priest (see *Ant.* 20.205).

3. Smallwood ('High Priests', pp. 27-28 and *Jews under Roman Rule*, p. 298) and Stern ('The Herodian Dynasty', p. 157) assume that Ananias offered bribes to Albinus. Note *Ant.* 20.213, where Josephus describes Ananias using bribes to maintain his high standing within the Jewish community. The basis of Ananias's wealth may lie in a dispute referred to by Josephus in *Ant.* 20.206-207. If so, we can

the sicarii chose his son as their first victim and then, once successful, other members of his household.[1]

It is certain that, by whatever means, Ananias convinced Albinus to help him. It is not recorded as being due to any official status he currently held, nor was Ananias represented by any formal body. Ananias dealt directly with Albinus, as a private citizen.

Here Josephus portrays Judaea in the early AD 60s as a territory in which money and personal connections were paramount to successful interaction in the public domain.[2] Moreover, a man who had previously held the high priesthood was able to maintain a high public profile without an official office.

assume that Ananias was counted among 'the chief priests' (οἱ ἀρχιερεῖς). This conflict within the priesthood appears to be the continuation, or re-emergence of a dispute that was mentioned as taking place while Ishmael was high priest.

1. Although the majority of texts read Ananus, the context of the story indicates that Ananias is accurate. See Smallwood ('High Priests', p. 27 n. 5) and Schürer (*History*, I, p. 469 n. 53). Note that Eleazar was an official connected with the Temple, implying that Ananias's family continued to be influential in Temple affairs after he was replaced as serving high priest.

2. Note the possible link between *War* 2.273-74 and *Ant.* 20.213-14. Important to note here is the reference to local councils and the description of Ananias in *War* as one of 'the powerful' (οἱ δυνατοί) of the revolutionaries. Presumably local councils existed in first-century AD Judaea and had some responsibility in terms of maintaining law and order. See Tcherikover ('Was Jerusalem a Polis?', p. 69). Note that the powerful applies to a type of person in this instance not only one group of people, good or bad. In *Ant.* Josephus indicates that the conflict was fought mainly by people connected with the high priesthood, past or present office holders and members of the Herodian family. Goodman (*Ruling Class*, pp. 143-47, 158-66) discusses in some detail the existence and identity of these groups. They appear to have been vying for influence within the community, using violence on some occasions.

Chapter 5

OPEN REBELLION AGAINST ROME: AD 66–70

1. *Trouble between the Jews and Greeks in Caesarea*

War 2. 286, Jewish youths attack Greek workshops near synagogue, 287, Florus intervenes, 'the powerful' (οἱ δυνατοί) Jews, including John, tax collector, bribe Florus, 289, further trouble between Greeks and Jews on sabbath, 291, Jucundus, the commander, intervenes, 292, twelve of 'the powerful' Jews, led by John, go to Florus, he arrests them.

At the time of the dispute between the local inhabitants, Caesarea was within the Roman province of Judaea. The incident was essentially a racial dispute between the Jews and Greeks living in Caesarea, although it was expressed through dissension over religious practices.

One aspect of Josephus's narrative requires some comment: the description of the Jewish participants. In defiance of the Jews, the Greeks decided to erect workshops around the synagogue. Josephus claims that it was angry youths who rose to the bait. Whether it was only the younger Jews who wanted to take direct action, however, is debatable, because later in the narrative, 'the powerful' Caesarean Jews are involved. It is possible that Josephus, in defence of the Jews generally, wanted to lay blame for the attack on an understandable minority. The more accurate scenario may be to suggest that most Jews in Caesarea demanded direct action, but that opinions differed regarding the type of action to be undertaken.[1]

The remainder of the narrative is clear. Four points should be noted from this incident, which took place outside Jerusalem. First, the

---

1. Josephus implies that the youths wanted physical action while the rest of the Jews opted for peaceful negotiations. Irrespective of any doubts held regarding this division, it is an insight into what Josephus understood to be acceptable practice. Whether relating the historical situation or his perception of it, Josephus displays a preference for negotiation via a small section of the community to win the favour of the procurator. Note that few scholars discuss this incident in any detail.

Roman procurator was involved in an inter-racial dispute. Elements of the Jewish and Greek communities in Caesarea were engaged in an argument over their respective freedom of activity.[1] Florus was recognized by the Jewish community as the appropriate person to resolve the dispute. The reference to Jucundus indicates that Florus relied upon others to deal with local day-to-day matters. Although specifically commissioned to deal with the issue at hand, however, Jucundus was unable to restore order.[2]

Secondly, the Jews were represented by a small section of their number, 'the powerful men'. It is probable that the two deputations sent to Florus consisted of the same men, especially as John is linked to both groups. On the second occasion it is specifically stated that John was the leading spokesman. Implicit in the references to John is that Jews collected taxes and that as a tax collector he was a respected member of the Jewish community in Caesarea. Presumably it was also believed that John would wield some influence over Florus.[3] Here,

1. This is not the first oubreak of trouble between the local inhabitants in Caesarea. In *War* 2.266-70, 284, Josephus narrates the dispute between Jews and Greeks for control of the city. The reference to Nero's decision immediately before narrating the synagogue incident suggests a connection between the two, or at least that Josephus wanted to portray one. Note that during the previous dispute the commander failed to resolve the matter, and that the Jews, apparently rich, pressed their case until Felix decided to refer the matter to Rome, sending 'the notable men' (οἱ γνώριμοι) (*War*; 'the first men' [οἱ πρῶτοι], *Ant.*) of both racial groups to represent their respective communities. Note also the racial trouble in Alexandria (*War* 2.487-98). Goodman (*Ruling Class*, pp. 18-19) points out that this trouble should not be automatically listed as a cause of the revolt. Although not necessarily constant, the existence of conflict may have only perturbed the Romans when physical violence took place. On this point see Goodman, *Ruling Class*, p. 173. In turn, this may partly explain the lack of activity by Florus.

2. It is possible that Josephus intended to negate the role played by Jucundus in an attempt to heighten his criticism of Florus. Zeitlin (*Rise and Fall*, II, p. 231) accepts Josephus's depiction of Florus as actively despising the Jews.

3. Goodman (*Ruling Class*, p. 141) states that John was a member of the deputation because he was a tax collector. Goodman believes that the Romans assumed John was part of the ruling class. We must remember that John was a Jewish representative, acceptable first and foremost among the Jews, for whatever reason they chose. He, and others, were unlikely to have been selected by the Romans to speak on behalf of the Jews. Note the earlier reference to the wealth of the Caesarean Jews. We cannot be certain, but the notable men of the previous dispute may be equated with the powerful men in this instance. If so, Josephus equated the two terms. There is no evidence in the narrative of this incident to suggest why twelve was the number chosen to represent the Jews.

'powerful men' were the spokesmen for the Caesarean Jews in a dispute that involved the Romans. There is no indication that these men were members or representatives of an institution. Furthermore, 'the powerful men' is applied to a 'type' of people from a city other than Jerusalem.

A third point to note is the persistence of the Caesarean Jews. Although Florus did nothing positive to help them after the first deputation, the Jews continued to address their requests to him. Part of the motivation for this persistence may have been that Florus had accepted a bribe. It is also likely that Florus remained the focus of attention simply because he was able to act as he saw fit. This point is indicated by Florus's subsequent actions, the arrest of the second deputation.[1]

Finally, the Caesarean Jews used whatever plausible means were necessary to achieve their aim. Recognizing that the Caesarean Greeks were within their legal rights to build the workshops, the Jews tried to employ other means to obtain favour with Florus, namely, the offer of money. Florus's acceptance of the bribe suggests that it was a legitimate practice.[2] This is particularly so since Josephus is ultimately critical of Florus because of his failure to fulfil his part of the deal.

2. *Florus in Jerusalem*

War 2. 293, Florus demands seventeen talents from Temple for imperial services, 295, mock collection of money by some Jews, 297, Jews meet Florus, 300, Capito threatens them, they disperse, 301, next day, 'the chief priests' (οἱ ἀρχιερεῖς), 'the powerful men' (οἱ δυνατοί) and 'the

---

1. Smallwood (*Jews under Roman Rule*, p. 289) describes the arrest as 'incomprehensible' while Goodman (*Ruling Class*, p. 153) views Florus's actions as a sign of his having lost confidence in the Caesarean ruling class. This may be correct, if we understand confidence in terms of acting as Florus desired. Josephus gives no reason for us to argue that these men no longer represented the views or desires of the Caesarean Jews as a whole. Irrespective of whether the charge as noted by Josephus was accurate, Florus could do essentially whatever he wanted with the Caesarean Jews. Note *War*. 2.293. The failure of the Jerusalem Jews to take any action may not necessarily be indicative of a lack of concern or interest. Jerusalem became the focus of attention soon after the arrest of the deputation when Florus demanded money from the Temple.

2. Note Goodman, *Ruling Class*, p. 149, who suggests that the use of bribery was 'the natural way' to obtain the support of the procurator. The existence of other incidents where bribery was used indicates that it was a legitimate means of obtaining influence. See *War* 2.273; *Ant.* 20.205; and possibly *Ant.* 20.119.

notable men' (οἱ γνώριμοι) see Florus, 302, he demands the practical jokers be handed over for punishment, the Jews refuse to comply, 305, troops sent to sack the Agora, 307, many Jews killed, 310, Bernice sends request for the troops to stop, 316, next day, 'the chief priests' and 'the powerful men' plead with the populace to stop their protest, 318, Florus tells 'chief priests' and 'the notable men' that the populace must greet the troops, 327, many Jews are killed, 330, Jews destroy porticoes between the Temple and Antonia, 331, Florus tells 'the chief priests' and *boule* that he will leave Jerusalem, 333, Florus informs Cestius that the Jews were rebelling, 'the rulers/magistrates' (οἱ ἄρχοντες) of Jerusalem and Bernice also write to Cestius, 336, 'chief priests', 'the powerful men' and *boule* meet Agrippa II at Jamnia, 340, Neapolitanus tours Jerusalem, all at peace, 342, Jews ask Agrippa and 'chief priests' to petition Nero regarding Florus, 405, Jews begin to rebuild porticoes, 'rulers/magistrates' and members of the *boule* levy the tribute arrears, 406, Agrippa tells the Jews to obey Florus, they refuse and ban Agrippa from Jerusalem, 407, Agrippa sends 'rulers/magistrates' and 'the powerful men' to Florus for the selection of tribute collectors.

Immediately after the disturbance at Caesarea in AD 66 Florus, the procurator, demanded that seventeen talents be handed over from the Temple treasury. This order marked the beginning of a series of actions which culminated in the Jews of Jerusalem forcing Agrippa II to leave the city. Although the narrative of events is relatively straightforward, some comment is required on the identity of the people involved in the machinations that followed the order.

It is important to note that personal interests may have been especially prevalent in this part of *The Jewish War*. These events immediately precede the outbreak of the revolt against Rome. As a result, one of Josephus's overriding concerns was to portray the majority of Jews as peaceful people, especially those men with whom he associated.[1]

Florus's demand was probably relayed to the Jews who administered the treasury. Although Josephus states that Florus claimed the money was required for imperial service, he later implies that greed was Florus's prime motivation. It is possible that the total required

---

1. For a detailed discussion of how personal bias may have affected what Josephus recorded and the manner in which he portrayed the events immediately prior to the revolt, see P. Bilde, 'The Causes of the Jewish War according to Josephus', *JSJ* 10 (1979), pp. 179-202 and Cohen, *Josephus in Galilee*, pp. 188-200.

was a shortfall in the tribute due, since later in the incident, Agrippa II remarks on the forty talents arrears in tribute. Whatever the motive, the Jews reacted angrily.[1] The specific response of a small number of Jews, making a mock collection, acted as a major turning point.[2] No further mention is made of the money and the central issue becomes the expression of loyalty to Florus and Rome.

From Josephus's detailed discussion of the negotiations we are able to develop a clear understanding of the main participants. The one person who is involved as a result of his own initiative is Florus, possibly influenced by pressing financial needs. He issued the original order and then decided to march on Jerusalem. During the few days that Florus stayed in the city, he made a number of demands. He ordered that the men who carried out the collection of money be turned over to him and that the Jews display their loyalty by assembling to welcome his troops from Caesarea.[3]

The other Romans mentioned are involved as a result of Florus's actions. His report that the Jews were rebelling necessitated the Syrian legate's investigation of the matter. Moreover, Florus renounced responsibility by turning the matter over to the senior Roman official in the region, Cestius. The two other Romans directly involved, Capito and Neapolitanus, were the assistants of Roman officials. The former acted as an envoy for Florus while the latter was sent to Jerusalem to make an initial report on the state of affairs in the city for Cestius.

---

1. Note that there is no indication of who was to deliver the money. Josephus's silence does not allow us to establish whether some members of the Jerusalem community were willing to hand over Temple treasury funds. Horsley ('High Priests', p. 48) uses the lack of reference to 'priestly aristocracy' leading the protest against the demand as evidence that they supported Florus, but is unable to provide any corroborating evidence. Most scholars who comment on the incident accept that the Jews had failed to pay all their tribute. For example, see Smallwood, *Jews under Roman Rule*, p. 289; Goodman, *Ruling Class*, p. 152; and Zeitlin, *Rise and Fall*, II, pp. 232-33. Cohen (*Josephus in Galilee*, p. 189) suggests that Florus may have been within his rights but that his demand was 'tactless'.

2. Goodman ('A Bad Joke in Josephus', *JJS* 36 [1985], pp. 195-99) has suggested that some, if not all, of the men who carried out the practical joke were members of the aristocracy, including Eleazar, son of Ananias. The resultant refusal to identify these men was an outright act of defiance.

3. Cohen (*Josephus in Galilee*, p. 188) suggests that Josephus has distorted this section of the narrative and that in fact the troops were arriving to help relieve the garrison trapped in the Antonia. The actions of the chief priests were, therefore, an attempt to prevent the Jews from hampering Florus's plans.

Detailed consideration of the identity and role of the Jewish participants is required. Josephus refers to the populace throughout the incident in a positive light. They gathered at the Temple to voice their general disapproval of the order. Later, they gathered to protest about the attack made by Florus's troops. After the speeches of certain Jews they expressed outward loyalty to Rome. Although the populace repelled the Romans attempting to enter the Temple, it was the rebels who destroyed the porticoes. In effect, the populace was a passive element in the dispute. This view, however, is contradicted in other parts of the narrative. Agrippa II appeals to the entire populace of Jerusalem to stop fighting and repair the physical damage. The Jewish appeal to Agrippa and 'the chief priests' to send an embassy to Rome also makes it apparent that at least some of the populace of Jerusalem were actively involved.[1] Although primarily responding to circumstances, the populace were an active and important element in the incident.

In the negotiations that took place, Jews other than the populace were involved. Josephus describes a number of people who participated in three different levels of negotiation: the people who carried out negotiations between the Jews and Romans; between the Jews; and the men involved as a result of Roman orders. I shall consider each level in turn, beginning with the men that Florus ordered to participate.

There are three occasions when Florus commanded Jews to perform a specific task. When he first entered Jerusalem Florus demanded that the men who collected the money be handed over for punishment. This task was delegated to 'the chief priests', 'the powerful men' and 'the notable men'. On the second occasion 'the chief priests' and 'the notable men' were told to gather the population together to welcome the troops travelling from Caesarea. Finally, when Florus decided to leave Jerusalem, he called together 'the chief priests' and the *boule*. He informed these men that they were to be responsible for keeping the peace and left them with the requested number of troops.

All negotiations initiated by Florus were carried out with a select group of people. They were the men Florus had chosen to convey his

1. Note Smallwood (*Jews under Roman Rule*, p. 291), who argues that an appeal to Nero was requested because the Jews did not trust Cestius; cf. Goodman ('A Bad Joke', p. 198), who claims that the request was an attempt by the Jews who protected the practical jokers to cover their guilt.

intentions to other Jews. Florus primarily demanded the presence and services of 'the chief priests'. The other Jews involved by Florus were prominent laymen. Josephus refers to 'the notable men' and 'the powerful men'. It appears that the two phrases were used as a means of emphasizing the idea that all respectable and important Jews were present. In the opinion of Florus, 'the chief priests' and the Jews who were 'powerful men'/'notable men' were the people who could influence the Jews of Jerusalem.

Florus also ordered the *boule* to participate. Josephus appears to be referring to a formal institution which was distinct from 'the chief priests'. Whether 'the powerful men'/'notable men' were members of the *boule* is not clear. The inclusion of the *boule* when Florus was preparing to depart is important. This was a formal stage in the proceedings at which Florus considered it appropriate to involve the *boule* of the city. In the previous meetings between Florus and the Jews he spoke only to a select group of individuals, priests and non-priests. Florus's decision to involve the *boule* in the final stage is probably related to his perception of its influence. Florus had not sought the assistance of the *boule* earlier because he believed that it had no effective influence in the community. As he was leaving the Jews in control of Roman troops, however, the official Jewish institution of government had to be involved. Florus had not developed confidence in the *boule*. He continued to perceive 'the chief priests' as the most prominent group within the Jewish community. Thus he informed the chief priests and the *boule* of his plans.

The suggestion that influence lay with particular groups of people rather than with institutions is confirmed by the second level of negotiations, discussions among the Jews. Early in the dispute 'the chief priests' and 'the powerful men' implore the populace to stop voicing their criticism of Florus. Later, 'the chief priests' assembled the populace to greet the soldiers arriving from Caesarea. This task was only achieved after much discussion and the vocal support of priests.[1] To win over the populace appeals were made to the name of each 'notable' citizen. The absence of prominent laymen on this occasion, therefore, is significant. It is possible that 'the chief priests'

---

1. The reference to priests here implies that Josephus did not believe that all the priesthood was represented by 'the chief priests'. It is also apparent that at this stage of the proceedings Josephus emphasizes the passive tendencies of some priests.

found themselves in a position of having to convince some of the 'notable men' as well as the populace. It appears that some of the men who encouraged the populace to cease their protests may have subsequently questioned the desirability of the advice they had offered.

When Agrippa returned from Alexandria there were further discussions among the Jews. 'The chief priests', 'the powerful men' and the *boule* went to meet him at Jamnia where they presented their version(s) of the situation. They are depicted as three distinct groups. The reference to these men as property owners suggests that Josephus recognized them as established, wealthy members of the Jewish community. The presence of 'the chief priests' and 'the powerful men' can be associated with the prominent role they played in the earlier events.

The *boule* was probably present to greet Agrippa on his official return to the region. Similar to the departure of Florus, this was a formal occasion. To Josephus, it was the presence of 'the chief priests' and 'the powerful men' that was significant in terms of resolving the dispute. Furthermore, the decision of these prominent Jews to seek Agrippa's involvement implies an acceptance of him in Jewish–Roman negotiations.

A further instance of Jewish interaction was the request by the populace that an embassy be sent to Nero. It is implied that by directing this request to Agrippa and 'the chief priests' the populace perceived these men as the most appropriate people to achieve their aim. Agrippa's response and consequent attempt to persuade the Jews against rebelling has probably been adapted by Josephus to highlight the reaction of the populace. They accepted some of Agrippa's advice, but the suggestion that Florus be recognized and obeyed until a replacement was sent, resulted in the Jews banishing Agrippa from the city.[1] An implication of the banishment is that Agrippa's prominence was associated with the acceptability of his advice. The populace sought his aid until they lost faith in his willingness to represent their perceived interests.

The 'rulers/magistrates' and the members of the *boule* later went to

---

1. Goodman (*Ruling Class*, p. 152) suggests that Agrippa was acting on behalf of the Romans, attempting to restore order in Jerusalem while the procurator was absent.

to the villages around Jerusalem to collect the tribute. This example of interaction between Jews is not an occasion of decision-making but one of fulfilling a practical administrative task. Before begin ning to interpret too much from this collection of taxes we should note that the circumstances were extraordinary. The tribute was in arrears by some forty talents and the Roman procurator had placed Jerusalem in the care of Jews. It was necessary for the Jews to perform this task. In this context it is possible that Josephus was referring to specific officials of some description, presumably 'magistrates'. Although they may have been associated with the *boule*, a distinction is drawn between them and the actual members of the *boule*.

The third level of negotiations consists of the occasions when Jews initiated discussions with the Romans. There are two examples of Herodians representing Jewish interests before Roman officials. First, when Florus sent his troops to attack the people in the Agora, Bernice attempted to intervene. Although unable to see him personally because of religious reasons, she sent a representative. Despite having no formal jurisdiction in Jerusalem, Bernice spoke on behalf of the community. Secondly, Agrippa befriended Neopolitanus and managed to persuade him to tour the whole of Jerusalem. Here Agrippa saw himself as a representative of the entire Jewish community.

The 'rulers/magistrates' of Jerusalem requested Cestius to inves-tigate the dispute. Aware of Florus's claims, the Jews chose to relay their version of what had taken place, seeking the assistance of the highest Roman authority in the region. It is probable that this was a formal report. Furthermore, Josephus was probably referring to officials, presumably the men involved in the collection of the tribute.

The other example of Jews initiating dialogue with Romans involves 'rulers/magistrates' and 'the powerful men'. These men were sent to Florus by Agrippa so that the procurator could choose the tribute collectors. It is possible that 'the rulers/magistrates' were the same men who collected the tribute in the villages around Jerusalem. On this occasion, 'the powerful men' were also to act in the capacity of tribute collectors. There is no obvious explanation as to why Agrippa was responsible for sending these men. It may even be that Agrippa in fact only advised rather than ordered the officials of

Jerusalem to present themselves before Florus.[1]

The 'chief priests' are central in Josephus's depiction of the Jews active in the negotiations. They were a homogeneous group recognized by Florus and the populace as the most influential Jews.[2] Other Jews aided 'the chief priests' at several stages in the incident. These men were some of the leading lay members of the community, 'the powerful'/'notable' Jews. As both groups appear to have been wealthy the main distinction we can make between 'the powerful men'/'notable men' and 'the chief priests' is in terms of membership of the priesthood. Although generally united in their approach to the situation in Jerusalem, some of 'the notable men' were not initially supportive of the order to greet the troops arriving from Caesarea. Furthermore, it appears that some of the men who made the mock collection of money were connected in some manner with the prominent Jews.[3] Throughout the incident 'the chief priests' are depicted as effective negotiators.[4]

The other recognizable negotiators are Agrippa and Bernice. Agrippa, in particular, played a significant role in representing the Jews. It appears that Agrippa's standing was based on his prestige. Thus, when he exhorted the Jews to submit to the rule of Florus,

1. For other references to Jews as tax collectors see *War* 2.287; Mt. 9.9, 19; Mk 5.27-28.

2. Several scholars have commented on who was left responsible for administering affairs in Jerusalem. E.P. Sanders (*Jesus*, p. 315) notes that it was 'the chief priests' and other leaders who took a major role in the negotiations between the Jews and Romans and that the *boule* was only formally present on one occasion throughout the time Florus was in Jerusalem. Efron (*Studies*, p. 315) simply points out that this part of Josephus's narrative establishes that there was a *boule* and magistrates in Jerusalem at this particular time. Smallwood (*Jews under Roman Rule*, p. 290) claims that the Jewish negotiators were members of the sanhedrin. Goodman (*Ruling Class*, p. 153) and Schürer (*History*, I, p. 485) state that 'the chief priests' and certain others were given the responsibility of restoring order in Jerusalem.

3. Goodman (*Ruling Class*, p. 172) and Cohen (*Josephus in Galilee*, p. 190) point out that not all 'chief priests' and lay leaders were pro-Roman. They refer to Eleazar and the Temple as a central part of what happened respectively. Smallwood (*Jews under Roman Rule*, p. 289) simply states that 'the chief priests' were the leaders of the peace party in Jerusalem, following Josephus's account.

4. Horsley ('High Priests', p. 48) views this incident as a time when Florus lost trust in the Jewish aristocracy. Horsley also believes that the populace were not under the influence of the aristocracy, who remained loyal to Rome and their own interests throughout the incident.

people opposed to such an action were able to exert their influence above that of Agrippa.

A final group of Jewish participants were 'the magistrates' and *boule*. These people became involved on formal occasions. They did not participate in any decision-making. Rather, they fulfilled administrative tasks and represented the Jews at official events. It is possible that a link did exist between the magistrates and the *boule*.[1]

The events that began with the demand for seventeen talents and culminated in Agrippa's forced departure from Jerusalem lead to four general observations pertinent to the administration of Judaea immediately prior to the revolt. First, Florus and the populace of Jerusalem acknowledged the existence of certain prominent Jews. This small section of the community is referred to by Josephus as 'the chief priests' and 'the powerful men'/'notable men'. Although they did not do everything demanded by Florus, they are portrayed as retaining the confidence of the populace and continue to be employed by the procurator. Despite being unable to make any detailed comment on the identity of these people, it is apparent that they were a select, wealthy section of the community who acted on an informal basis. Indeed, the actual negotiations between Florus and the Jews were almost entirely carried out on an informal basis.[2]

The second point is that 'the chief priests' above any other group were the focal point of the Jewish leadership. These men held the respect of the community irrespective of whether or not they held any formal civic administrative status in Jerusalem. The extent to which they were able to influence the populace, however, may have been partly determined by the course of action they proposed.

---

1. The presence of 'magistrates' in Jerusalem before the war is attested in *War* 6.303-305. Note that they also fulfil an administrative task on this occasion. See also *War* 2.273.

2. Goodman ('A Bad Joke', p. 198) suggests that this incident was a major break-down in relations between the Romans and the Jewish aristocracy. Florus lost faith in the aristocracy and it lost faith in him. The resultant lack of co-operation was interpreted to be a sign of open revolt. In presenting this approach, however, Goodman's explanation (*Ruling Class*, p. 153) that Florus turned Jerusalem over to the men he had completely lost faith in because there was nothing else to do follows Josephus but does not appear to be an adequate explanation. Regardless of whether Florus expected more co-operation and was greatly angered by what had happened, he retained enough confidence in them to place a cohort of auxiliaries at their disposal to maintain order in Jerusalem.

Thirdly, there was a council in Jerusalem in the AD 60s referred to by Josephus as the *boule*. In this incident the *boule* functioned by fulfilling administrative tasks and acting as the official representative of the Jews in Jerusalem on formal occasions.[1] At no stage does Josephus link the *boule* in any manner with the decision-making process.

Finally, the initial protest made by the Jerusalem community implies a degree of independence. Irrespective of the reason why Florus ordered money to be removed from the Temple treasury, it roused Jews into making a public protest and at least one act of mockery. With reference to the Temple the Jerusalem community believed foreign intervention was not acceptable, whatever the political structure in the territory.

3. *Cessation of Sacrifices Offered for Foreigners*

War 2.409, Eleazar, son of Ananias, captain, persuades the Temple ministers to stop the sacrifices offered for foreigners, 410, 'the chief priests' (οἱ ἀρχιερεῖς) and 'the notable men' (οἱ γνώριμοι) argue for their retention, priests refuse to reconsider the matter.

An incident narrated only in *The Jewish War* is the cessation of sacrifices in honour of Rome and Caesar.[2] This incident took place while Florus was still procurator of the province in AD 66. This was the first action connected with the revolt which was independently undertaken by the Jews and expressed public rejection of the Romans. Apart from its significance in terms of the revolt, the incident reflects three important points regarding the administration of Palestine.[3]

---

1. Tcherikover ('Was Jerusalem a Polis?', pp. 67-69) argues that *boule* is only used in the strict sense of a *boule* similar to the Greek polis in *War* 2.405. Elsewhere, in *War* 2.301, 318, 331, Josephus equates *boule* with 'the notable men' and 'the powerful men'. As a result, Tcherikover believes it is appropriate to equate this *boule* with the sanhedrin of Jerusalem, which combined with 'the chief priests' to function as the 'supreme Jewish authority'. Josephus's narrative of this incident, however, does not support the idea that *boule* and 'the powerful men'/'notable men' are to be equated.

2. The incident may be narrated in *b. Git.* 56a. C. Roth ('The Debate on the Loyal Sacrifices, AD 66', *HTR* 53 [1960], p. 93) dismisses *b. Git.* 56a as 'legendary', although he does discuss the possible role played by Simon and other Pharisees.

3. Smallwood (*Jews under Roman Rule*, p. 292 n. 120) notes the fact that Josephus fails to provide a date for when the sacrifices were stopped. Goodman

It must be noted that this part of Josephus's narrative was subject to great personal and political self-interest. Josephus was concerned to lay responsibility for the end of the sacrifices on as few people as possible, and particularly not on people with whom he associated. As a result, any of Josephus's explicit observations or comments regarding this incident will be tempered by what we can learn from other related aspects of the narrative.[1]

In this incident it is notable that control over Temple events is depicted as primarily dependent on what those officiating believed should happen. These ministers had the final say as to whether or not the sacrifice was offered, irrespective of other opinions, and the number of influential advisors. Apparently these ministers were so independently minded as to ignore the demands of at least some of 'the chief priests'.[2]

Secondly, specific Jews tried to influence the course of action taken. Josephus speaks of Eleazar, son of Ananias, and the revolutionaries advocating the end of sacrifices. It is apparent that Eleazar, as the captain, was connected with the Temple. Part of his influence may have also been physical force.[3] The reference to the revolutionaries

(*Ruling Class*, p. 152) places the event in May–June 66. For the details regarding these sacrifices see Thackeray, *Josephus*, II [Loeb], p. 483. It is difficult to explain why Josephus gave no chronological indication of when the incident took place. It is unlikely that he was lacking information as he was present in Jerusalem and lists himself among those disapproving of the action. Rather, the explanation may lie in Josephus's general vagueness regarding the beginning of the revolt. Claiming that the trouble in Caesarea was the first sign of the war (*War* 2.285) he trivialized the situation and placed the focus of attention on Florus's actions. Josephus passed over the decision to stop the sacrifices without going into much detail.

1. See section 2, above, and section 4 below. Rajak (*Josephus*, pp. 78-103) and Cohen (*Josephus in Galilee*, pp. 84-100) also comment in detail on Josephus's major personal interests in this section of the narrative. Note Josephus's description of people responsible for what happened (*War* 4.409, 560; 5.53).

2. This part of the narrative may, in fact, be an example of Josephus's distortion of the situation. It is possible that the men who offered the sacrifices were also among the people who debated whether the sacrifices should be ceased. This, however, does not necessarily mean that people like Ananias and Eleazar should automatically be included among the particular Temple ministers mentioned here. Some division may have existed but it is possible that Josephus has extended this to suit his interests.

3. The status of the captain of the Temple is difficult to establish. Here he is presented as a leading representative of a particular opinion. Therefore, although he may officially be subordinate to the high priest that does not mean he was always in

appears to be part of an attempt to place responsibility for the rebellious action in the hands of an extreme group of Jews who remain faceless.[1]

The other group of people seeking to influence the priests were 'the chief priests' and 'the notable men'. These men argued that the sacrifice should be continued. Although 'the chief priests' and the 'notable men' may have wanted to replace Florus, they did not agree with making such an independent statement as ceasing the sacrifice.[2] Josephus, therefore, claims that prominent members of the community, priests and laity, opposed the plan suggested by Eleazar. The extremity of Josephus's division, however, may be a slight distortion.[3] There is no doubt that opposing views were expressed

agreement with him. Note Thackeray, *Josephus*, II [Loeb], p. 482, and Mantel, 'High Priesthood', p. 273. Rhoads (*Revolution*, p. 100) questions whether Eleazar was a Pharisee or Sadducee, while Mantel ('High Priesthood', p. 273) assumes that the captain was a Pharisaic priest. We have no reason to seek a particular relationship between Eleazar and the Sadducees or Pharisees. His actions in this instance do not necessarily reflect that of any particular religious group.

1. Zeitlin (*Rise and Fall*, II, p. 238) describes this group as extremist on the basis that Josephus's account can be accepted as being accurate; cf. Rhoads, *Revolution*, pp. 98-99, who proposes that some of Eleazar's associates were priests. See also Goodman, *Ruling Class*, pp. 154-55, 158-59.

2. Roth ('Debate', pp. 96-97), based on a discussion of the rabbinic material, concludes that the 'priestly experts' were opposed to ending the sacrifices, although most Pharisees were probably 'non-committal'; cf. Alon, 'Attitude of the Pharisees', pp. 45-46. Note Zeitlin, *Rise and Fall*, II, p. 239, who claims that the Hillelites should be included in this category of people.

3. Some comment is required on the question of motivation. According to Rhoads (*Revolution*, p. 99) it was a sign of class struggle. Lower priests and leaders of the populace were pitched against traditional high priestly authorities, a conflict which could be dated back to the time of Felix (*Ant.* 20.180-81, 205-207). Rhoads also believes that the refusal of Eleazar to let his opponents into the Temple (*War* 2.425) indicates a nationalistic aspect to the action. Goodman (*Ruling Class*, p. 156) views Ananias and others as attempting to smother Eleazar's popular support. He accepts that Eleazar had been a leading citizen since AD 62. He suggests (p. 158) that the action was a bid for popular support by Eleazar as most of his supporters were Temple priests (*War* 2.451). He also states that this was not an isolated incident (p. 170). It is likely that Eleazar had been developing his support among the populace by displaying a strong nationalistic Jewish stance in relations with Rome. Note the other signs of factionalism when Ananias strove to increase his public status (*Ant.* 20.205), while 'the chief priests' took tithes from other priests (*Ant.* 20.207). The earlier reference to fighting in *Ant.* 20.180 is mirrored in *Ant.* 20.213 where a number of groups are described as gathering together armed bands of followers. It is possible that the question of whether to end the sacrifices for foreigners should be

regarding the continuation of the sacrifice. The leading spokesman for
the cessation was the son of a high priest. Father and son, therefore,
opposed one another. Similarly, it is possible that some of Eleazar's
associates were among 'the chief priests' and influential laity. What is
clear is that the people mentioned were not noted for a link with an
institution. In fact, influence is centred primarily on members of
Ananias's family in this instance.

The third point to note is in terms of how influence was determined.
The majority of priests chose, for whatever reason, to accept
Eleazar's argument. It is possible that they did so out of loyalty or
because of physical pressure placed on them by the captain. Whatever
the case, some of 'the chief priests' and 'the notable men' provided the
Temple ministers with the opportunity to oppose Eleazar. Irrespective
of the prestige of these men Eleazar held the upper hand in this
instance because his view, and that of his associates, was approved by
the Temple ministers.[1]

4. *Events in Jerusalem during the Revolt*

War 2.411, 'the powerful men' (οἱ δυνατοί), 'the chief priests' (οἱ
ἀρχιερεῖς) and 'the notable' (οἱ γνώριμοι) Pharisees confer, 418, they
petition Agrippa II and Florus, 422, 'the powerful men', 'chief priests'
and people favouring peace occupy upper city, 426, upper city captured,
428, 'the powerful men' and 'chief priests' flee, 434, Menahem proclaims
himself king, 442, Ananias and Ezekias killed, 448, Menahem and
followers killed, 533, 'the notable men' of the people led by Ananus
invite Cestius into Jerusalem, 562, Jews who fought Cestius gather in the
Temple to appoint additional generals, namely, 563, Joseph, son of
Gorion and Ananus, the high priest, 566, Jesus, son of Sapphas, one of
'the chief priests', Eleazar, son of the high priest Ananias, Niger, 567,
Joseph, son of Simon, Manasseh, John the Essene, 568, John, son of
Ananias, Josephus, son of Matthias, 626, John of Gischala wants to
remove Josephus, 627, 'the powerful men' of the people and some of 'the
rulers/magistrates' (οἱ ἄρχοντες) join against Josephus, 630, Josephus
returns envoys (named in 628, Joesdrus, son of Nomicus, Ananias, son
of Sadok, Simon and Judas, son of Jonathan) to Jerusalem, 648, Ananus

placed within this context, and be seen primarily as an extension of it, in which the
groups had to decide which course of action they would support.

1. Note Agrippa II's absence, despite the fact that he was custodian of the
Temple. This may, in part, be explained by his rejection by the Jews in Jerusalem
(*War* 2.406).

and the powerful men prepare Jerusalem, 3.138, Josephus seeks guidance from 'the leading men' (οἱ ἐν τέλει) in Jerusalem, 4.140, Antipas, one of 'the most powerful men' (οἱ δυνατώτατοι) and treasurer, 141, Levias, Syphas and other 'eminent/distinguished men' (οἱ ἐπίσημοι) killed, 150, 'the leading men' in conflict with one another, 153, high priest elected by lot, 155, Phanni, 159, 'the most respected men' (οἱ προύχειν δοκοῦντες) of the people, Gorion, son of Joseph, and Simon, son of Gamaliel, address 'assembly' (ἐκκλησία) and talk to individuals, 160, supported by the most prominent of 'the chief priests', Jesus, son of Gamalas, and Ananus, 235, Idumaeans march on Jerusalem, 238, Jesus, the 'high/chief priest' next in seniority to Ananus, talks to the Idumaeans, 316, Ananus and Jesus killed, 334, mock trial, 335, of Zacharias, 336, seventy 'leading men' of the people summoned, 340, they declare Zacharias not guilty, 360, Niger is killed, 572, Idumaeans talk with 'chief priests', 573, they seek the support of Simon, 574, they decide that Matthias, the high priest, should talk to Simon, 5.527, Simon has Matthias, son of Boethus, killed, 532, he also has Ananias, son of Masbalus, one of 'the eminent/distinguished' men, and Aristeus, the secretary of the *boule*, executed, 6.114, Jesus and Joseph, 'chief priests', sons of 'chief/high priests', three of Ishmael, four of Matthias, one of another Matthias, leave Jerusalem, many others join these 'chief priests', 318, priests surrender in the Temple, 322, their execution is ordered by Titus.

Life 21, Josephus talks with 'chief priests' and 'the first men' (οἱ πρῶτοι) of the Pharisees, 28, 'the first men' of Jerusalem send Josephus to Galilee, 62, Josephus writes to the *synedrion* of Jerusalem for information, 190, John of Gischala sends Simon and Jonathan, son of Sisenna, to Simon, son of Gamaliel, to get the 'common council' (κοινόν) of Jerusalem to remove Josephus, 193, 'chief priests', Ananus and Jesus, agree to help them, 194, Ananus speaks of 'chief priests' and 'the first men' of the people supporting Josephus in the dispute, 197, the envoys sent were Jonathan and Ananias, both Pharisees, Jozar, a priest and Pharisee, and Simon who was descended from high priests, 309, people angry at Ananus and Simon, acting without sanction of the 'common council', 310, 'the first men' of Jerusalem confirm Josephus's command.

The events that followed the cessation of sacrifices in honour of foreigners and the subsequent administration of affairs in Jerusalem until the final capture of the city in AD 70 constitute the penultimate events to examine. The aim here is not to consider in any detail how the military campaign progressed. Rather, my attention is focused on identifying the people and/or institutions important in controlling the

affairs of state in Jerusalem during the revolt. We are dependent on
Josephus's *The Jewish War* and *Life of Josephus* for our literary
record of these events. As in the two previous cases, Josephus's perso-
nal involvement makes it important to view his accounts with caution.
I shall proceed first by examining the initial preparations made for
war and then comment on the structure of the administration prior to
AD 68 on the basis of information contained in the attempt to remove
Josephus from his command. In the latter part of this case I shall
briefly consider the situation in Jerusalem after the demise of
Ananus.[1]

Those in favour of war were able to gain the upper hand in
Jerusalem. What is of interest here is the identity of the people who
decided to sue for peace and those who chose the path of war.
According to Josephus 'the powerful men', 'the chief priests', 'the
notable'/'first' Pharisees and a number of the populace opposed the
war.[2] Ananias, the high priest, was the main protagonist of this
faction, with the support of his brother, Ezekias, Costobar and Saul,
Antipas, Simon, the son of Ananias, and Philip and Dorius. Agrippa
II's support for this group is implied by Josephus. In other words,
certain men who had an active role in pre-war negotiations attempted
to prevent armed conflict by means of reconciliation and then by
seeking the aid of Agrippa II and Florus.[3]

---

1. Josephus's knowledge of events inside Jerusalem after his surrender was
obtained while he resided within the Roman camp. However biased their accounts
may have been, Josephus was able to learn of some of the events that took place in
the city from the people who deserted (*War* 6.115). Scholars have been quick to
acknowledge the personal interests of Josephus in the narration of the war. Whether
the extent of criticism levelled at Josephus by such scholars as Cohen (*Josephus in
Galilee*, p. 181) is warranted, is debatable. Other scholars who devote detailed
sections of their work to the war narrative legitimately express the need for caution.
See, for example, Rajak, *Josephus*, and Goodman, *Ruling Class*. The central issue
is how much emphasis should be placed on the analytical statements in comparison to
the actual narrative of events.

2. Although the cessation of sacrifices did not make full-scale revolt inevitable,
this, combined with the repulsion of Roman troops, left the Jews of Jerusalem faced
with a major decision: whether or not to opt for open revolt. There may have been
much discussion and variation in opinion with regard to how either course of action
should be implemented. Goodman (*Ruling Class*, p. 209) argues that the start of the
revolt is one of the few clear examples of when the prominent Jews were actually in
dispute regarding a matter of policy.

3. By requesting military assistance it appears that the main motivation for these

A select number of Pharisees should also be included in this pro-peace group. These men are described in *The Jewish War* as 'the notable' and in the *Life of Josephus* as 'the first' Pharisees. In this instance, 'the first' and 'the notable' are equated in meaning. This is the first occasion since the time of Herod that Josephus refers explicitly to Pharisees in his narrative of events. Clearly, Josephus relieves certain Jews of responsibility for the outbreak of the revolt.[1] While the specific reference here to the 'notable'/'first' Pharisees may reflect the historical situation, it may also have been included to show that members of the school of thought with which Josephus associated himself rejected war.[2]

The Jews arguing for peace were eventually overwhelmed by the Jews who favoured war, among whom revolutionaries shoulder much of the blame for the outbreak of fighting. Among this group of revolutionaries, it is important to note that Josephus names several who stood out for their involvement in the initial campaign against the Romans. They included Gorion, son of Nicomedes, Judas, son of Jonathan, Ananias, son of Sadok, Niger, Monobazus, Cenedaeus, and Silas. Josephus also refers to Simon, son of Gioras, Eleazar, son of Simon, and to Menahem, who laid claim to overall control of the uprising. Internal division among the Jews in favour of the war resulted in Menahem and many of his followers being killed.[3]

---

prominent men was peace under Roman rule, not simply peace for its own sake. It should be noted that they were not automatically declared the enemies of the rebellion. Although Ananias and Ezekias were murdered, Saul and Costobar were allowed to leave the city as free men while Antipas was killed by the zealots later in the war in Jerusalem.

1. Concern about Roman reaction is expressed in *War* 2.418. For Josephus's interest in blaming a specific section of the Jewish community see *War* 4.128-37, 150, 385-88; 5.53; 6.214-16.

2. There is no reason to doubt that people who described themselves as Pharisees, any less than any other Jews, were faced with having to choose between rebellion and peace. Note that Alon (*Jews in their Land*, I, p. 93) presents the Pharisees as being split into three sub-groups as a result of the revolt. C. Roth ('The Pharisees in the Jewish Revolution', *JSS* 7 [1962], pp. 66-67) believes that the importance of being linked with the Pharisees at the beginning of the revolt was minimal. A question not addressed in any detail by these scholars, or by those who refer to the prominence of the Pharisees within the Jewish community, is why most of the populace were able to be convinced that they should fight the Romans when Josephus informs us that the prominent Pharisees were opposed to the revolt.

3. Some of the populace and Temple ministers also favoured war (*War* 2.417,

The notion of destructive revolutionaries instigating the revolt is complicated by Josephus's references to Ananus, son of Jonathan, and 'the notable men' of the people. These men offered to open the gates of Jerusalem for Cestius. The plan was discovered and Ananus and his supporters were discharged from defending the walls. The absence of any reference to punishment suggests that extremist, pro-war tendencies were not rigidly dominant.

With Cestius defeated and, for the moment, no Roman authority able to intervene in Jerusalem, the city was in Jewish hands. Rejoicing over their victory, most Jews in Jerusalem appear to have accepted the path of war and independent rule. The appointment of men to command the war effort was the next positive step taken by the Jews to assert their independence after the cessation of the sacrifices. Although the *Life of Josephus* only notes the appointment of Josephus in Galilee several details are provided in *The Jewish War*.[1]

Josephus ascribed the control of the early fighting to a few individuals, presumably men with some military experience, and/or armed followers. Now, with the immediate threat from Roman troops and those of Agrippa II removed, the Jews were in a position to make permanent appointments. It is implied in the account in *The Jewish War* that control of the war was exercised from Jerusalem, in particular, by the people who made the appointments. All areas of Palestine were catered for, including territory officially under the jurisdiction of Agrippa II.

The Jewish War and the *Life of Josephus* differ regarding who made the appointments and whence the authority to do so was derived. In the *Life of Josephus*, Josephus states that he was appointed commander of Galilee by the first men of Jerusalem. In *The Jewish War* Josephus gives no such detail. The people who met to choose the generals were those who fought against Cestius and the Jews of Jerusalem who decided to support the war after the defeat of the

---

422). See Horsley and Hanson, *Bandits*, pp. 211-16, for a detailed examination of the part played by the sicarii in the early stages of the revolt.

1. There is some dispute as to whether these were additional appointments, as indicated by Josephus (*War* 2.563). See Goodman (*Ruling Class*, pp. 163-68). The minting of coins immediately after the outbreak of the revolt indicates that some form of organization was in existence. See C. Roth, 'The Historical Implications of the Jewish Coinage of the First Revolt', *IEJ* 12 (1962), p. 37 and Meshorer, *Coinage*, II, p. 99.

Roman legate. The implication appears to be that it was a general gathering of Jews in the Temple. There is no indication in *The Jewish War* that it was a formal meeting.

The apparent differences regarding the identity of the people who appointed the generals are readily explained. In the *Life of Josephus*, Josephus appears to have primarily sought to defend both his appointment as general of Galilee and the people responsible for selecting him. Josephus attempts to fulfil this task by interpreting his commission as a peace-orientated one, made by the group of people previously described as being opposed to the war. As a result, it is possible that the reference to the first men was a necessary detail due to Josephus's interests rather than his concerns for veracity.

The version in *The Jewish War* is not so much a different interpretation as a generalized, somewhat vague account of the event. The problem for Josephus in *The Jewish War* was that he was one of the generals. Therefore, although he may have wanted to lay blame for the revolt outside his social circle, he could not state outright that the men involved in the process of appointing the generals were evil or power-hungry revolutionaries. Thus, Josephus avoids identifying the people responsible for making the appointments.[1]

Some of the generals listed were accustomed to life in the public sphere. Several of the others listed appear only once in the works of Josephus. For example, Joseph, son of Simon, Manasseh, John, son of Ananus, and Jesus, son of Sapphas play no further part in the narrative. It is possible that these men may also previously have been prominent in public affairs although they were not named. The reference to Jesus is important. According to Josephus he was one of 'the chief priests'. There is, however, no record of this Jesus holding the office of high priest. It appears, therefore, that Josephus uses 'chief priests' as a reference to people who did not hold a direct link with the high priesthood in this instance.

Josephus lists five other generals for whom he provides further information. The first of these is Eleazar, the son of the high priest

---

1. Note the difference regarding Josephus's terms of reference in Galilee between *Life* 28–29 and *War* 2.569-72. Cohen (*Josephus in Galilee*, pp. 200-206) indicates that the *War* version probably reflects the historical situation more than the *Life*; cf. Bilde (*Flavius Josephus*, pp. 38-52, 179). On the attitude of Galilaeans towards the war see Freyne (*Galilee*, pp. 80-81).

Ananias, who had been prominent prior to the revolt.[1] The second general is John, the Essene. The only extra detail we have regarding John is that he died later in the war fighting the Romans. That he was designated an Essene indicates that some Essenes chose direct involvement in the revolt at the outset. The third general, Josephus, the author, was a priest and related to the royal line of Aristobulus. The two remaining generals listed were given responsibility for affairs in Jerusalem. They were Joseph, son of Gorion, and Ananus. It is possible that Joseph was the person referred to when Simon, son of Gamaliel (*War* 4.159), spoke to the populace in AD 68. We have no details regarding his family or personal status. The other general, Ananus, is referred to by Josephus as high priest, a position he briefly held in AD 62.

These men, at least three of whom participated in public affairs prior to the revolt, may not have been zealous in their opposition to Rome, but they were willing to act as commanders of the Jewish forces. It is not possible to determine whether or not the gathering of Jews in the Temple was intended to be a chance for nominees to be publicly acclaimed or actually appointed. It is apparent, however, that at least some support from the populace was considered appropriate.[2]

In combination, elements of the accounts in the *Life of Josephus* and *The Jewish War* suggest that at the outbreak of the revolt a leading role was taken by people who had some public standing prior to the revolt. These men had the confidence of the populace in controlling the campaign against Rome. Furthermore, the idea that some form of machination took place is indicated in *The Jewish War* by the reference to the inability of Eleazar, son of Simon, to obtain a post.[3]

1. It is generally accepted that Hudson's rendering of the text as Ananias rather than Neus is accurate.
2. The involvement of prominent Jews is further supported by the references to 'the first men' confirming Josephus's appointment (*Life* 310) and the assistance 'the powerful men' rendered to Ananus in preparing Jerusalem for war (*War* 2.648).
3. Note that Eleazar, son of Simon, was later able to obtain power as leader of the zealots. Another person unable to feature among those men given a commission was Simon, son of Gioras. Goodman (*Ruling Class*, pp. 163-69) accurately highlights that factional fighting among men previously prominent in the public sphere was the basis for the negotiations to determine who was given what command. Note also his detailed account of the people to be identified with each faction. Many scholars argue that the change was an indication that moderate Jews came to the forefront. See Horsley, 'The Zealots. Their Origin, Relationship and Importance in the Jewish

Clarification of the administrative structure of Jerusalem during the early part of the war can be obtained from the account of the protest lodged against Josephus. For this incident the *Life of Josephus* provides greater detail than *The Jewish War*, although both versions agree in the basic outline of what happened. A complaint against Josephus was registered in Jerusalem. In part, this may have been necessitated because Josephus held a strong position in Galilee. More importantly though, it suggests that Jerusalem was chosen as the place to present the protest because the source of Josephus's authority lay in that city.[1]

In *The Jewish War* Josephus claims that the complaint was ignored by the people of Jerusalem, because they favoured him. In the *Life of Josephus*, the protest is registered discreetly with a select few. Both versions enhance the characterization of Josephus. It is probable, however, that neither account alone exactly represents what happened. In *The Jewish War* 'the powerful men' and some of 'the rulers/ magistrates' hear and support the complaint. In the *Life of Josephus*, Josephus states that the emissaries of John sought the aid of Simon, son of Gamaliel, who was asked to have the 'common council' (κοινόν) of Jerusalem remove Josephus from his command. To achieve this aim, Simon called upon the support of a group of people headed by Ananus and Jesus, son of Gamalas, the most eminent of 'the chief priests'. It appears that Simon believed that in order to remove Josephus he required the assistance of the most influential group of Jews in Jerusalem.[2]

Revolt', *NovT* 28 (1986), pp. 171-73; Rajak, *Josephus*, p. 129; and Rhoads, *Revolution*, pp. 151-52. This approach fails to acknowledge the consistent involvement of prominent Jews throughout the revolt and that there was not a clearly definable radical element in the Jewish community in Jerusalem in AD 66.

1. Note that the attempt to remove Josephus was dependent on financial and military aid from Jerusalem. This may, in part, indicate that the envoys sent to Galilee did not intend to assist John of Gischala but possibly intended to place their own candidate in command. See Goodman, *Ruling Class*, pp. 183-85, who argues that it was an extension of the factional fighting in Jerusalem. Note also the involvement of Pharisees and priests in the mission to Galilee. There remains some debate as to the reason why an attempt was made to replace Josephus when he appears to have been accepted by the majority of Galilaeans. See Freyne, *Galilee*, p. 244. Cohen (*Josephus in Galilee*, p. 231) argues that the incident marks the Pharisaic attempt to gain power in Jerusalem. S. Freyne ('Galilee–Jerusalem Relations according to Josephus's Life', *NTS* 33 [1987], p. 603) also views the dispute between John and Josephus as a Pharisaic–priestly conflict.

2. Note that Simon was described as a member of a prominent Pharisaic family

We cannot establish if these men continued to act informally or whether they required the support of a formal institution. In *The Jewish War* Josephus simply states that the populace was angry when Josephus returned the envoys sent by Simon and Ananus. It is implied that the envoys were sent without the general approval of those in the city. The lack of any reference in either text to punishment for the perpetrators appears to indicate that, irrespective of whether the action was authorized, little could be, or was intended to be, done against the offenders.

The account in the *Life of Josephus* is important in clarifying the issue of authorization. Jonathan, the envoy from Jerusalem, claimed he had been commissioned by the 'common council'. It would appear, therefore, that after obtaining the support of Ananus and Jesus, Simon presented the protest against Josephus to this 'common council'. Similarly, when Josephus sent emissaries to Jerusalem to argue in his defence, they were to address the 'common council' of Jerusalem. Jonathan may have perceived the support of Simon, Ananus and Jesus to be an indication of the wishes of the 'common council' without necessarily obtaining formal approval.

Two elements of the administrative structure in Jerusalem are featured in this incident. The first of these is the 'common council', a specific institution. It was involved in the organization of the war and it possibly came into existence with the advent of the war as its terms of reference appear to have been linked with the revolt.[1] Furthermore, several people appear to have been able to obtain a prominent position within the 'common council'. Its membership may have been diverse, yet it appears that the number of members was limited.[2]

(*Life* 191). See Roth, 'The Pharisees', p. 67, and Alon, 'The Attitude of the Pharisees', p. 44, regarding the extent of Simon's involvement. We are unable to establish when Simon became involved and whether he represented a different faction to that in which Ananus and Jesus were prominent. See Goodman, *Ruling Class*, pp. 183-85. The emergence of Jesus, son of Gamalas, high priest AD 63–64, supports the notion of internal wrangling to decide who should take a leading role in managing the revolt.

1. See *Life* 190; cf. *Life* 310.

2. This is inferred from the distinction between Jesus' and Simon's addresses to the Jewish community as a whole in an 'assembly' in Jerusalem. It was, however, to the 'common council' that Josephus referred his case (*Life* 266). It may be plausible to suggest that the magistrates who assisted Ananus (*War* 2.653) are linked with the common council.

The executive is the second element of the administrative structure mentioned. It acted as the main authority for dealing with the day-to-day direction of affairs. This executive is referred to at other stages of the narrative as 'the leading men' (*War* 3.138)/*synedrion* (*Life* 62) and 'the first men' of Jerusalem (*Life* 309). These men were contacted when an immediate response was required. Whether this status was due to formal appointment or personal prominence is difficult to determine. Furthermore, this executive acted on its own initiative.[1] A gathering of the populace expressed support for or disapproval of certain decisions. Formal resolutions were probably instituted by the 'common council'. At the same time, however, important decisions that required immediate attention were controlled by a smaller executive, not necessarily formally appointed or directly accountable to anyone.

There is an overt bias in the narrative of Josephus which tends to result in depicting those who held a high public profile in the pre-war years as being strongly in favour of peace in AD 66. The narrative of events, however, indicates that the people who took a leading role in the early part of the war included some of those men who had participated in public affairs before the war (*War* 2.428, 556).

Increased tension regarding the state of affairs in the revolt resulted in civil war and the death of Ananus and Jesus. This growing tension was evident in the election of the high priest by lot and the execution of Antipas and his colleagues. The new high priest, Phanni, came from a family not previously associated with the office. This break from tradition as well as his appointment by election appear to have angered Ananus, an ex-high priest, and his followers. Antipas and the other 'eminent men' were put to death probably because of a lack of firm conviction in support of the rebel cause.

These events took place while Ananus and Jesus were still officially in command in Jerusalem, yet indicate that they did not have complete control of affairs. It is possible that underlying this tension were concerns for the overall state of affairs in the war and differing opinions regarding the appropriate response of the Jews to the isolation of

---

1. It is possible that Ananus, Jesus and Simon were among this inner executive. Note Smallwood, *Jews under Roman Rule*, p. 298, who argues that the sanhedrin was the executive of the government, and that the 'popular assembly' held ultimate authority (p. 300).

Jerusalem.[1] These disturbances soon gave way to civil war which concluded with the murders of Ananus and Jesus and the command of Jerusalem passing into the hands of several rival factions.

According to Josephus these extremist groups were led by disreputable individuals. Furthermore, the associates of Ananus and Jesus no longer featured in the events in Jerusalem. The notion of chaos is enhanced by the description of fighting between the factions for outright control of Jerusalem. The narrative of events between AD 68–70, however, and the continued production of coinage, some of reasonably high quality, until AD 70 suggests that certain semblances of stability and systematic organization remained in operation throughout the revolt.[2]

The departure of certain Jews, and the recording of several executions and a trial suggest that disorder was rife in Jerusalem. The narration of these incidents, however, indicates that such a view is not entirely accurate. Josephus cites one particular example of a mock trial, the case of Zacharias, son of Baris. The zealots allegedly tried Zacharias simply because they were tired of indiscriminate killing. This idea is apparently contradicted by the later narrative where Gorion and Niger are killed without any mention of recourse to a trial. What appears most likely is that trials were held, not necessarily in every case, but when those in control of affairs wanted to assert their power. This appears to be supported by Josephus's account of the

1. For discussion of the origin and purpose of the zealots see Horsley, 'The Zealots'. pp. 159-92, and Horsley and Hanson, *Bandits*, pp. 216-41; cf. Hengel, *Die Zeloten*, pp. 61-76, 319-83, and T.L. Donaldson, 'Rural Bandits, City Mobs and the Zealots', *JSJ* 21 (1990), pp. 39-40, who directs attention to the possible significance of an urban element in the rise of the zealots. Most scholars view the zealots as attempting to alter the political structure in Jerusalem. See Horsley, 'The Zealots', pp. 175-90, and Rajak, *Josephus*, pp. 132-36; cf. Goodman, *Ruling Class*, pp. 193-206. The notion that it was a civil war is dependent on an acceptance of the view that the upper-class Jews ceased to participate in the administration of affairs in the city.

2. See Meshorer, *Coinage*, II, pp. 99-123. Note also *War* 5.568 and the continuation of Temple services throughout the revolt. The recent findings in Wadi Fara also suggest that some degree of preparation and organization was involved in the war against Rome. See J. Patrich, 'Hideouts in the Judaean Wilderness', *BARev* 15 (1989), pp. 32-42. Note also the provision for ritual bathing in at least one of the caves (p. 39), indicating a desire to maintain some ritual practices by the rebels who occupied the caves. We must wait for further reports before we can confirm that the caves were used by Simon and his associates as suggested by Patrich (p. 42).

trial. The judges returned a not guilty verdict, which is slightly puzzling considering they were supposedly told what to do by the zealots. Even more puzzling, the judges were not punished for this verdict. Josephus unrealistically claims that their release was to be a warning to the populace. Certainly, the opinion of these men was of little value. Zacharias was killed and we have no further references to the use of such trials in Jerusalem. The contradiction in this account suggests that Josephus has manipulated it to present a negative picture of the zealots.

At some point in time after Simon, son of Gioras, entered Jerusalem in AD 69 several prominent men were killed. One of Josephus's main motives in citing these particular executions was to highlight the brutality and unpredictability of the zealots. By mentioning that his father was imprisoned, however, Josephus's account suggests that the murderers were selective in whom they killed. Their motive was not simply indiscriminate murder. This point is indicated by the status of some of the men listed. Among Simon's victims was a priest named Ananias, son of Masbalus, who was one of 'the eminent/distinguished men'. Apparently there were fifteen other such men killed. More significantly, however, Simon had Matthias, son of Boethus, descended from high priests, and three of his sons, executed. Another person whose death was ordered by Simon was Aristeus, the secretary of the *boule*. The high public standing of the victims and some of the participants in the trial(s) and executions is an important feature in these references. This strongly suggests that the deaths of Ananus and Jesus did not mark an end to the involvement of men other than those who belonged to the extremist revolutionary factions.[1]

The account of several individuals leaving Jerusalem late in the war reinforces the point that it was not only extremist revolutionaries who remained active in Jerusalem. Joseph and Jesus left the city, as did three sons of Ishmael, four of Matthias and one of another Matthias.

---

1. Goodman (*Ruling Class*, pp. 206-207) alone acknowledges the consistent involvement of prominent members of the Jewish community in the war. Other scholars, such as Rajak (*Josephus*, p. 132), Horsley ('The Zealots', p. 175) and P.A. Brunt ('Josephus on Social Conflicts in Roman Judaea', *Klio* 59 [1977], p. 152) explain away the references to prominent Jews, highlighting the radical control of government without questioning what these people were still doing in Jerusalem after the death of Ananus and Jesus. Donaldson ('Rural Mobs', pp. 19-40) also fails to give due attention to these references in his discussion of the role of 'urban bandits' in Jerusalem before and after the removal of Ananus.

These men are linked with the group referred to as 'the chief priests' and are joined by numerous other citizens.[1] Although these people are narrated as ending their association with the rebel cause in one way or another, they had for several years shown passive, or in some cases, active support for the rebellion.

Josephus's personal involvement in the revolt appears to have directly affected the content and direction of his narrative of the events in Jerusalem during AD 66–70. Despite such personal interest we are able to draw together several aspects of how the city was administered during the revolt. It appears that there was a formal institution which functioned in Jerusalem, the 'common council'. This institution was probably separate from the pre-war *boule* and possibly replaced it. We are not able to determine whether the 'common council' ceased to exist after AD 68. It was, however, particular individuals, sometimes working in alliance, who held the greatest influence regarding what decisions were taken and whether they were carried out. Moreover, many of these influential people were from the same group that had been prominent prior to the revolt and, in some instances, the same people. Although many of 'the notable men'/ 'powerful men' and 'chief priests' opposed the war, other members of this stratum of society appear to have chosen to take up arms against the Romans, some by taking a leading role in the fighting with popular backing. The declining fortunes of the Jewish military efforts were matched by a move toward more extremist attitudes and a greater emphasis on the influence of particular individuals. There is, however, evidence of prominent Jews remaining among the rebels until AD 70.[2] Furthermore, the notion that individuals took a leading role was not a new feature of Jerusalem in AD 68. What probably marked individuals prominent in the later part of the revolt as being different from their earlier counterparts was that they were less willing to negotiate and share power with others.

1. The reference to these men leaving Jerusalem enhanced Josephus's prestige as an effective negotiator. The presence of 'chief priests' in Jerusalem is also indicated by the reference to the Idumaeans having joined with the chief priests against the zealots (*War* 4.572-73).

2. See Goodman (*Ruling Class*, pp. 200-206) regarding the possible respectable social background of Eleazar, son of Simon, Simon, son of Gioras and John of Gischala. While reviewing Goodman, J. Geiger ('The Causes of the Jewish War', *JRA* 2 [1989], pp. 292-93) clearly outlines the debate that remains regarding the alleged background of Simon.

5. *Revolt of Tiberias against Josephus*

War 2.632, Tiberias seeks aid from Agrippa II, 639, Josephus orders the ten 'most powerful men' (οἱ δυνστώτστοι), then fifty 'notable men' (οἱ γνώριμοι) of the *boule* to appear before him, 641, eventually he captures all 600 members of the *boule* and 2000 citizens.

Life 155, Tiberias seeks Agrippa II's aid, 168, Josephus orders ten leaders of the people to appear before him, 169, eventually he captures the whole *boule* and 'the first men' (οἱ πρῶτοι) of the people, including Justus and Pistus.

The revolt of Tiberias against Josephus is the final incident to consider in detail. The incident took place during the Jewish revolt against Rome, after Josephus had been sent from Jerusalem to command Galilee.[1] At the same time, however, Agrippa II was officially sovereign of Tiberias and other parts of Galilee (*War* 2.252; *Ant.* 20.159). Thus, when the people of Tiberias decided to oppose Josephus's overlordship they turned to Agrippa.

Josephus's two accounts are very similar, presenting the order of events without any contradiction. The variation in the description of people involved in the revolt, however, requires comment. Moreover, care is required in the interpretation of Josephus's narrative of the events taking place in Galilee. It is possible that aspects of the account have been doctored to highlight Josephus's prowess and innocence.[2]

Josephus refers to three groups of people in the two texts. The first group is described as the ten 'most powerful men' of Tiberias in *The Jewish War* and as ten leaders of the people in the *Life of Josephus*. The second group in *The Jewish War* are the fifty 'notable men' of the *boule* and all the members of the *boule* in the *Life of Josephus*. Finally, Josephus speaks of all 600 members of the *boule* and 2000 citizens being captured in *The Jewish War*, while in the *Life of*

---

1. There is some debate based on discrepancies between Josephus's *War* and *Life* as to whether Josephus was commissioned to prepare the region for war or to prevent the region from going to war. Despite the alleged intentions ascribed to himself, Josephus's actions tend to support the view that he was sent to Galilee as a general with orders to fight the Romans and any Jews opposed to the conflict. See Cohen, *Josephus in Galilee*, pp. 200-206, and Rajak, *Josephus*, pp. 130, 157-58.

2. For a detailed examination of the possible influences at work in Josephus's narrative of events in Galilee see Cohen, *Josephus in Galilee*, pp. 146-73, and Rajak *Josephus*, pp. 181-231.

Josephus Josephus refers to all 'the first men' of the people and the whole *boule*.

Three points should be noted regarding the way Josephus describes these participants. First, when referring to the members of the *boule* that he captured Josephus does not provide the same amount of detail in the *Life of Josephus* as in *The Jewish War*. He does, however, indicate that these men were captured in stages. Secondly, the difference in terms used to describe the ten people initially captured probably reflects a change in linguistic style rather than a possible alteration in meaning.[1] Finally, the terms used to describe the third group of people captured also appear to reflect a shift in emphasis rather than a change in meaning. In the *Life of Josephus* Josephus makes his point by referring to particular people and their high standing. In *The Jewish War*, however, he emphasizes the number of people captured. These alterations do not affect the meaning of the passage, nor do they present a major problem for understanding the order of events or the people who were involved.

Two main observations can be made regarding the administration of Tiberias from this incident. In turn, these observations may be of value for our perception of the administrative structure in Palestine as a whole. First, Tiberias had a formal administrative institution. According to Josephus it was a *boule* with 600 members. Josephus connects this *boule* to the revolt against him, but gives no details regarding its function.[2] Josephus's consideration that the capture of its members was a means of regaining control of Tiberias, suggests that

1. Stern ('Province of Judaea', p. 345) states that the ten leading men were a financial committee. T. Rajak ('Justus of Tiberias', *CQ* ns 23 [1973], p. 347 and *Josephus*, p. 40) and Tcherikover ('Was Jerusalem a Polis?', p. 67 n. 13) point out that the link between the ten men and the finances of the city was not established by the mid-first century AD and that these men from Tiberias were the most eminent men who represented their community. Note also the reference to ten men on a number of other occasions in the narrative of Josephus. See, for example, *Life* 67, 68, 296, where reference is made to ten 'first men' of Tiberias. Note that they are accompanied by another person, Capella. In *Ant.* 20.194 the ten 'first men' assist Ishmael and Helcias. See above, Chapter 4, section 4. Note that Josephus portrays other towns in the region by referring to influential individuals (*War* 4.18, 413, 416).

2. Rajak ('Justus', p. 346) notes that Josephus provides no information regarding the means by which membership of the *boule* was determined. Rajak ('Justus', p. 346) and Freyne (*Galilee*, p. 129) have noted that the presence of a *boule* and chief magistrate indicate that Tiberias was similar to a Greek polis in a political structure.

he perceived the *boule* to be important. I cannot, however, comment conclusively on whether the *boule* at Tiberias was the focal point of the city's administration.

The second observation is Josephus's perception of the power structure at Tiberias. His success in preventing the revolt of Tiberias suggests that he correctly understood the situation in the city, selecting particular people and in a specific order. This order of priority included the ten most influential of the city, the *boule*, in which there was an order of importance, and other prominent citizens who were outside the *boule*.[1]

The people Josephus wanted under his control first and foremost were not members of the *boule*. Furthermore, Josephus then selected people from within the *boule* whom he, and presumably the people of Tiberias, recognized as being the most influential of that institution.[2] It is implied, therefore, that membership of the *boule* was not a pre-requisite for being influential in Tiberias. Membership of the *boule* alone did not necessarily make a person important in public affairs. In Tiberias public prestige and influence were not dependent on holding any formal administrative position.[3]

1. How the chief magistrate fitted into this scheme of affairs is not clear. Note Rajak ('Justus', p. 346), who suggests that he may have been elected by popular vote. The reference to the first men of the *boule* requesting Agrippa II's aid against Josephus (*Life* 381) reinforces the idea that there was some form of hierarchy within the *boule*.

2. There are several people mentioned by Josephus in terms of affairs in Tiberias (*Life* 33–36) about whose role in the incident we remain uncertain. It is possible that Jannaeus and Dassion, whom Josephus describes as two of the first men of Tiberias (*Life* 131) were still with Agippa II.

3. Note that Josephus does not make any further reference to the seventy men he appointed to assist him (*War* 2.570; *Life* 79). Furthermore, Silas fails to forewarn Josephus of the events in Tiberias (*Life* 89–90, 272; *War* 2.610). Rajak ('Justus', p. 347) remarks on the fact that Jospheus is silent about what these men supposedly did in the incident.

Chapter 6

SYNTHESIS

The preceding assessment of the case studies has been intentionally disparate. This approach has enabled the incidents to be examined in chronological order with the prime concern being to establish which people and/or institutions actually participated in decision-making.[1]

By reserving overall assessment until now this study avoids problems associated with relying on one particular source above all others.[2] I am consequently in a position to question the degree to which participation in the decision-making process was routinely delegated to Jews, and/or assumed by certain Jews to be their prerogative. Furthermore, there is an opportunity to comment on certain issues raised in the introduction of this study, such as the concept of a distinction between political and religious issues and the ability of Jews to convict and execute people in the first century AD.

This synthesis will establish what are the consistent and the extraordinary elements within the twenty-one studies. I shall then consider specific aspects of the administration. For example, the identity of any particular family(s) or institution(s) that may have been prevalent, the possible prominence of any religious group, possible tools of diplomacy, delineations in duty that may have existed, whether there was a relationship between the success of the Jews, the identity of those involved and the issue(s) at stake, and the possible motivation of social groups or individuals involved in the decision-making process. I shall conclude by discussing the broader issue of the Jewish ruling class's interests and its relationship with the remainder of the Jewish community.

Among the Jews residing in Palestine there were always some who vied for acknowledgment as the prominent and influential. The quest

1. It is not assumed that information from one part of the 100 BC–AD 70 period necessarily pertains to the entire period.
2. See Cohen, 'Political and Social History', pp. 37-41.

for a prominent role in the community was occasionally expressed by a bid to obtain outright control of the administration through revolt against the existing head of state, or through petitioning when the leadership of Palestine was vacant. For example, during the reign of Alexander Jannaeus a large number of Jews rallied together in an effort to remove the king. Similarly, after the Roman settlement that restored Hyrcanus, several attempts were made to remove him by Aristobulus and his relatives (*War* 1.158-78; *Ant.* 14.79-97, 100-103). The death of Herod was also used by several individuals as an opportunity to claim authority before the arbitration of the Roman emperor (*War* 2.20-22; *Ant.* 17.224-27). Other Jews saw Herod's death as a chance to claim leadership by the use of force (*War* 2.55-65; *Ant.* 17.269-84). The revolt against Rome marks a further occasion when a number of Jews claimed outright control of the rebel cause (*War* 4.556-84).[1]

For the most part, the Jews seeking prominence were content to stand under the official head of state, whether Jewish or Roman. The main preoccupation of these Jews was to obtain a position of privilege and public status. In effect, such a position resulted in involvement in certain administrative tasks. Of greater significance, though, was the opportunity for those successful in the machinations to participate actively in decisions regarding policy.

Two clear examples of this vying for prominence exist in the first century BC. Early in the reign of Salome Alexandra a group which included Pharisees successfully obtained a position of favour, while men previously associated with Alexander Jannaeus, whose main spokesman was Aristobulus, were forced to withdraw from Jerusalem. Initially a dispute to seek the queen's approval, it eventually erupted into open rebellion by those who had been forced to take a low public profile. Later, when Hyrcanus was the ethnarch, Antipater and his sons manoeuvred themselves into a prominent position as Hyrcanus's main stewards. The legitimacy of this position was actively challenged by a number of Jews wishing to supplant Antipater's family.

Rivalry to acquire a privileged status within the Jewish community continued during the first century AD. Between AD 6 and the early AD 50s some rivalry may be inferred from the frequent changes made in

---

1. Note also the protests addressed to Antony against Herod and Phasael (*War* 1.242-45; *Ant.* 14.302-305, 324-29) and the request made by Jews and Samaritans that Archelaus be removed by Augustus (*War* 2.111-13; *Ant.* 17.342-44).

the office of high priest. Dissatisfaction with the incumbents may have influenced the Roman prefects, and then the Herodians, to change the high priest (*Ant.* 18.34-35; 20.16, 197). Similarly, the willingness of the head of state to change the high priest may have been viewed as an opportunity by others to increase their prominence (*Ant.* 20.213).[1]

From the mid-AD 50s there is much evidence of people vying for prominence. Certain members of the Jewish community formed alliances and engaged in intermittent conflict. Central among these men were Ananias, Ananus, Saul, Costobar and Eleazar, son of Ananias.[2] It appears that the conflict between these men did not spread to involve the entire Jewish population. Furthermore, at no stage was there a direct attack on the official head of state; at issue was prominence within the Jewish community. An expression of this conflict coincided with Ananus's trial and execution of several Jews. This event was viewed by rivals as an opportune occasion to successfully challenge Ananus's worthiness as high priest. There were also divisions among the priests who resided in Jerusalem, through which a few were able to increase their wealth.

The Jews seeking prominence were frequently united in the advice they offered. The protest regarding the Temple wall, the control of the high priests' vestments and the machinations in the case against Jesus suggest that prominent, influential Jews willingly argued the same plan of action. On a few occasions, however, it is evident that not all prominent Jews were in agreement over the particular issue requiring resolution. For example, Eleazar opposed his father in the dispute regarding the offering of sacrifices on behalf of foreigners. Although many of the cases present the Jews as a united group, it should be acknowledged that this may occasionally be as much the intention of the author as it is an accurate account of the incident.

During the first centuries BC and AD certain men continually disputed the right to hold first place among the Jewish community.

---

1. Note also the case of Joazar. Initially ousted from office by Archelaus (*Ant.* 17.339) he was reinstated as high priest and assisted Quirinius in carrying out the census (*Ant.* 18.3). His support may have been used by others, such as the house of Ananus, to assert their claims for prominence. On the career of Joazar, see Goodman, *Ruling Class,* pp. 139-40 and Smallwood, 'High Priests', pp. 17-21.

2. See Goodman, *Ruling Class,* pp. 137-227. This is the first major critical assessment of the identity of factions within the Jewish nobility which is based on a detailed analysis of the events recorded by Josephus.

The existence of this conflict implies that there were more people seeking prominence than the community required. Furthermore, changes in personnel did not alter the principle of rivalry. This observation raises three important issues: first, the reason why Jews should want to attain a position of prominence; second, identifying the social groups to which the Jews who sought to obtain prominence belonged; third, how were prominence and influence perceived in Palestine in the first centuries BC and AD? I shall return to these issues at a later point.

In the incidents examined there is much information that enables us to clarify the means by which decisions were made and actions taken, especially for events in the first century AD. Two main tools of diplomacy were used throughout the period, violence and negotiation. On several occasions a combination of the two is evident.

The incidents which were resolved entirely by the use of violence are comparatively few in number. This is in marked contrast to the degree of violence associated with the revolt of AD 66–70. There are only two definite and one possible example of the exclusive use of violence. The dispute over Alexander Jannaeus's right to rule outright was expressed through open defiance and resulted in armed conflict. This revolt was finally subdued by the king's capture of the rebels and consequent harsh exaction of justice.[1] Secondly, the protest over the aqueduct during Pilate's term as prefect was resolved by violence. Opposition to Pilate's decision was easily quashed by the use of troops in the city.[2] The death of Stephen may be a further example of a decision being reached by violence. If not the outcome of a trial, it appears that Stephen's death was the result of mob action which received passive support from prominent Jews.

It is notable that only in the aqueduct incident is it possible to argue that violence was chosen by preference. There is no evidence that Pilate tried but failed to appease the protesters. Rather, the impression

1. The subsequent Pharisaic antagonism against Alexander Jannaeus's advisors in connection with the execution of the 800 suggests that the king alone was not to blame.

2. Note also the harsh manner in which Pilate dealt with the Samaritans (*Ant.* 18.85-87). His subsequent removal from office by Vitellius suggests that violence was not always sanctioned (*Ant.* 18.88-89). P.W. Barnett ('Under Tiberius All Was Quiet', *NTS* 21 [1974–75], pp. 546-71) notes that violence was used on only a few isolated occasions before the reign of Agrippa I.

is that the prefect decided from the outset that he would deal with the protest swiftly by the use of force. The revolt against Alexander Jannaeus, by its nature, however, required the king to protect himself, assuming he wanted to retain his position. Uncertainty regarding the details of the account of Stephen's death does not allow us to comment on the relation of the action taken to other possible attempts to resolve the case.

The majority of studies indicate that negotiation was a legitimate and effective means of reaching a decision. This practice took place in incidents involving Jews alone, those where Jews were in dispute with the Romans, and those involving other ethnic groups. Negotiations took place in Palestine and/or Rome.

Negotiation alone was the vehicle by which solutions were obtained in thirteen of the examples considered. In many of these incidents acts of violence were an integral part, as a direct cause of the dispute or as a threat used in the resolution of the dispute. For example, Roman interest in Paul was aroused by the attack on him. Similarly, the kidnapping of his son meant that Ananias was forced to negotiate with the procurator. The execution of James at the instigation of Ananus signalled the outbreak of protests against the high priest. Examples of violence being used as a threat include the trial of Herod. There seems little doubt that Sextus Caesar made it clear to Hyrcanus that he would be wise to ensure that Herod was not convicted. Similarly, in the protest against Pilate's introduction of military standards, the prefect commenced by indicating his willingness to use his troops if the Jews did not disperse immediately. Also, in the dispute regarding Gaius's order, Petronius indicated that he had at his disposal a large number of troops to suppress any proposed Jewish resistance.

Whatever the circumstances, the reliance on negotiation by Jews and, when they were involved, by Romans, is apparent. In disputes between Jews and Romans it was normally the former who instigated negotiation. The one exception to this practice is the incident con cerning the statue of Gaius, when Petronius actively sought the assistance of certain Jews to implement his instructions. Having failed to achieve his aim initially, it is notable that Petronius continued to seek a solution through negotiation. At no stage in the preceedings does it appear that the legate viewed the Jewish unwillingness to comply with the order as tantamount to rebellion.[1]

There are a numerous examples of the reliance on negotiation, whether the head of state was Jewish or Roman. The actions associated with the trial of Herod revolve around negotiations in which Hyrcanus was the central figure. The demands to have Herod brought to trial were all addressed to Hyrcanus, as were the subsequent requests for a retrial. Even Sextus Caesar chose to intervene through Hyrcanus.

There are four incidents from the first century AD when negotiation was employed in disputes involving only Jews. In the two hearings against Peter and John the men who decided the fate of the disciples viewed violence as an option but they also recognized that it was viable to arbitrate without turning to violence in the first instance. It is also apparent that the disciples acknowledged the power and authority of those who admonished them. In the debate over ceasing the sacrifices offered on behalf of foreigners and in Josephus's quelling of a revolt in Tiberias, circumstances probably dictated the use of negotiation to reach a solution. The Jews who wanted to end sacrifices for foreigners may have been a greater physical force than their opponents, leaving negotiation as one of the few viable options for the latter. Similarly, Josephus was not able to call on enough troops to employ violence as a means of ending the uprising in Tiberias. In both incidents, though, it is possible that negotiation may have been preferred. As the Romans gathered in strength Josephus probably desired a quick end to the rebellion. Furthermore, irrespective of any threats Josephus may have made, it is notable that the people of Tiberias did negotiate. Similarly, to maintain the offering of sacrifices it is possible that willing participation was preferred over forced acceptance of the practice.

The proceedings that resulted in the death of Jesus constitute one of the first of many incidents displaying a willingness by Jews and Romans to negotiate a settlement. We are not able to determine whether or not the formal involvement of the Roman prefect was actively sought because of a legal limitation imposed on the Jews. At no point in the incident did the Jews attempt to remove Jesus themselves. Moreover, irrespective of opinions regarding the legal rights of the Jews, Jesus' opponents were able to convince the prefect that the offence warranted his attention.

---

1. Note also that the opposition to the census was not viewed as a significant risk to security (*War* 2.118; *Ant.* 18.4-10).

Another example of negotiation being preferred took place when Pilate was prefect. Despite Pilate's initial contempt for the Jewish requests to remove military standards from Jerusalem, he was eventually willing to interact with the Jews. It is notable that this incident was resolved in a different manner to that regarding the aqueduct. Presumably Pilate was willing to use whatever means he considered most appropriate to resolve the issue at hand.

Reliance on negotiation is also evident in the Jewish refusal to comply with Fadus's order to place the high priests' vestments under his control. The Jews successfully requested that the procurator and legate allow them to plead their case before the emperor in Rome. Claudius's subsequent support of the Jewish case suggests a degree of flexibility in the manner in which stability in the province was maintained. Similarly, confidence in negotiations is apparent from the Temple wall incident. Rather than attempt to resolve the dispute among themselves, the group of Jews opposed to Agrippa II took their case directly to the Roman procurator. Although it was clear to them that Agrippa II would not concede to their view, it is notable that the Jews readily acknowledged that they could seek and expect Roman support. Furthermore, this view was vindicated by the procurator's decision to refer the case to Rome.

After the intervention of the tribune in the case against Paul the incident came under Roman jurisdiction. Initially the Jews opposed to Paul readily adapted to the circumstances and recognized that their wishes might be achieved through negotiation. Although a few Jews grew impatient with the lack of progress, negotiation was the only plausible approach in the legal circumstances of the case.

Negotiation was also employed by the opponents of Ananus after the execution of James. It is possible that these men did not have the power to take direct action against him. Even if this was the case, they recognized that other peaceful channels existed by which they could press their demands. Appeals were made to the new Roman procurator, Albinus, and to Agrippa II. This referral to a higher authority succeeded.

An important insight into the recognition of negotiation as an effective tool of diplomacy is the kidnapping of Ananias's son by the sicarii. The ability of certain Jews to negotiate with the procurator on an informal basis was astutely recognized by the sicarii. They surmised that Ananias would be able to meet their demands by winning favour with the procurator.

Three important observations are evident from the reliance on negotiation as a diplomatic tool. First, negotiation was employed in issues that were instigated by Roman and by Jewish actions. The majority of incidents were the result of a Roman initiative where the Jews sought a particular decision. Furthermore, the Jews acknowledged Roman involvement as arbitrators. Secondly, failure to achieve their aim did not necessarily result in the Jews resorting to violence. Thirdly, the reliance on negotiation indicates a belief that it was a mutually accepted process. Jews and Romans expected that issues would be discussed. It is implied, therefore, that what happened in Palestine was not dependent on Roman policy alone.

Five of the cases form a further group in which decisions were reached by a combination of violence and negotiation. In these cases it is apparent that the first alternative in an effort to reach a solution was negotiation. Furthermore, despite the fact that violence was employed, negotiation was not automatically cast aside. For example, during the reign of Salome Alexandra the Jews opposed to the advisors of her late husband reacted violently when the queen failed to comply with all their demands. The men facing persecution responded by negotiating protection from the queen and accepting a reduction in their prominence in Jerusalem.

In the Galilaean–Samaritan dispute, negotiation was interspersed by violence in an attempt to seek a solution. Throughout the incident the preference of all interested parties appears to have been to rely on negotiation. The Jews requested the Roman procurator to arbitrate. His failure to understand the intensity of Jewish feeling, however, resulted in some Jews seeking justice by attacking Samaritan settlements. The procurator then restored control by the use of violence. Samaritans and then Jews subsequently requested the legate to resolve the dispute. The remainder of the incident involved negotiations between all three groups in Palestine and then in Rome.

The racial fighting between Jews and Greeks in Caesarea was also dominated by negotiation. To ensure a favourable resolution the Jews requested the assistance of the procurator, offering Florus a bribe in return for his support. Despite the failure of Florus to fulfil his bargain, the Caesarean Jews did not reject the principle of negotiation.

Having decided to quit Caesarea, they repeated their attempt to obtain Florus's support.

The visit of Florus to Jerusalem in AD 66 and the events in the city during the war also display a mixture of violence and negotiation. Initially Florus demanded that certain Jews hand over the men responsible for insulting the procurator through their mock collection of money. The failure of the Jews to respond positively to this approach resulted in Florus ordering his troops to attack the Jewish crowd. This attack, however, did not signal the end of negotiations. Rather, a number of Jews continued to negotiate with the procurator. At the same time the Jewish community called upon a select number of their own to represent them as the dispute escalated to involve the Syrian legate. This process continued until the majority of Jews decided that direct action was the only plausible remaining option to deal with the Romans in Palestine.

It is notable that Jewish confidence in negotiation did not end with the defeat of the legate. Members of the Jewish community continued to employ a mixture of negotiation and violence in their internal relations. After the removal of Menahem the Jews present in Jerusalem engaged in a certain amount of politicking to appoint their generals. Later in the revolt negotiation was matched by physical violence in the conflict between prominent figure-heads within the rebel force, Ananus, Jesus, son of Gamalas, Simon, son of Gamaliel, Eleazar, son of Simon, John of Gischala and Simon, son of Gioras.

Considering the above comments it can be stated that it was routinely expected by the head of state, whether Roman or Jewish, that there would be some members of the Jewish community willing and/or able to participate in the process of negotiation. Similarly, many Jews expected that such a process was available for use when and where it was deemed necessary.

The varying use of negotiation and/or violence necessitates a consideration of what determined the use of different solutions. Where violence was the only diplomatic tool employed, it is possible to find explanations in the circumstances that were peculiar to that incident. In the revolt during Alexander Jannaeus's reign violence was the natural process by which both sides interacted. The right of the head of state to rule was challenged. The king did not wish to compromise his position by entering into discussion with those who directly undermined him. Similarly, those who opposed Alexander

Jannaeus committed themselves to asserting their cause by violent means. The use of violence reflected the king's desire to assert publicly his strength and superiority and the total commitment of his opponents. Only when Alexander Jannaeus found himself on the verge of defeat did he attempt to seek a negotiated settlement. Assuming there was no trial, the account of Stephen's death can be explained by the tacit approval to remove him given by prominent Jews. The opponents of Stephen believed that they were sanctioned to ignore a strictly legal course of action.[1]

An important incident resolved by violence alone is the protest regarding the aqueduct while Pilate was prefect. Despite the apparent desire of the Jews who protested in a peaceful manner, Pilate did not hesitate to use physical force. Two interrelated features of the incident indicate why Pilate responded as he did. First, the protest against Pilate's instructions was not immediate. In the other incidents where Jews responded negatively to a Roman order they did so without any delay. The second feature is the apparent absence of any prominent Jews amongst the protesters. Although Josephus does not identify the protesters, it does appear that at least some of the Jews who held a prominent position in Temple affairs conceded to Pilate's order. In the knowledge that the Jews who protested were not ardent enough in their cause to respond spontaneously against his instructions, and in the belief that they were not supported by prominent members of the community, Pilate decided that physical force was an appropriate means of dealing with the situation.

The incidents where decisions were reached entirely by negotiation are readily explained. Negotiation was the accepted practice. This attitude prevailed when there was either a Jewish head of state or direct Roman rule. Implicit in this was a belief among the Roman administrators that certain members of the Jewish community could speak on behalf of the entire population. The Jewish populace also acknowledged the possibility of negotiating a decision through the agency of a select few within their number. Furthermore, Roman willingness to adhere to a peaceful approach is evident on a number of occasions. Pilate threatened the Jews but eventually conceded to their petition regarding the effigies. Fadus accepted that the question of who

---

1. If Stephen's death was the result of mob action it is probable that it would have been viewed as a destabilizing action by prominent Jews, if not the Romans. Thus it would have warranted some response unless the 'mob' already had implicit approval.

should control the high priests' vestments could be resolved in Rome before the emperor. Even Petronius, with direct orders from Gaius, was receptive to seeking a peaceful resolution by negotiating with the Jews.

A number of related factors shaped the incidents where violence and negotiation were combined. Underlying several of the incidents was the notion that neither party would compromise their position without a struggle. Failure to achieve the desired outcome in the first instance necessitated the use of another channel to achieve the desired aim. For example, because the Jews refused to assist him by naming the men who mocked him, Florus decided to use physical force to assert his dominance. Similarly, believing that Cumanus was not receptive to demands for justice, some Jews took matters into their own hands to exact punishment upon the Samaritans.

Two further significant factors relate to the role played by those Jews seeking to act as intermediaries between the Jewish community and the Roman officials. First, from a Roman perspective the use of negotiation and violence may reflect how the Jewish negotiators were perceived. For example, Florus may have regarded the Jewish reluctance to comply with his demands as a sign that the Jewish representatives no longer intended to negotiate. Similarly, from a Jewish perspective, lack of confidence in their representatives influenced the resolution of certain incidents. In the dispute that followed the attack on Galilaean pilgrims, faith in the commitment of prominent Jews to uphold the Jewish cause was questioned. It was, therefore, important that the prominent Jews be able to maintain an effective influence within the Jewish community and that they be willing to participate in negotiations, irrespective of the outcome.

The other factor that encouraged the mixture of violence and negotiation was the personal attitude of Roman administrators. Jewish determination to argue a particular case aroused different reactions in the officials. Only Florus appears to have viewed Jewish unwillingness to concede ground as an impasse that required the response of violence. Fadus and Longinus, as well as Petronius, however, were willing to remain committed to negotiation when the Jews refused to comply with their demands. Although negotiation was the natural option for making decisions, certain factors continued to necessitate the added use of violence.

It should also be noted that negotiation took numerous forms. Jews and Romans used threats as a means of forwarding their cause. For the Jews the prime threat was that of passive protest irrespective of the consequences. From the Roman perspective it was the threat of using physical force. Bribery and the taking of hostages were also employed.

The involvement of prominent Jews in resolving disputes was important, for their participation meant that violence alone was not employed. It follows that we should identify who these prominent people and/or institutions were. The use of several different sources means that some of the terminology may vary. Differences may exist because the people and/or institution(s) described varied, or because authors referred to the same people and/or institution(s) with different terms. Furthermore, the Jewish participants in the events cannot always be identified by name. It is also possible that the people and/or institutions involved may have varied according to the nature of the issue.

There are seven distinct groups of Jews referred to in the cases studied. The first of these to consider is the priests, who are mentioned in all but two of the cases. No information is provided to identify the people who protested against Pilate's actions. We can speculate that prominent Jews connected with the Temple consented to Pilate's demands for money to help in the construction of the aqueduct. Whether any priests participated in the protest against the introduction of the effigies remains uncertain.[1]

The other study where priests are not mentioned relates to an incident that took place outside Jerusalem. The embassy of Caesarean Jews that addressed Florus only included men from that city. Furthermore, Josephus describes the men as 'the powerful men' (οἱ δυνατοί) a term that he uses for members of the laity.

In two studies we are not able to identify the priests involved with certainty. According to Philo's account of the protest over Gaius's order, priests participated in the negotiations with the legate Petronius. The role of priests when the Samaritans intruded into the Temple precinct is also uncertain. Because the text of Josephus is corrupt we are unable to state conclusively that it was priests who initiated measures to prevent such an action being repeated.

In all the other cases, members of the priesthood participated in the

---

1. Note that it was 'the first men' (οἱ πρῶτοι) who petitioned Vitellius (*Ant* 18.121).

decisions that were taken. Individual priests, especially the serving and/or a previous high priest are mentioned in many instances. The serving high priest is integral to the three first-century BC studies. In the revolt during Alexander Jannaeus's reign and in the trial of Herod, the office of high priest was held by the head of state. There is no reason to suggest that Alexander Jannaeus and Hyrcanus participated solely as head of state or high priest. Although some of the critics of Alexander Jannaeus may have demanded the separation of the high priesthood from the head of state, the rebellion was designed to replace Alexander Jannaeus, not just restrict the type of office he held. Furthermore, if the main concern was the separation of the two functions, some explanation is necessary for why Aristobulus and Hyrcanus did not bow to pressure to split the offices.

In the other first-century BC study, the office of high priest was separated from the head of state. Salome Alexandra bestowed the office upon her eldest son, Hyrcanus. Josephus's narrative of Hyrcanus's involvement in the incident deliberately casts doubt on his ability to wield much influence and maintain a prominent position. There is little doubt, however, that Hyrcanus opposed Aristobulus. As a representative of the administration commissioned by Salome, it is understandable that Hyrcanus should participate in whatever efforts were undertaken to quell the attempts of Aristobulus to usurp the throne.

The involvement of the serving high priest is well-attested throughout the years that a Roman prefect/procurator acted as head of state. In the trial of Jesus the high priest is presented as a leading spokesman within the Jewish discussion regarding the line of action to be taken. Similarly, he is mentioned in the two hearings against Peter and John, presiding over the second hearing. Although it is difficult to establish the details with accuracy, it is possible that the high priest was involved in the machinations that led to the death of Stephen. If there was some form of approval given, it may have been from the high priest who is narrated as being prominent throughout the incident. The high priest also features in the case against Paul. The Roman centurion apparently recognized him as the leading spokesman among Paul's opponents. The protest regarding the height of the Temple wall is a further incident where the high priest is prominent. Ishmael led the Jewish deputation that travelled to Rome. Although not initially involved in the Galilaean–Samaritan dispute, the high priest was designated by Quadratus as one of the key Jews to be held responsible. Finally, in the trial of James, the high priest instigated the entire incident. Ananus's responsibility for what happened was made apparent by Agrippa II's decision to depose him.

Men who at some time held the office of high priest are also named in the studies. It is possible that an ex-high priest was prominent in discussions regarding what was to be done about Jesus. In the Galilaean–Samaritan dispute two ex-high priests, with the serving high priest, appear to have been set aside by Quadratus as the leading Jewish representatives. It is also notable that the sicarii targeted an ex-high priest in their attempt to secure the release of associates. Ananias was acknowledged as a man who had sufficient funds and persuasive powers to win influence with the Roman procurator. The prominence of Ananias is further attested in Josephus's references to factional fighting in Jerusalem in the early AD 60s. Finally, the ex-high priests, Ananus and Jesus, were two of the most prominent persons in the city in the early part of the revolt.

A group of priests, described by the term 'the chief priests' (οἱ ἀρχιερεῖς), are also prominent in the first-century AD studies. The trial of Jesus is the first of many references to 'the chief priests'. These men helped determine what to do about Jesus and encouraged Pilate to take decisive action. In the two hearings against Peter and John, 'the chief priests' assisted in deciding how to proceed against the apostles.

The involvement of 'chief priests' is attested in the protest over the high priests' vestments. They are also involved in the case against Paul, deciding what to do and negotiating with various Roman officials. In a similar vein, during Florus's visit to Jerusalem, 'chief priests' negotiate with the procurator and with the Jewish community in the city. The subsequent decision to cease offering sacrifices on behalf of foreigners and the events in Jerusalem during the revolt also indicate the prominence of 'chief priests'. It is notable in these last three studies that 'the chief priests' were not always in agreement with the majority opinion of the Jews, nor with one another.

It is evident that the serving high priest was able to play a prominent part in the administration. During the first century BC, the involvement of the high priest was, in part, a reflection of the fact that he was often the head of state. In the first century AD the high priest continued to function as a representative of the Jews, whether in disputes between Jews or with Roman officials. With the office separated from the position of head of state under Roman rule, the high priest should be viewed as the chief spokesman among a group rather than a leader with several assistants. In some instances it is even possible that he was simply one of an association of men involved in a dispute.

Some men who previously held the office of high priest were also prominent. The Romans adopted the practice initiated by Herod, changing the incumbent when it was considered appropriate. The increased turnover of office-bearers resulted in several deposed men remaining alive and active. The prominence of the ex-high priest was, therefore, a new phenomenon of the first century AD. Furthermore, to have been deposed from the office did not necessarily mean that a person's participation in public affairs ceased. It is also possible to infer that priests other than the serving high priest could be prominent. This point is further indicated by the numerous references to 'chief priests'. Unfortunately the terminology used in the sources does not enable us to present a precise definition. The few names we have, however, leave little doubt that the term 'chief priests' referred to more people than just the serving or ex-high priests. On this basis the translation 'chief priests' is used to describe the group of prominent priests.[1]

Despite their established position within the community, 'chief priests' only appear in the first century AD. Three hints regarding the identity of the group 'chief priests' are contained in the cases studied. First, in the narrative of events in Jerusalem during the war Josephus indicates that there was a sense of hierarchy within the group. Of those 'chief priests' still in Jerusalem two ex-high priests, Ananus and Jesus, were the most prominent. We can only speculate upon the basis on which this hierarchy was determined. The second hint is contained in the account of Ananias's influence within the community. Certain priests increased their wealth at the expense of other priests. It is plausible to suggest that the wealthy priests were also 'the chief priests'. The final hint is derived from the names of the men included

---

1. The existence of a group of prominent priests is attested elsewhere in Josephus's narrative (*Apion* 1.29) and in the New Testament (Mt. 2.4; Jn 12.10). Similarly, see S.N. Mason, 'Priesthood in Josephus and the Pharisaic Revolution', *JBL* 107 (1988), pp. 658-59, who notes that the priests remained the guardians of the law in the first century AD. See *War* 2.417.

in the group. Most of the 'chief priests' named are connected with the high priesthood. They either held the office themselves, as in the case of Ananus and Ananias, or are described as being related to someone who held the office, namely, the sons of Ishmael.

There is no reason to believe that 'the chief priests' were always men who held official posts, or that they were a formal group. Instead, 'the chief priests' acquired their prominence and public status. They were dynamic members of the priesthood who held interests outside the realm of religious instruction and ritual. More importantly, 'the chief priests' were primarily individuals linked with the high priesthood. Some of the people associated with the office were prominent in their own right. These three groups of priests, however, also combined to form one powerful group of prominent Jews.

Several specific comments regarding these priests are pertinent. First, these men participated in matters that involved interaction between the Romans and the Jews and in issues that only concerned sections of the Jewish community. Secondly, the individual serving as high priest was not necessarily dependent on group support to participate in any negotiations regarding what decisions were to be made. Although the high priest may have been accompanied by 'the chief priests', as in the trial of Jesus, his participation was acknowledged in its own right. Thirdly, not all those who served as high priest were automatically prominent in affairs of government. It was not the office itself, therefore, that enabled a person to hold a prominent place within the Jewish community. Nor was it the only channel open to members of the priesthood if they wished to participate in public affairs. Furthermore, holding the office did not require the high priest to become a prominent spokesman for the Jews. Finally, 'the chief priests' were normally united in the line of action they proposed. There is evidence, however, that apart from rivalry to obtain prominence within the group, some division in matters of policy did exist.

The prominence of these priests is related to two factors. First, the increased turnover in the number of high priests encouraged competition for the office. More priestly families than were necessary sought to increase their status within the community.[1] Associated with the

---

1. See Smallwood, 'High Priests', pp. 14-34, and M. Stern 'Aspects of Jewish Society: The Priesthood and Other Classes', in Safrai and Stern (eds.), *The Jewish People*, II, pp. 605-607, for further discussion of the families involved.

increased turnover was the introduction of direct Roman rule. Men who had previously assisted and advised the Jewish heads of state may have believed that it was possible to have more direct participation in affairs of government. Others, presumably outside the old sphere of advisors, may have seen the change in circumstances as an opportunity to press their own interests to hold prominence. Secondly, the priests believed that it was appropriate and legitimate for them to become involved in a variety of issues. Their interests were not restricted in strict terms to matters relating only to Temple worship. At the same time the Jewish community willingly recognized 'the chief priests', incorporating the serving high priest and ex-high priests, as being capable of representing them in the decision-making process.

No other Jews participating in the decision-making process are directly associated with the priesthood. The influential lay Jews are referred to by a variety of terms in the studies. During the reign of Alexandra Salome 'the elders' (οἱ πρεσβύτεροι) seek the queen's assistance in dealing with Aristobulus. These 'elders' were some of the men who had obtained prominence under the auspices of the queen. The narrative of Herod's trial indicates that Josephus used 'the first men' (οἱ πρῶτοι) and 'the leading men' (οἱ ἐν τέλει) as synonymous terms. These men requested Hyrcanus to take action against Herod. During the trial of Jesus the terms 'elders' and 'the rulers' (οἱ ἄρχοντες) describe the men who helped determine what action the Jews would take. Jewish 'elders' were also involved in the first hearing against Peter and John. The terms the 'powerful men', 'leading men', 'first men', 'the notable men' (οἱ γνώριμοι) and 'elders' are used to describe the same group of Jews involved in the protest against Gaius's order. In the petition to retain control of the high priests' vestments reference is made to 'the first men'. In the Galilaean–Samaritan dispute 'the notable' Galilaeans and 'the powerful' Jews and Samaritans are mentioned. Furthermore, a distinction is drawn between 'the most powerful men' (οἱ δυνατώτατοι) and the remainder of the influential men of each community. In the petition regarding the height of the Temple wall, ten of 'the first men' travelled to Rome to assist in presenting the Jewish case. In the trial of Paul, the terms 'elders' and 'the first men' describe non-priests. During the dispute in Caesarea the Jews were represented by 'the powerful men' of their number. Similarly, in the dispute in Jerusalem regarding the offering of sacrifices for foreigners, some of the Jews who argue for their retention are 'the notable'/'powerful' Jews. During Florus's visit to Jerusalem 'the powerful'/'notable' Jews participate. The influential laity are also mentioned in connection with the revolt. Early in the war 'the powerful' Jews are referred to as leaving the city. Later, however, some of 'the powerful men' are still present in Jerusalem.

We have, therefore, a large number of terms used in the sources to describe the influential laity. The 'first men', 'leading men', 'powerful men', 'elders', 'rulers', 'notable men', 'most powerful men' and 'the eminent/distinguished' (οἱ ἐπίσημοι)/'the respected men' (οἱ προύχοντες) refer to the same group of people. The variety of terms used probably relates to the specific author's preference and changes in style. Thus, for Josephus, 'the powerful men' and 'the notable men' feature mainly in the earlier text, *The Jewish War*, while 'the first men' appears in *Antiquities of the Jews* and the *Life of Josephus*. Furthermore, the terms describe a sub-section of people within several ethnic groups.[1] They do not refer to a specific official group of

---

1. Examples of other usages: (1) 'the notable men', *War* 2.270, Jews and Greeks of Caesarea; 2.612 and 'rulers' opposing Josephus captured. (2) 'The most eminent/distinguished men', *Ant* 15.278, Herod talks to them regarding images; 20.114, arrested by Cumanus; 20.178, with the fairminded men go to Cumanus. (3) 'Rulers/magistrates', *War* 2.612, and 'the notable men' opposing Josephus captured; 2.652, of Idumaea raise troops; 4.516, of Idumaea; *Ant*. 15.256, Herod appoints Costobarus, in Idumaea; Lk. 14.1 of the Pharisees; Jn 3.1, Nicodemus; 7.26; 12.42, of Jews. (4) 'Elders', Acts 11.30; 15.2, 4, 6, 22, 23; 16.4, of Christians; Acts 20.17, of Antioch church; Lk. 7.3, of Jews. (5) 'The leading men', *War* 1.243, 100 of them protest to Romans regarding Herod and Phasael (= *Ant*. 14.302, 'the powerful men'); 1.331, of Jericho, Herod dines with them; 1.360, of Syria; 2.81, a *synedrion* of them, Romans (= *Ant*. 17.301, 'the first men'); 4.150, in Jerusalem, at dispute with one another; *Ant*. 14.302, protest to Romans regarding Phasael and Herod (= *War* 1.242, 'the powerful men'); 17.37, of Tiberias; 17.160, of Jews summoned by Herod to Jericho. (6) 'The powerful men', *War* 1.242, protest to Romans regarding Herod and Phasael (= *Ant*. 14.302, 'the leading men'); 1.491, talk with Alexander (499); 1.512, with Herod escort Archelaus; 1.574, Soaemus one of them of Petra; 2.274, of rebel party dealing with Albinus; 2.570, of Galilee; 4.18, regarding Chares and Joseph of Gamala; 4.413, of Gadara send embassy to Romans; *Ant*. 14.11, Antipater gets them to support Hyrcanus; 14.302, 100 of them protest to Romans regarding Herod and Phasael (= *War* 1.243, 'the leading men'); 14.450, Galileans rebel against them. (7) 'The first men', *War* 4.416, Dolesus, of the people at Gadara; *Ant*. 14.9, Antipater's family of the Jews in Babylon; 15.6, Herod kills forty-five of them of Antigonus' party; 15.253, Costobarus one of them of Idumaea; 17.301, *synedrion* of them, Roman (= *War* 2.81, 'the leading men'); 17.342, of

people within the Jewish community. In other communities these men were the 'influential'. In Jewish society, however, they were 'influential lay men'. Most of the influential laity appear to have been wealthy. Furthermore, some of them may have been officials. In one sense they were a constant element. Prominent lay people were actively involved in public affairs throughout the first centuries BC and AD. It is also probable that the influential laity remained a consistent, stable element in Jewish society. It is apparent, however, that these men did not always agree with one another. Furthermore, the presence of a sense of hierarchy suggests internal competition for prominence among their number.

The third group of Jews who participated in public affairs held a formal position. This included specific named officials and 'magistrates'. In the debate regarding the Temple wall, the Temple treasurer, Helcias, is among the Jewish representatives. Later the position was held by Antipas. The other official mentioned on several occasions is the captain of the Temple. In the dispute regarding offering sacrifices for foreigners, Eleazar, the son of Ananias, was prominent while holding the position. The captain was probably also involved in the arrest of Jesus and of the apostles Peter and John. On these occasions the captain was in charge of a *quasi* formal police force for the Jewish community in Jerusalem. The other individual official linked with Jerusalem is the secretary of the *boule*, who was executed by the rebels. While it is plausible to surmise that people held these positions throughout the first century AD, if not before, only a few of the individuals holding these offices were considered relevant to the narrative of events. It appears that their importance did not necessarily depend on the official position they held.

Jews and Samaritans who protest to Romans regarding Archelaus; 18.121, of Jews who protest to Vitellius regarding effigies; 20.2, of Peraeans, they did not approve of fighting with Philadelphians; 20.4, Fadus arrests four of them; 20.53, money sent to them of Jerusalem by Izates; 20.180, fighting between those of the people, 'chief priests' and priests; 20.182, of the Jews in Caesarea; 20.183, of the Syrians in Caesarea; *Life* 21, regarding Menahem's associates; 56, Varus orders seventy of them from Ecbatana to answer a charge; 67, of the *boule* of Tiberias sent for by Josephus; 131, two of them from Tiberias, Jannaeus and Dassion; 220, Josephus dines with them of Galilee; 296, ten of them with Capella from Tiberias; 305, of Galilee summoned by Josephus to Tarichaeae; 313, of Gadara who oppose Josephus; 410, of Syria, they send Justus to Vespasian; Acts 28.17, of Jews in Rome.

Outside Jerusalem, the chief magistrate of Tiberias, Justus, is referred to in relations between the city and Josephus (*War* 2.599; *Life*
278, 294). It was an office acquired by appointment rather than
hereditary claims, which allowed him to issue orders and instruct
certain men to gather in a meeting (*boule*). Whether this office also
existed in Jerusalem is debatable. If there was a chief magistrate in the
city, he was never considered prominent enough to warrant a mention
in one of the incidents. Furthermore, although it is possible that the
position existed in cities other than Tiberias, the one other incident
involving Jews in a city outside Jerusalem, the trouble in Caesarea,
specifically mentions a tax collector, who was not noted for holding
any formal position.

The other officials mentioned because they fulfilled certain administrative functions are 'the magistrates'. During Florus's visit to
Jerusalem and the events in the city during the war Jewish
'magistrates' carry out specific tasks.[1] The nature of the 'magistrates'
involvement in these two studies is important in explaining their
absence from the majority of the incidents. These men were not
involved in reaching any of the decisions. Although they may have
been in league with the influential laity and prominent members of the
priesthood they only fulfilled administrative tasks. Their absence from
most incidents, therefore, is probably due to the function they
performed. 'Magistrates' were a formal group within the community
who fulfilled a necessary, if somewhat mechanical role within the
system of government. Their existence implies that the Jews
participated in the functioning of government in Palestine during
direct Roman rule.

'Scribes' (οἱ γραμματεῖς) are referred to in two incidents recorded
in the New Testament. In the trial of Jesus and the first hearing against
Peter and John 'the scribes' form a separate group within the Jewish
community. They appear to have been distinguished by their learning
and their role as teachers, presumably in aspects of Jewish religion.
The 'scribes' are not central to the outcome of either incident. Rather,
the references to them may reflect a desire to show that Jesus and
Peter and John were opposed by all aspects of Jewish society, the

---

1. See also *War* 6.303-305, where 'the magistrates' liaise with the procurator.
The seventy men appointed by Josephus do not appear to have taken any significant
part in the events that he narrates. I cannot establish whether they were to supplement
or replace the existing authorities in Galilee.

priesthood, lay teachers, and influential laity.[1]

Pharisees and Sadducees are referred to in several incidents. During the reign of Salome Alexandra the Pharisees obtained a position of prominence, becoming the queen's main advisors at the expense of the associates of her late husband. This prominence was challenged when Aristobulus led an uprising late in the region. We are also informed that some Pharisees were among the men who rebelled against Alexander Jannaeus. The next case in which Pharisees actively participated is the second hearing against Peter and John.[2] A Pharisee named Gamaliel addressed the men present and convinced them that the apostles should not be severely punished. It is implied that Gamaliel's participation was at the invitation of the serving high priest.

Pharisees and Sadducees are also involved in the initial proceedings against Paul. The Pharisees and Sadducees were requested to assist the tribune by defining the exact nature of Paul's offence. Josephus criticizes Ananus for his allegiance to the Sadducees in the account of the trial of James. The acknowledgement of Ananus as a Sadducee, however, is not important in determining the outcome of the incident. Furthermore, it is probable that Ananus's opponents were not opposed to him because he was a Sadducee, but were keen to undermine his personal dominance. Finally, Pharisees and Sadducees participate in the events in Jerusalem during the war. In AD 66 'the notable' Pharisees opposed the cessation of sacrifices for foreigners. Later in his narrative Josephus refers to Simon, a Pharisee, taking a leading role in association with Ananus, a Sadducee. In other words, a Pharisee and a Sadducee worked in common cause against the Romans.[3]

---

1. Another possibility is that increased prominence in a later generation was imposed upon the narrative of the text. If so, however, it is slightly strange that they are only referred to in two of the incidents. Saldarini (*Pharisees*, pp. 241-76) also concludes that 'the scribes' were not an 'autonomous group' with independent power and influence.

2. Pharisees are also mentioned as opposing Jesus during his ministry. See Mt. 21.15, 45-46; 22.15; Mk 3.6; 12.13; Jn 7.32; 8.3; 11.47-57; cf. Lk. 13.41. During the reign of Herod there is evidence that Pharisees were involved in an attempt to subvert the regime. See *Ant.* 17.44-45.

3. The involvement of Pharisees in the war is further indicated by the reference to the envoys sent from Jerusalem to remove Josephus (*Life* 197). There is no reason to argue that a Pharisaic 'party' was attempting to obtain power in Jerusalem, as suggested by Cohen (*Josephus in Galilee*, p. 231). These men are referred to as

It is important to note editorial interests in these incidents. Luke used Gamaliel's speech to highlight that God's justice would legitimize Christianity. In Paul's case the squabbling of the Pharisees and Sadducees highlighted the notion that the Jews had no united case against him. Describing Ananus as a Sadducee in the trial of James, Josephus speaks of the high priest's cruelty and lack of popularity. The reference to the notable Pharisees opposing the end of sacrifices for foreigners indicates that some Pharisees, with whom Josephus was associated, wanted to prevent matters from deteriorating into open revolt.

A notable feature of these references is that allegiance to a religious group did not entitle men to a prominent role in the decisions that were made. Nor was 'membership' an important requirement in attaining influence and prominence. It is possible, therefore, to state that the summary statements of Josephus regarding the status of the Pharisees and Sadducees do not necessarily reflect the historical situation. The notion that Pharisees held the confidence of the populace and that Sadducees were forced to concede to the former's views simply on the basis that they adhered to the doctrines of a particular religious group is not relevant to the historical account of which Jews participated in decision-making (*War* 2.166; *Ant.* 13.298; 18.15-17).[1]

Members of the Herodian family constitute the final section of the Jewish community to note. Herodian involvement in Palestinian affairs was maintained at times other than when a family member was the head of state in the first century AD. As the custodian of the Temple, Herod of Chalcis and then Agrippa II were able to maintain the practice of changing the high priest when it was deemed necessary. Other requests relevant to the Temple were directed to the Herodian custodian. The Temple wall dispute, however, indicates that the Jews

being in league with Ananus. See also Saldarini, *Pharisees*, pp. 101-106, 281, and Schwartz, 'Josephus and Nicolaus', pp. 167, 170.

1. As indicated by Goodman, *Ruling Class*, pp. 209-10. In his major study incorporating sociological concepts Saldarini (*Pharisees*, pp. 132, 277-88, 298-301) concludes that the Pharisees and Sadducees did function as social and political groups that competed for prominence with many other groups. Although he clarifies a number of misconceptions, in attempting to elaborate upon the roles played by the Pharisees, scribes and Sadducees, Saldarini consistently notes the lack of detailed information available for such a study without questioning the possible implications of such a scarcity of material.

did not believe that the custodian was the only authority to whom they could refer matters related to the Temple.

Herodian involvement was not dependent on holding an official position within Roman-controlled territory. In several cases members of the Herodian family represented the Jewish cause in discussion with Romans. Some Herodians probably supported the request that Pilate remove the effigies from Jerusalem.[1] Later, in the protest over Gaius's order, relatives of Herod Agrippa spoke with Petronius. Furthermore, these discussions were held in Tiberias, territory controlled by Agrippa I. In Rome Agrippa I attempted to persuade the emperor to cancel the order. Agrippa II intervened in the Galilaean–Samaritan dispute when the representatives were sent to Rome. Claudius specifically associated the success of the Jewish appeal with Agrippa II's involvement. As custodian of the Temple, Agrippa II was drawn into the trial of James. Whether motivated by a sense of injustice or a desire to attack Ananus's public prominence, his opponents requested Agrippa II to punish the high priest.[2]

Herodians were also involved in the visit of Florus to Jerusalem. Initially, Bernice tried to mediate with Florus. On his return from Alexandria, Agrippa II was requested to assist in the negotiations and to present a Jewish complaint against the procurator in Rome. Agrippa II's split with the Jews of Jerusalem came when he proposed a course of action that the majority found unacceptable. Implicit in the rejection of Agrippa II is the notion that he had previously expressed views that received popular approval. Acceptance of the Herodian family in the Jewish community, therefore, was based on more than their assimilation into Roman society. During the war several Herodians remained in Jerusalem. Josephus indicates that Antipas held the office of Temple treasurer, indicating at least an involvement in the functioning of government. It is apparent, therefore, that Herodians were accepted as active participants by the Jewish community.

A number of references in the studies are made to institutions which

1. Herodians are referred to as opposing Jesus. See Mt. 22.16; Mk 3.6; 12.13.

2. It is possible that Saul and Costobar were among Ananus's opponents. Note B-Z. Rosenfeld, 'The "Boundary of Gezer" Inscriptions and the History of Gezer at the End of the Second Temple Period', *IEJ* 38 (1988), pp. 235-45, who suggests that we can identify a family that was closely associated with the Herodians that remained prominent throughout the first century AD.

have generated scholarly discussion without much consensus being achieved. A great deal of clarification and qualification is possible, despite the lack of complete documentation. Two issues require examination: identifying the institution(s) that existed; and establishing the nature of its/their involvement in the functioning of government, especially in relation to the people outlined above.

Although there is evidence of a formal Jewish institution prior to the period of direct Roman rule reference to such a body in this study occurs only in cases from the first century AD.[1] This institution is referred to by the terms *boule* and *gerousia*. Variations in terminology probably reflect an alteration in the institution's functioning, or the authors' reliance on terms with which they were familiar. In the trial of Jesus, Joseph of Arimathaea is described as a member of the *boule*. Later, in the protest over Gaius's order, Philo refers to the *gerousia*. The Jerusalem *boule* is also mentioned in connection with the protest regarding the high priests' vestments, although there remains a possibility that the format of Claudius's letter did not specifically relate to the situation in Jerusalem. The references to the *boule* in the visit of Florus to Jerusalem and the events in the city during the war, however, confirm the existence of the formal institution. The members of the *boule* greeted Agrippa II and were called into the presence of Florus immediately prior to his departure from the city. Josephus also names the secretary of the *boule* and refers to the *boule* chamber in the context of other events that took place during the revolt.

The reference to the *boule* of Tiberias is important. The existence of a *boule* in Tiberias neither proves nor disproves that Jerusalem had a *boule*. What is notable is that there was a hierarchy within the Tiberias *boule* and that prominence was not necessarily linked with membership of the institution. It is possible that similar circumstances existed in Jerusalem. The *boule* in Tiberias, with 600 members, however, was the council of a polis. In Jerusalem we can make no such equation.[2] Rather, it is possible that the use of *boule* in connection

---

1. Josephus is consistent with 1 Macc. 12.6 in describing the Hasmonaean institution as the *gerousia*. See *Ant.* 13.166, 169. He also agrees with Philo in referring to the Alexandrian Jewish institution as the *gerousia*. See *War* 7.412 and *Flacc.* 74. Note also *Ant.* 5.135, referring to the period prior to the judges.

2. Although arguing from a different perspective I am in agreement with Tcherikover ('Was Jerusalem a Polis?', p. 72) that the reference to the *boule* is not a

with the Samaritans is of more relevance to the situation in Jerusalem. This council is not the *boule* of a city, but of the Samaritan people (*Ant.* 18.8). Similarly, the Jerusalem *boule* may have acquired such status.[1]

The *boule* dealt directly with matters pertinent to Jerusalem and with issues connected with the capital city, such as Gaius's order and the control of the high priests' vestments, which were relevant to the entire Jewish populace. It is in these circumstances that the Jerusalem *boule* may have assumed the status of a national institution.

It is difficult to determine when this *boule* was instituted. Josephus's silence about its origin is puzzling. Although it is possible that AD 6 marked its inauguration, the *boule* may have already been in existence when Coponius arrived. Changes to the size and function of the institution may have occurred, but the Jerusalem *boule* of the first century AD was most likely the successor, possibly by several generations, of the older *gerousia*.

After the outbreak of revolt, we hear of a new institution, the 'common council' (κοινόν). The *boule*, therefore, was replaced at some point in time early in the revolt by the 'common council'. The deliberate change in terminology may indicate that the new institution was different in character and function.[2] What form this change took is difficult to ascertain. It is plausible to argue that the people who decided to fight the Romans believed that the *boule* did not represent a broad enough range of the populace. If so, it can be inferred that the *boule* was not entirely satisfactory. The principle of having a formal institution may have remained constant, while the practical application of the principle altered.

We have few details regarding the members of the *boule* and of the 'common council'. In the narrative of Florus's visit to Jerusalem a distinction is drawn between the influential laity, 'chief priests' and the *boule*. Although some members of these groups may have served on the *boule*, it is not necessary to assume that all members of the *boule*

sign that Jerusalem was a polis.

1. Note that the term is also used for the Senate in Rome (*Ant.* 18.1) and in reference to local institutions (*War* 2.273). Other references to the Tiberias *boule* are located in *Life* 67, 69, 313, 381.

2. There is no reason to support Cohen (*Josephus in Galilee*, p. 182 n. 2) that Josephus was inconsistent in his use of terminology regarding institutions in this instance.

were also influential Jews. This notion is supported by the situation in Tiberias. There is no reason automatically to equate membership of the *boule* with influential status in Tiberias. Several prominent individuals, including Simon and Ananus, are associated with the 'common council'. It should be noted, however, that the 'common council' did not always concur with the plans of these men. I am unable to make any comment regarding terms of office or positions within the *boule* or 'common council', with the exception of a secretary in the former.[1]

We have sufficient information to state that there was a formal institution in Jerusalem during the first century AD known as the *boule*. It is possible that this *boule* was the successor of an institution that pre-dates the first century AD. The Jerusalem *boule* acquired the character of a national institution on the basis that numerous issues which pertained to the city were relevant to the interests of all Jews. With the outbreak of the revolt, the *boule* in Jerusalem was replaced by a new institution, the 'common council', which was probably intended to be more representative of the populace.

Two further institutions described by the same term, *synedrion*, are referred to in the cases. They function for specific tasks, to try people and to offer advice on what action to take.[2] Although not permanent institutions, they were the embodiment of a principle and, as such, were formal instruments of government sanctioned by the leading figure, whether Jewish or Roman. Furthermore, they should not be confused with, or assumed to be associated with, the *boule*. I will examine each body in turn, commencing with the *synedrion* which functioned to offer advice.

During the protest over Gaius's order, Philo states that Petronius called a *synedrion* of his associates to discuss the pending crisis regarding the agricultural strike and the Jewish refusal to comply with Gaius's instructions. Although the *synedrion* did discuss and express

---

1. I am unable to comment with any certainty on the possible location of the *boule* chamber and to establish any significance in the mishnaic reference to the Chamber of Hewn Stone.

2. Note that the *synedrion* was not the only form of court. See *War* 1.530; *Ant.* 16.393, where Herod uses an 'assembly' (ἐκκλησία) of people to try Trio and Trypho; and *War* 1.654, where the golden eagle incident is resolved. The term 'assembly' referred to a gathering of the populace, not to a specific institution. See *Ant.* 19.332. Note also the use of *synedrion* to describe the gathering where Herod informed Jews of his intentions regarding his grandchildren (*War* 1.559). In the parallel passage, *Ant.* 17.15, there is no such reference.

support for Petronius's proposed plan of action, it only served as a means by which Petronius obtained advice. The term *synedrion* is also used by Philo to describe the thought process of Petronius.

There are other examples of this consultative *synedrion* in Josephus's narrative. In each case the leader, a Roman, calls upon associates to assist in determining what course of action to pursue. Augustus held a *synedrion* to consider who should succeed Herod. The final decision was made by Augustus (*War* 2.25, 38, 81, 93-100 *Ant.*; 17.301, 317-20).[1] During the siege of Jerusalem, Titus held a *synedrion* of his generals to discuss whether to attack the Jews. It was Titus who made the decision (*War* 6.243).[2]

The more common body referred to as *synedrion* was a place of arbitration, that is, a court. Most of the examples are trials of individuals on a capital charge. For example, in the version of Herod's trial in *Antiquities of the Jews*, Josephus states several times that the trial was to be heard before the *synedrion*. It is probable that despite Josephus's introduction of the involvement of the *synedrion* in his narrative, the trial was resolved by Hyrcanus alone. Irrespective of this imposition, it is evident that Josephus knew of courts, called *synedria*, which the ruler could formally convene. In the trial of Jesus the Jewish *synedrion* participated in the decision to seek Pilate's involvement. In this instance the *synedrion* is not recorded as voting to come to a decision. Rather, it is presented as agreeing with the views of the serving high priest. The *synedrion* is also involved in the two hearings against Peter and John. Although not necessarily capital cases, I cannot establish if the *synedria* were legally restricted in what action they could take. The leading figure in both hearings is the serving high priest.

Doubt remains regarding the reference to the *synedrion* in the account of Stephen's death. Although it is plausible that there was no formal hearing against Stephen, it is apparent that Luke believed a system existed in which the leading figure could convene a body to try an accused person. The *synedrion* also features in the case against Paul. According to the Jews the *synedrion* was the appropriate Jewish body to decide the case against him. Furthermore, the Roman tribune in Jerusalem is described as being aware of the institution's existence

---

1. See also *Ant.* 15.358.

2. Note that the *synedrion*/'first men' who acted as an executive during the early part of the war are noted for their role as a source of advice (*War* 3.138; *Life* 62).

and its function as a court. The final case where the *synedrion* functions as a court is the trial of James. Josephus specifically states that this was a court of judges convened by the leading figure to decide the fate of James and certain other men.

The use of *synedrion* to describe a formal court, and thus an instrument of government that could be convened by a leading figure, is attested elsewhere in the sources. During the reign of Herod several important cases were decided by *synedria*. In each instance the men convened were chosen by Herod. The reference to the *synedrion* in the trial of Hyrcanus shows that this body was perceived to be a legitimate means of deciding a case. It should be noted, however, that the *synedrion* was not the only means available for trying capital cases. Furthermore, Herod probably only used the *synedrion* in a few major trials (*War* 1.537-39, 620; *Ant.* 15.173; 16.356; 17.46, 93, 106, 132).

The court could deal with issues other than capital cases. In Mt. 5.22 the *synedrion* is described as the forum for a case of false witness. The most notable example, however, is when Agrippa II and the *synedrion* decided the request of the Levites (*Ant.* 20.216-18). It is implied that responsibility for allowing the desired changes lay with Agrippa II rather than being the result of an independent solution arrived at by members of the *synedrion*. Furthermore, this indicates that more than one person could convene the court *synedrion*. In other words, there was not one permanent head of the court. Rather, the identity of the leading figure(s) depended on the particular circumstances (Jn 11.47-53).[1]

It is notable that the definite article is used in connection with the court in seven of the cases (*Ant.* 14.167; Mk 14.55; Mt. 26.59; Acts 4.15; 5.21; 6.12; 22.30). Although these references appear to be to a specific permanent institution, either its members or the place, the

---

1. Philo (*Leg. Gai.* 349–50) provides a description of how a court should act in his account of Gaius's response to the Jewish delegation from Alexandria. The leader, in this case the emperor, should have called together associates who would hear the petition and then provide the emperor with advice as to the judgment. It is notable that Philo describes these associates with the term *synedrion* (*Leg. Gai.* 349, 350). Note also the possibility that the *synedrion* described above might equate with the concept of *consilium* in Rome. See J.A. Crook, *Consilium Principis* (Cambridge: Cambridge University Press, 1955), pp. 21-52, 105, and Millar, *Emperor*, pp. 110-22. Crook's point (p. 33) regarding the difficulty of establishing a rigid division between the judicial and administrative functions of the *consilium* may also apply to the situation in Palestine.

synedria described are the embodiment of a principle. They represent a recognized process by which trials could be formally judged. Thus, Josephus refers to Herod's claim that Hyrcanus was condemned by an acceptable legal means, the *synedrion*. Similarly, in Herod's trial the context for Samaias's speech was a recognizable institution.

The frequent use of the definite article in the New Testament can be attributed to two factors, each author's perception of what happened and deliberate editing by them. The prominence of certain social groups among the people with whom Christians came into conflict influenced the New Testament account of events. Inadvertently, their prominence was perceived to be a sign of permanency. The attitude of the evangelists also appears to have influenced the presentation of the court. The overall impression is that the Christians were opposed by all aspects of judicial Jewish authority. There existed, therefore, a tendency to emphasize the official nature of the opposition to Christianity within the framework of a total rejection of the new teaching. In these contexts the use of the definite article intensified the significance of the court within the Jewish administration.[1]

The identity of the people associated with the two bodies is important. There was no concept of permanent membership. Rather, the participants were determined by the appropriate leading figure. The consultative *synedrion* consisted of whoever the leader decided was relevant. Petronius called upon members of his staff with him in Tiberias, while Titus gathered together his officers. Members of each court *synedrion* were also determined by the leading figure. Thus Herod decided which of his associates would assist him. The reference to a '*synedrion* of judges' (συνέδριον κριτῶν) in the trial of James may suggest that there was a section of the community from whom it was expected that the members of the court *synedrion* would be gathered. Some qualification of this suggestion is necessary. It is apparent that the men who served on the *synedrion* assisted the person who appointed them. Thus Ananus called together people who would concur with his wishes.

---

1. For discussion of the use of *synedrion* in earlier Greek literature, compare Zeitlin, 'Political Synedrion', pp. 109-11, and 'Synedrion in the Judeo-Hellenistic Literature', pp. 307-15, with Wolfson, 'Synedrion', pp. 303-305. In the context of the above outline it is apparent that both scholars are partly correct. *Synedrion* was used in the sense of a court and of a conference without referring to a specific permanent institution.

References to participants in the New Testament support two previously noted observations. First, in each instance, reference to the court was an isolated embodiment of a principle. Secondly, the members of each *synedrion* were decided upon by the leading figure, not drawn from a pre-determined group. There is confusion in the narrative of the trials of Jesus and Paul regarding the people involved in the court. Distinctions are drawn between the court, the chief priests and influential laity, suggesting that the former had a separate identity. It is apparent that the members were determined by the leading figure, who also decided what role the *synedrion* would play. Furthermore, the court's status was directly linked to the person that commissioned it.[1]

A few brief comments are necessary regarding the involvement in the administration of the two bodies referred to by the term *synedrion*. Both were *ad hoc* bodies that were commissioned for specific tasks. Their importance was derived from the leading figure, who was responsible for their existence. Of the two, it was the court *synedrion* that obtained a higher profile. Its decisions in trials were sanctioned and formalized because it was a legitimate forum of government with the blessing of the leading figure to act in the particular circumstances being considered.

The involvement of the *boule* of Jerusalem in the administration took two forms. First, the *boule* was an official element in the administration of Palestine, possibly viewed as the institutional head of the Jews. Thus, it became involved at certain official stages of the negotiations with Florus, greeting the king when he returned from Egypt and appearing before Florus when he decided to quit the city. This status, however, did not enable the *boule* to influence what decisions were taken. In fact, it is notable that the *boule* is not mentioned in any of the cases in connection with the decision-making process. This absence may help explain its demise and replacement by the 'common council' during the revolt. Secondly, the *boule* dealt with practical administrative tasks, possibly in association with 'the magistrates'. Thus, the members of the *boule* took responsibility for collecting the tax arrears from the district surrounding the city. It is

---

1. The significance of the terminology used to refer to Gabinius's division of Palestine is difficult to establish. It does not appear that Josephus was referring to institutions. See *War* 1.170; *Ant.* 14.91. Note that *synedrion* in Mt. 10.17; Mk 13.9 also refers to a trial court.

now apparent that the institution depicted in *m. Sanh.* did not exist during the period examined. It remains debatable whether we should even attempt to associate this institution with any historical period.[1]

It is possible to outline the Jews involved in the decision-making process. In the first century BC the influential laity and other non-priests were intermittently prominent, primarily in the restricted sense of being advisors. This restriction was in part due to the official head of state's dominating affairs. Although subject to a variety of external influences, especially foreign military pressure, the head of state involved members of the Jewish community in whatever capacity he/she wished in internal affairs. Salome Alexandra gave prominence in public affairs to certain Pharisees rather than to the men who had advised her late husband. This prominence, however, was not permanent and it was subject to the overall control of Salome. Similarly, Hyrcanus acceded to the demands of some of the influential laity that Herod answer for his actions in Galilee. It was Hyrcanus, however, who decided what would happen to Herod.

The years that followed the death of Herod appear to have been a period of change. Men previously restricted to the role of advisor began to seek a higher profile in public affairs. The extension of the practice of changing the high priest whenever it was considered appropriate under Roman rule was regarded in a positive light by some Jews. It was believed that these changes increased the opportunity for Jews to directly influence the decisions taken regarding their country by participation in negotiation. It is important to note, however, that the Jews who participated did so more in the form of protest against Roman plans rather than by the innovation of policies. Two elements within the Jewish community, 'the chief priests' and the influential laity, were prominent in the administration. There was no division between religious and civil affairs. Together 'the chief priests' and influential laity represented the entire community in any issue involving Jewish–Roman negotiation, and were prominent in decisions that did not directly concern the Romans.[2] The 'chief priests' were the more important of the two groups, with a high priest often acting as the leader of the Jews. The predominance of 'the chief

---

1. Rather than speculate on the possible audience and setting of *m. Sanh.* here I intend to examine these and other aspects of the text in a future study.

2. See also Acts 9.1, 14, 21; 22.5, where reference is made to the appointment of Saul by Jewish authorities.

priests', the majority of whom were connected with the high priesthood, is also reflected in the concentration of the office in the hands of a select number of families. It should be noted that these high priests were not always united. There was competition for prominence within their own group and occasional differences of opinion in matters of policy. Similarly, although normally in agreement, some of the influential laity occasionally disagreed with the 'chief priests' over what should be done.

Divisions within the influential laity and 'chief priests', and between the two, existed because of various individuals' desire to obtain seniority. Such rivalry, however, did not diminish the ability of men associated with either group to hold prominent status within the Jewish community.

Members of the Herodian family came to the assistance of the Jewish cause in a number of the cases where the Jews were negotiating with the Romans. In part, familiarity with Roman society may have made the Herodians obvious candidates. Irrespective of the reason, and whether or not they were holding direct control, the Herodians were accepted as legitimate representatives of Jewish interests by both Romans and Jews.

The motivation of these men is open to debate. It is unlikely that idealism or, at the other extreme, greed, can be viewed as their prime concern. The silence regarding Pilate's decision to use Temple funds to build the aqueduct might suggest a degree of self-interest. Similarly, some of the men who argued for obedience to Florus may have feared for their lives. The protest against Fadus's order, however, indicates a concern to uphold certain Jewish traditions. In the context of their immediate surroundings the influential laity and 'chief priests' appear to have acted in the belief that they understood what was best for the community as a whole. It is understandable that the course of action proposed would also agree with the personal interests of these men, especially in internal matters. They believed, too, that to preserve the Jewish community they had to maintain their prominent position in society. Although not always in agreement, the chief priests and influential laity held a common belief that actions they proposed were for the benefit of the whole community.

The social grouping of the prominent men remained constant. Two factors were the basis of this prominence. First, the influential laity and 'chief priests' were expected to participate in the administration.

Apart from their wealth and education, the laity had previously been advisors to heads of state. The 'chief priests' already held prominent positions in Temple affairs. As a result it was expected that these groups would want to represent Jewish interests and be capable of so doing. Furthermore, it is possible that it was with the introduction of direct Roman rule that the 'chief priests' developed their identity as a group concerned with public affairs. Their status, however, was not predestined.

Many individuals and groups attempted to obtain prominence within the Jewish community. Although most of these men were able to express their views, they failed to gain widespread appeal.[1] It is in this context that the second factor is pertinent. Attaining and then maintaining prominence was dependent on acceptance within the community. It was important that the Romans regarded the negotiators as capable of controlling the Jewish community and as men with whom they were willing to deal. Acceptance within the Jewish community, however, was equally important. The prominent Jews were not able to ignore popular opinion. Instead, it was necessary to express views that found some popular acceptance, or reflected popular views. The nature of authority is indicated in the tense events of AD 66. Agrippa II proposed a course of action unpalatable to the majority of Jews in Jerusalem and was forced to retreat from the city. Similarly, 'the chief priests' and influential laity who favoured peace were also forced to reconsider their options, having lost their prominence with the populace at the expense of those favouring rebellion.[2]

---

1. A number of people may be included in this category. For example, Judas, the Galilaean (*War* 1.118; *Ant.* 18.4-10, 23-25; Acts 5.37); Jesus, son of Ananias (*War* 6.300-309); Theudas (*Ant.* 20.97-99; Acts 5.36); the Egyptian (*War* 2.261-63; *Ant.* 20.169-72; Acts 21.38). It is possible that John the Baptist and Jesus were viewed in a similar manner.

2. Goodman (*Ruling Class*, p. 212) argues that obtaining the confidence of the procurator was the basis of power before AD 66. Reliance on violence and popular support developed immediately before and during the revolt (p. 215). On a more general level, Goodman clearly highlights the existence of factions within the ruling class. While agreeing that much emphasis should be placed on the factional fighting to explain the situation in Judaea, the reliance on negotiation that we have observed suggests the need to alter our perception of the ruling classes' power base. Some of the prominent Jews failed to retain public confidence. As Goodman points out, however, several prominent Jews were involved in affairs in the revolt as leaders of the new independent Jewish state. The consistency with which elements of the

It is important to distinguish between practical involvement in administrative tasks and participation in the decision-making process. There was a formal institution referred to as the *boule*, later replaced by the 'common council'. Although it was the official figurehead in Jerusalem, this institution only fulfilled administrative tasks. Further instruments of the government were the two bodies referred to by the term *synedrion*. The consultative *synedrion* was a forum for discussion of specific issues while the court *synedrion* judged cases. Both were operated whenever the appropriate leading figure deemed it to be necessary.

It was people in the Jewish community who attained their prominence for reasons other than membership of any institution who were important in decisions that were reached. The 'chief priests', among whom the serving high priest featured as the leading spokesman, and the influential laity, represented the Jewish community. They did so on a routine basis, whether in response to a Roman order or as part of a Jewish initiative. Furthermore, they did not distinguish between supposedly religious and political issues. On a few occasions these groups were assisted by members of the Herodian family. Religious groups, such as the Pharisees, however, were not prominent.[1] The question of Jewish ability to try and execute people for capital offences under direct Roman rule remains unsettled. Although the Jews

influential laity and 'chief priests' were able to remain prominent indicates that they argued for status quo in a manner with which the community sympathized. As a result, the emphasis placed on popular opposition to the ruling class by such scholars as Brunt ('Josephus', pp. 150, 152) and Horsley ('The Zealots', pp. 174-76) requires major qualification. Similarly, the notion that *the* Jewish ruling class is an example of the general Roman practice of Romanizing the local elite is not substantiated by the events examined.

1. The Pharisees did obtain some prominence over other aspirants during the reign of Salome Alexandra. Note the debate centred on Josephus's summary statements regarding the importance of the Pharisees. See Smith, 'Palestinian Judaism', pp. 183-97, and D. Goodblatt, 'The Place of the Pharisees in First Century Judaism: The State of the Debate', *JSJ* 20 (1989), pp. 12-30; cf. Schwartz, 'Josephus and Nicolaus', pp. 157-71. The assessment of actual events supports the approach of Smith and Goodblatt in their analysis of the summaries. Note also Mason, 'Josephus on the Pharisees', pp. 468-69, who argues that Josephus was critical of the Pharisees in both texts. Unfortunately Mason does not then proceed to question the accuracy of the summary statements, but accepts that the Pharisees dominated public opinion.

operated within the Roman judicial system they probably retained the right of trial and execution.

Despite their continued prominence, the 'chief priests' and influential laity did not operate a committee government. Within each group there were certain prominent individuals who tended to influence the views of the chief priests and influential laity as a whole.[1]

A structure of administration operated in Palestine in which the Jews played a practical and essential part. With the exception of determining who should be head of state, certain Jews had an active routine part in what decisions were made.[2] They also perceived themselves as maintaining a high degree of self-determination. At the same time the Romans held the right as military masters to intervene in issues that were deemed appropriate, normally in the guise of a negotiated settlement. In measures initiated by the Romans the Jews expressed an independent view and found a general willingness in the Roman administration to hear that view in the interests of stability.

1. In a broad sense, therefore, Josephus's statements about the type of government may be accurate (*War* 1.170; *Ant.* 14.91; 20.251; *Apion* 2.185). The Jews were led by priests under an aristocratic form of leadership (*Ant.* 4.223; 5.135; 6.36, 268; 11.111; 20.229).

2. It is possible that Jonathan did indicate some form of approval of Felix's appointment. See *Ant.* 20.162. The willingness of Jews to rely on negotiation and to participate routinely in the administration may, in part be related to the idea that the Romans tended to display a passive, conservative approach to the governing of the provinces. See Millar, *Emperor*, pp. 379, 384, and P. Garnsey and R. Saller, *The Roman Empire, Economy, Society and Culture* (London: Duckworth, 1987), pp. 197, 202-203; cf. p. 170 regarding the Roman attitude toward the Jews.

CONCLUSION

Because it is event-based, this study is unique among discussions of the administration of Palestine during the first centuries BC and AD. This approach has enabled me to clarify many aspects of how the administration functioned, especially in terms of which Jews participated in the decision-making process. Consequently, it has important implications for scholarly understanding of what actually happened in the governing and administration of the late Second Temple Jewish community in Palestine, and leads us to challenge many established ideas.

Institutions existing in this period were not significant in decision-making. There is evidence for a *boule/gerousia* in Jerusalem during the first centuries BC and AD. Thus *boule/gerousia* was an official institution, recognized as representative of the community on formal occasions. It was, however, only an active participant in the sense that it fulfilled administrative tasks, possible in association with 'magistrates' (οἱ ἄρχοντες). The origins of this institution are uncertain, though it probably dated from before the first century AD. It was replaced by the 'common council' (κοινόν) during the revolt.

Two further instruments of government could be activated by a leading figure whenever it was deemed appropriate. Both these bodies are described by the term *synedrion* in Josephus's works and the New Testament. One acted as an advisory body while the other was a means of arbitration, normally in a capital offence trial. Neither was a permanent institution, let alone a 'representative national body'. Their membership was determined on an *ad hoc* basis by one of the leading figures. Hence, all scholarly discussion of whether one, two or three permanent institutions known by the title *synedrion* existed is irrelevant.

The Jews important in the decision-making process were the influential laity and 'the chief priests' (οἱ ἀρχιερεῖς). In the first century AD it was predominantly 'the chief priests' that took a leading

role in affairs. Combined, these men represented the Jewish community and upheld the status quo. Occasionally they were assisted by
Herodians, who sought to maintain a prominent role throughout the
first century AD. The prominent priests and influential laity believed it
was appropriate for them to take a leading role in all public affairs.

There was no distinction between political and religious issues.
Furthermore, religious groups were rarely important in administration. The Pharisees, as a group, were prominent as advisors only
during the reign of Salome Alexandra. At all other times it was
individuals, leaders among 'the chief priests', influential laity and
occasionally Herodians, who dictated Jewish affairs. The sociopolitical
context in which Christianity began, therefore, was primarily centred
around the priesthood.

Negotiation was the favoured means for reaching a decision. This
situation is especially evident in Jewish–Roman relations. There are
only a limited number of occasions where dogmatic arbitrary decisions were made. It was expected that negotiations would take place to
seek a solution. The willingness of Jews to participate in negotiations
was based on a desire to protect the status quo. This reliance on
negotiation reinforces the view that provincial administration of the
early principate actively sought the involvement of local inhabitants.

The prominence of Jews was based on three related factors: an
alignment with the sentiments of the community as a whole; an
expectancy that certain men would represent the interests of the community; and acceptance within Roman circles. We have no evidence of
any long-standing tension between prominent Jews and the remainder
of the community. The consistency with which 'the chief priests' and
select Jews identified as the influential laity featured in the decision-
making process indicates that the majority of Jews were willing to
heed their advice. In general, these men retained the respect and trust
of the community.

Under Roman rule the Jewish community maintained its identity
and sense of independence in terms of administrative affairs. It is even
possible that the advent of direct Roman rule provided greater opportunity for certain Jews to participate actively. The Jews expected to be
able to negotiate and were expected to do so. Similarly, in many
instances, the Jews made decisions without interference. Although
Rome held overall control through its military power, it was not a
relationship of master–servant. Jews retained their sense of commu-

nity identity and interacted with the Romans as a subsidiary partner on the basis that the territory should remain loyal in friendship to Rome. The revolt of AD 66–70 was, therefore, not inevitable.

BIBLIOGRAPHY

1. Texts

Augustine, *In Iohannis Evangelium*, Tractatus CXXIV (Corpus Christianorum, Series Latina, 36; Turnholti: Typographi Brepols Editores, 1954).
Babylonian Talmud (ed I. Epstein; London: The Soncino Press, 1935–1971).
Eusebius, *Historia Ecclesiastica* (trans. and ed. K. Lake: LCL; London: Heinemann, 1926).
—*Demonstratio Evangelica*, (trans. and ed. W.J. Ferrar; New York: Macmillan, 1920).
Greek New Testament (ed. K. Aland, M. Black, C.M. Martini, B.M. Metzger and A. Wikgren; London: United Bible Societies, 3rd edn, 1966).
Josephus, *Works* (trans. and ed. H.St.J. Thackeray, R. Marcus and L. Feldman; 10 vols.; LCL; London: Heinemann, 1926–1965).
The Mishnah (trans. H. Danby; Oxford: Clarendon Press, 1933).
Philo, *Works* (trans. and ed. F.H. Colson and G.H. Whitaker; 10 vols.; LCL; London: Heinemann, 1929–1943).
Sifre Deuteronomy (trans. R. Hammer; Yale Judaica Series, 24; New Haven: Yale University Press, 1986).
Tacitus, *Annals*, Books 4–6, 11–12 (trans. J. Jackson; LCL; London: Heinemann, 1937).
—*Histories* (trans. and ed. C.H. Moore; LCL; London: Heinemann, 1931).

2. Secondary Works

Aberbach, M., 'The Conflicting Accounts of Josephus and Tacitus Concerning Cumanus' and Felix' Terms of Office', *JQR* 40 (1949), pp. 1-14.
Albright, W.F. and C.S. Mann, *Matthew* (AB, 26; New York: Doubleday, 1971).
Allen, J.E., 'Why Pilate?', in *The Trial of Jesus. Cambridge Studies in Honour of C.F.D. Moule* (ed. E. Bammel; SBT, II, 13; London: SCM Press, 1970), pp. 78-83.
Alon, G., 'Did the Jewish People and its Sages Cause the Hasmonaeans To Be Forgotten?', in *Jews, Judaism and the Classical World* (ed. G. Alon; trans. I. Abrahams; Jerusalem: Magnes Press, 1977), pp. 1-17.
—'The Attitude of the Pharisees to Roman Rule and the House of Herod', in *Jews, Judaism and the Classical World* (ed. G. Alon; trans. I. Abrahams; Jerusalem: Magnes Press, 1977), pp. 18-47.
—'The Burning of the Temple', in *Jews, Judaism and the Classical World* (ed. G. Alon; trans. I. Abrahams; Jerusalem: Magnes Press, 1977), pp. 252-68.
—*The Jews in their Land in the Talmudic Age*, I (trans. I. Abrahams; ed. G. Levi; Jerusalem: Magnes Press, 1980).
Applebaum, S., 'The Zealots: The Case for Revaluation', *JRS* 61 (1971), pp. 155-70.
Aune, D.E., *The New Testament and its Literary Environment* (Philadelphia; Westminster Press, 1987).
Avi-Yonah, M., *The Holy Land, From the Persian to Arab Conquests* (Grand Rapids: Baker Book House, 1966).
Balsdon, J.P.V.D., 'Notes Concerning the Principate of Gaius', *JRS* 24 (1934), pp. 13-24.

Bammel, E., 'The Trial Before Pilate', in *Jesus and the Politics of His Day* (ed. E. Bammel and C.F.D. Moule; Cambridge: Cambridge University Press, 1984), pp. 415-51.
—'The *titulus*', in *Jesus and the Politics of his Day* (ed. E. Bammel and C.F.D. Moule; Cambridge: Cambridge University Press, 1984), pp. 353-64.
—'Crucifixion as a Punishment in Palestine', in *The Trial of Jesus. Cambridge Studies in Honour of C.F.D. Moule* (ed. E. Bammel; SBT, II, 13; London: SCM Press, 1970), pp. 162-65.
Baumgarten, A.I., 'The Name of the Pharisees', *JBL* 102 (1983), pp. 411-28.
Beare, F.W., *The Gospel according to Matthew* (Oxford: Basil Blackwell, 1981).
Beavis, M.A., 'The Trial before the Sanhedrin (Mark 14.53-65): Reader Response and Greco-Roman Readers', *CBQ* 49 (1987), pp. 581-96.
Bevan, E., *Jerusalem under the High Priests* (London: Edward Arnold, 1904).
Bickerman, E., *From Ezra to the Last of the Maccabees* (New York: Schocken Books, 1947).
—'Utilitas Crucis', in *Studies in Jewish and Christian History*, Part 3 (ed. E. Bickerman; Leiden: Brill, 1986), pp. 82-138.
—'The Warning Inscriptions of Herod's Temple', in *Studies in Jewish and Christian History*, Part 2 (ed. E. Bickerman; Leiden: Brill, 1980), pp. 210-24.
Bilde, P., 'The Causes of the Jewish War according to Josephus', *JSJ* 10 (1979), pp. 179-202.
—'The Roman Emperor Gaius (Caligula)'s Attempt to Erect his Statue in the Temple of Jerusalem', *Studia Theologica* 32 (1978), pp. 67-93.
—*Flavius Josephus between Jerusalem and Rome* (JSPSup, 2; Sheffield: JSOT Press, 1988).
Blinzler, J., 'The Jewish Punishment of Stoning in the New Testament Period', in *The Trial of Jesus. Cambridge Studies in Honour of C.F.D. Moule* (ed. E. Bammel; SBT, II, 13; London: SCM Press, 1970), pp. 147-61.
—*The Trial of Jesus* (Maryland: The Newman Press, 1959).
—'The Trial of Jesus in the Light of History', *Judaism* 20 (1971), pp. 49-55.
Bokser, B.M., 'Jacob N. Epstein's *Introduction to the Text of the Mishnah*', in *The Modern Study of the Mishnah* (ed. J. Neusner; Leiden: Brill, 1973), pp. 13-36.
—'Jacob N. Epstein on the Formation of the Mishnah', in *The Modern Study of the Mishnah* (ed. J. Neusner; Leiden: Brill, 1973), pp. 37-55.
Bosker, B.Z., *Judaism and the Christian Predicament* (New York: Alfred A. Knoff, 1967).
Brandon, S.G.F., 'The Death of James the Just: A New Interpretation', in *Studies in Mysticism and Religion, Presented to G.G. Scholem* (ed. E.E. Urbach, R.J. Zuri Werblowsky, C. Wirazubshi; Jerusalem: Magnes Press, 1967), pp. 57-69.
—*The Fall of Jerusalem and the Christian Church* (London: SPCK, 2nd edn, 1968).
—*Jesus and the Zealots* (Manchester: Manchester University Press, 1967).
—'The Trial of Jesus', *Judaism* 20 (1971), pp. 43-48.
—*The Trial of Jesus of Nazareth* (London: Batsford, 1968).
Brawley, R.L., *Luke–Acts and the Jews* (SBLMS, 33; Atlanta: Scholars Press, 1987).
Brown, R.E., *The Gospel according to John (XIII–XXI)* (AB, 29a; New York: Doubleday, 1970).
Bruce, F.F., *Men and Movements in the Primitive Church* (Exeter: The Paternoster Press, 1979).
—*New Testament History* (London: Oliphants, rev. edn, 1971).
—*The Acts of the Apostles* (London: The Tyndale Press, 2nd edn, 1952).
Brunt, P.A., 'Josephus on Social Conflicts in Roman Judaea', *Klio* 59 (1977), pp. 149-53.
—'The Romanization of the Local Ruling Classes in the Roman Empire', in *Assimilation et résistance à la culture gréco-romaine dans le monde ancien. Travaux du VIe Congrès*

International d'Etudes Classiques, Madrid, Septembre 1974 (ed. D. Pippidi; Bucharest: Editura Academiei, 1976), pp. 161-73.

Büchler, A., *Das Synedrion in Jerusalem und das grosse Beth-Din in der Quaderkammer des Jerusalemischen Tempels* (Vienna: Alfred Holder, 1902).

Buehler, W.W., *The Pre-Herodian Civil War and Social Debate, Jewish Society in the Period 76–40 BC and the Social Factors Contributing to the Rise of the Pharisees and the Sadducees* (Basil: Friedrich Reinhardt, 1974).

Cadbury, H., *The Making of Luke–Acts* (London: SPCK, 2nd edn, 1958).

Carcopino, J., 'Encore le rescrit impérial sur les violations de sépulture', *Revue Historique* 156 (1931), pp. 88-92.

Cassidy, R.J., *Society and Politics in the Acts of the Apostles* (New York: Orbis Books, 1987).

Catchpole, D.R., 'The Problem of the Historicity of the Sanhedrin Trial', in *The Trial of Jesus. Cambridge Studies in Honour of C.F.D. Moule* (ed. E. Bammel; SBT, II, 13; London: SCM Press, 1970), pp. 47-65.

Cohen, S.J.D., 'The Political and Social History of the Jews in Greco-Roman Antiquity: The State of the Question', in *Early Judaism and its Modern Interpreters* (ed. R.A. Kraft and G.W.E. Nickelsberg; Philadelphia: Fortress Press, 1986), pp. 33-56.

—*Josephus in Galilee and Rome* (Leiden: Brill, 1979).

Cohn, H., 'Reflections on the Trial of Jesus', *Judaism* 20 (1971), pp. 10-23.

Cole, R.A., *The Gospel according to St Mark* (Leicester: Inter-Varsity Press, 1961).

Conzelmann, H., *Acts of the Apostles* (trans. J. Limburg, A.T. Kraabel and D.H. Juel; Philadelphia: Fortress Press, 1987).

—*The Theology of St Luke* (trans. G. Buswell; London: Faber & Faber, 1960).

Cook, M.J., *Mark's Treatment of the Jewish Leaders* (NovTSup, 51; Leiden: Brill, 1978).

Crook, J.A., *Consilium Principis* (Cambridge: Cambridge University Press, 1955).

Davies, P.S., 'The Meaning of Philo's Text about the Gilded Shields', *JTS* ns 37 (1986), pp. 109-14.

Dibelius, M., *Studies in the Acts of the Apostles* (trans. and ed. H. Greevan; London: SCM Press, 1956).

Doble, P., 'The Son of Man Saying in Stephen's Witnessing: Acts 6.8–8.2', *NTS* 31 (1985), pp. 68-84.

Donaldson, T.L., 'Rural Bandits, City Mobs and the Zealots', *JSJ* 21 (1990), pp. 19-40.

Doyle, A., 'Pilate's Career and the Date of the Crucifixion', *JTS* 42 (1941), pp. 190-93.

Dunn, J.D.G., *Unity and Diversity in the New Testament* (London: SCM Press, 1977).

Efron, J., *Studies in the Hasmonaean Period* (trans. N. Handelman; Leiden: Brill, 1987).

Ehrhardt, A., *The Acts of the Apostles* (Manchester: University of Manchester Press, 1969).

Ehrman, B.D., 'Jesus' Trial before Pilate, John 18.28–19.16', *BTB* 13 (1983), pp. 124-31.

Enslin, M.S., 'The Temple and the Cross', *Judaism* 20 (1971), pp. 24-31.

Falk, Z.W., *Introduction to Jewish Law of the Second Commonwealth*, Part 1 (Leiden: Brill, 1972).

Farmer, W.R., 'Judas, Simon and Athronges', *NTS* 4 (1957–58), pp. 147–55.

—*Maccabees, Zealots and Josephus* (New York: Columbia University Press, 1956).

Fitzmyer, J.A., 'Crucifixion in Ancient Palestine, Qumran Literature and the New Testament', *CBQ* 40 (1978), pp. 493-513.

—*The Gospel according to Luke (X–XXIV)* (AB, 28a; New York: Doubleday, 1985).

Flusser, D., 'A Literary Approach to the Trial of Jesus', *Judaism* 20 (1971), pp. 32-36.

Fortna, R.T., 'Jesus and Peter at the High Priest's House: A Test Case for the Question of the Relation between Mark's and John's Gospels', *NTS* 24 (1978), pp. 371-83.

Freyne, S., *Galilee: From Alexander the Great to Hadrian, 323 BC to 135 CE* (Wilmington, DE: Michael Glazier, 1980).

—*Galilee, Jesus and the Gospels. Literary Approaches and Historical Investigations* (Dublin: Gill & MacMillan, 1988).

—'Galilee–Jerusalem Relations according to Josephus's Life', *NTS* 33 (1987), pp. 600-609.

Friedländer, I., 'The Rupture between Alexander Jannai and the Pharisees', *JQR* 4 (1913–14), pp. 443-48.

Fuks, G., 'Again on the Episode of the Gilded Roman Shields at Jerusalem', *HTR* 75 (1982), pp. 503-507.

Garnsey, P., *Social Status and Legal Privilege in the Roman Empire* (Oxford: Clarendon Press, 1970).

—'The Criminal Jurisdiction of Governors', *JRS* 58 (1968), pp. 51-59.

—'The *Lex Iulia* and Appeal under the Empire', *JRS* 56 (1966), pp. 167-89.

Garnsey, P. and R. Saller, *The Roman Empire, Economy, Society and Culture* (London: Duckworth, 1987).

Geiger, J., 'The Causes of the Jewish War', *JRA* 2 (1989), pp. 291-93.

Geller, M.J., 'Alexander Jannaeus and the Pharisee Rift', *JJS* 30 (1979), pp. 202-11

Giblin, C.H., 'John's Narration of the Hearing before Pilate (John 18.28–19.16a)', *Bib* 67 (1986), pp. 221-39.

Goodblatt, D., 'The Place of the Pharisees in First Century Judaism: The State of the Debate', *JSJ* 20 (1989), pp. 12-30.

Goodchild, R.G., 'The Coast Road of Phoenicia and its Roman Milestones', *Berytus* 9 (1948), pp. 91-127.

Goodman, M., 'A Bad Joke in Josephus', *JJS* 36 (1985), pp. 195-99.

—*The Ruling Class of Judaea. The Origins of the Jewish Revolt against Rome AD 66–70* (Cambridge: Cambridge University Press, 1987).

—*State and Society in Roman Galilee, AD 132–212* (New Jersey: Rowman & Allanheld, 1983).

Gordis, R., 'The Trial of Jesus in the Light of History', *Judaism* 20 (1971), pp. 6-9.

Grant, M., *Herod the Great* (London: Weidenfeld & Nicholson, 1971).

Grant, R.M., 'Eusebius, Josephus and the Fate of the Jews', in *Society of Biblical Literature 1979 Seminar Papers*, II (ed. P.J. Achtemeier; Missoula, MT: Scholars Press, 1979), pp. 69-86.

—'The Trial of Jesus in the Light of History', *Judaism* 20 (1971), pp. 37-42.

Green, W.S., 'Abraham Goldberg', in *The Modern Study of the Mishnah* (ed. J. Neusner; Leiden: Brill, 1973), pp. 225-41.

Grundmann, W., 'The Decision of the Supreme Court to Put Jesus to Death (John 11.47-57) in its Context: Tradition and Redaction in the Gospel of John', in *Jesus and the Politics of His Day* (ed. E. Bammel and C.F.D. Moule; Cambridge: Cambridge University Press, 1984), pp. 295-318.

Guillet, P.E., 'Entrée en scène de Pilate', *CCER* 24 (1977), pp. 1-24.

Guttmann, A., *Rabbinic Judaism in the Making* (Detroit: Wayne State University Press, 1970).

Haenchen, E., *The Acts of the Apostles* (rev. trans. R.McL.Wilson; Oxford: Basil Blackwell, 1971).

Halivni, D.A., 'The Reception Accorded to Rabbi Judah's Mishnah', in *Jewish and Christian Self-Definition. II. Aspects of Judaism in the Greco-Roman Period* (ed. E.P. Sanders with A.I. Baumgarten and A. Mendelson; London: SCM Press, 1981), pp. 204-12.

Hare, D., *The Theme of Jewish Persecution in the Gospel according to St Matthew* (Cambridge: Cambridge University Press, 1967).

Harvey, A.E., *Jesus on Trial. A Study in the Fourth Gospel* (London: SPCK, 1976).

Hengel, M., *Acts and the History of Earliest Christianity* (trans. J. Bowden; London: SCM Press, 1979).

—*Between Jesus and Paul. Studies in the Earliest History of Christianity* (trans. J. Bowden; London: SCM Press, 1983).

—*Crucifixion* (trans. J. Bowden; London: SCM Press, 1977).

—*Die Zeloten* (Leiden: Brill, 1961).

—*The Johannine Question* (trans. J. Bowden; London: SCM Press, 1989).

Hill, D., 'Jesus before the Sanhedrin–On What Charge?', *IBS* 7 (1985), pp. 174-86.

Hoehner, H., *Herod Antipas* (Cambridge: Cambridge University Press, 1972).

—'Why Did Pilate Hand Jesus over to Antipas?', in *The Trial of Jesus. Cambridge Studies in Honour of C.F.D. Moule* (ed. E. Bammel; SBT, II, 13; London: SCM Press, 1970), pp 84-90.

Hoenig, S., '*Dorsh Halakot* in the Pesher Nahum Scrolls', *JBL* 83 (1964), pp. 119-38.

—*The Great Sanhedrin* (Philadelphia: Dropsie College, 1953).

Hopkins, K., 'Rules of Evidence', *JRS* 68 (1978), pp. 178-86.

Horsley, R.A., 'Ancient Jewish Banditry and the Revolt against Rome, AD 66–70', *CBQ* 43 (1981), pp. 409-32.

—'High Priests and the Politics of Roman Palestine', *JSJ* 17 (1986), pp. 23-55.

—*Jesus and the Spiral of Violence. Popular Jewish Resistance in Roman Palestine* (San Francisco: Harper & Row, 1987).

—'The Sicarii: Ancient Jewish Terrorists', *JR* 59 (1979), pp. 435-58.

—'The Zealots. Their Origin, Relationship and Importance in the Jewish Revolt', *NovT* 28 (1986), pp. 159-92.

Horsley, R.A. and J.S. Hanson, *Bandits, Prophets, and Messiahs. Popular Movements in the Time of Jesus* (Minneapolis, MN: Winston Press, 1985).

Jagersma, H., *A History of Israel from Alexander the Great to Bar Kochba* (trans. J. Bowden; London: SCM Press, 1985).

Jeremias, J., *Jerusalem in the Time of Jesus* (trans. F.H. and C.H. Cave; London: SCM Press, 1969).

Jones, A.H.M., *The Criminal Courts of the Roman Republic and Principate* (ed. J.A. Crook; Oxford: Basil Blackwell, 1972).

—*The Herods of Judaea* (Oxford; Oxford University Press, 1938).

—*Studies in Roman Government and Law* (Oxford; Basil Blackwell, 1960).

Kennard, J.S., Jr, 'The Jewish Provincial Assembly', *ZNW* 53 (1962), pp. 25-51.

Kingsbury, J.D., 'The Religious Authorities in the Gospel of Mark', *NTS* 36 (1990), pp. 42-65.

Klausner, J., 'Judah Aristobulus and Jannaeus Alexander', in *The World History of the Jewish People*. 1st series, VI. *The Hellenistic Age* (ed. A. Schalit; Jerusalem: Massada Publishing Co., 1972), pp. 222-41.

—'Queen Salome Alexandra', in *The World History of the Jewish People*. 1st series, VI. *The Hellenistic Age* (ed. A. Schalit; Jerusalem: Massada Publishing Co., 1972), pp. 242-54.

Kraeling, C., 'The Episode of the Roman Standards at Jerusalem', *HTR* 35 (1942), pp. 263-89.

Lampe, G.W.H., 'AD 70 in Christian Reflection', in *Jesus and the Politics of His Day* (ed. E. Bammel and C.F.D. Moule; Cambridge: Cambridge University Press, 1984), pp. 153-71.

Leaney, A.R.C., *The Jewish and Christian World, 200 BC to AD 200* (Cambridge Commentaries on Writings of the Jewish and Christian World, 200 BC–AD 200, 7; Cambridge: Cambridge University Press, 1984).

Le Moyne, J., *Les Sadducéens* (E Bib; Paris, 1972).

Loftus, F., 'The Anti-Roman Revolts of the Jews and the Galileans', *JQR* 68 (1977–78), pp. 78-98.

Longenecker, R.N., *The Acts of the Apostles* (The Expositor's Bible Commentary, 9; Grand Rapids: Zondervan, 1981).

Maccoby, H., *Early Rabbinic Writings* (Cambridge: Cambridge University Press, 1988).

McCullough, W.S., *The History and Literature of the Palestinian Jews from Cyrus to Herod, 550 BC to 4 BC* (Toronto: University of Toronto Press, 1975).

McLaren, J., 'Jerusalem to Pella–the Evidence in Question' (unpublished MA thesis, University of Melbourne, 1985).

Maier, P., 'The Episode of the Golden Roman Shields at Jerusalem', *HTR* 62 (1969), pp. 109-21.

Mann, C.S., *Mark* (AB, 27; New York: Doubleday, 1986).

Mantel, H., 'The High Priesthood and the Sanhedrin in the Second Temple Period', in *The World History of the Jewish People*. 1st Series, VII. *The Herodian Period* (ed. M. Avi-Yonah; Jerusalem: Massada Publishing Co., 1975), pp. 264-81.

—*Studies in the History of the Sanhedrin* (Harvard Semitic Series, 17; Cambridge, MA: Harvard University Press, 1961).

Marshall, I.H., *The Acts of the Apostles* (Leicester: Inter-Varsity Press, 1980).

Martin, R.P., 'The Life-Setting of the Epistle of James in the Light of Jewish History', in *Biblical and Near Eastern Studies. Essays in Honour of William Sanford LaSor* (ed. G.A. Tuttle; Grand Rapids: Eerdmans, 1978), pp. 97-103.

Mason, S.N., 'Josephus on the Pharisees Reconsidered: A Critique of Smith/Neusner', *Studies in Religion (Sciences Religieuses)* 17 (1988), pp. 455-69.

—'Priesthood in Josephus and the Pharisees', *JBL* 107 (1988), pp. 657-61.

—'Was Josephus a Pharisee? A Re-Examination of *Life* 10–12', *JJS* 30 (1989), pp. 31-45.

Merritt, R.L., 'Jesus, Barabbas and the Paschal Pardon', *JBL* 104 (1985), pp. 57-68.

Meshorer, Y., *Ancient Jewish Coinage*, I & II (New York: Amphora Books, 1982).

Michaels, J. Ramsey, 'John 18.31 and the "Trial" of Jesus', *NTS* 36 (1990), pp. 474-79.

Millar, F., *The Emperor in the Roman World (31 BC–AD 337)* (London: Duckworth, 1977).

—'The Emperor, the Senate and the Provinces', *JRS* 56 (1966), pp. 156-66.

Morris, L., *The Gospel according to St Luke* (Leicester: Inter-Varsity Press, 1974).

Munck, J., *The Acts of Apostles* (AB, 31; rev. W.F. Albright and C.S. Mann; New York: Doubleday, 1967).

Naveh, J., 'Dated Coins of Alexander Jannaeus', *IEJ* 18 (1968), pp. 20-25.

Neusner, J., *Method and Meaning in Ancient Judaism* (Missoula, MT: Scholars Press, 1979).

—(ed.) *The Study of Ancient Judaism*. I. *Mishnah, Midrash, Siddur* (New York: Ktav, 1981).

Neyrey, J., *The Passion according to Luke* (New York: Paulist Press, 1985).

O'Neill, J.C., 'The Charge of Blasphemy at Jesus' Trial before the Sanhedrin', in *The Trial of Jesus. Cambridge Studies in Honour of C.F.D. Moule* (ed. E. Bammel; SBT, II, 13; London: SCM Press, 1970), pp. 72-77.

Overstreet, R.L., 'Roman Law and the Trial of Christ', *Bibliotheca Sacra* 135 (1978), pp. 323-32.

Patrich, J., 'Hideouts in the Judaean Wilderness', *BARev* 15 (1989), pp. 32-42

Porton, G.G., 'Hanokh Albeck on the Mishnah', in *The Modern Study of the Mishnah* (ed. J. Neusner; Leiden: Brill, 1973), pp. 209-24.

Rabin, C., 'Alexander Jannaeus and the Pharisees', *JJS* 7 (1956), pp. 3-11.

Rajak, T., *Josephus: The Historian and his Society* (London: Duckworth, 1983).

—'Justus of Tiberius', *CQ* 23 (1973), pp. 345-68.

Reicke, B., 'Judaeo-Christianity and the Jewish Establishment, AD 33–66', in *Jesus and the*

Politics of His Day (ed. E. Bammel and C.F.D. Moule; Cambridge: Cambridge University Press, 1984).

—*The Roots of the Synoptic Gospels* (Philadelphia: Fortress Press, 1986).

—'Synoptic Prophecies on the Destruction of Jerusalem', in *Studies in New Testament and Early Christian Literature* (ed. D.E. Aune; NovTSup, 33; Leiden: Brill, 1972), pp. 121-34.

Rhoads, D., *Israel in Revolution: 6–74 CE: A Political History Based on the Writings of Josephus* (Philadelphia: Fortress Press, 1976).

Richards, E., 'Acts 7. An Investigation of the Samaritan Evidence', *CBQ* 39 (1977), pp. 190-208.

—'The Political Character of the Joseph Episode in Acts 7', *JBL* 98 (1979), pp. 255-67.

Rivkin, E., *A Hidden Revolution* (Nashville: Parthenon Press, 1978).

—'Beth Din, Boulé, Sanhedrin: A Tragedy of Errors', *HUCA* 46 (1975), pp. 181-99.

—*What Crucified Jesus?* (Nashville: Abingdon Press, 1984).

Robinson, J.A.T., *Redating the New Testament* (London: SCM Press, 1976).

—*The Priority of John* (ed. J.F. Coakley; London: SCM Press, 1985).

Rosenfeld, B-Z, 'The "Boundary of Gezer" Inscriptions and the History of Gezer at the End of the Second Temple Period', *IEJ* 38 (1988), pp. 235-45.

Roth, C., 'The Constitution of the Jewish Republic of 66–70', *JSS* 9 (1964), pp. 295-319.

—'The Debate on the Loyal Sacrifices, AD 66', *HTR* 53 (1960), pp. 93-97.

—'The Historical Implications of the Jewish Coinage of the First Revolt', *IEJ* 12 (1962), pp. 33-46.

—'The Pharisees in the Jewish Revolution of 66–73', *JSS* 7 (1962), pp. 63-80.

—'The Zealots in the War of 66–73', *JSS* 4 (1959), pp. 332-55.

Safrai, S. and M. Stern (eds.), *The Jewish People in the First Century* (2 vols; CRIANT; Assen: Van Gorcum I, 1974, II, 1976).

Saldarini, A.J., *Pharisees, Scribes and Sadducees in Palestinian Society* (Edinburgh: T. & T. Clark, 1989).

Sanders, E.P., *Jesus and Judaism* (London: SCM Press, 1985).

Sanders, E.P. and M. Davies, *Studying the Synoptic Gospels* (London: SCM Press, 1988).

Sanders, J.T., *The Jews in Luke–Acts* (London: SCM Press, 1987).

Sandmel, S., 'The Trial of Jesus: Reservations', *Judaism* 20 (1971), pp. 59-74.

Schalit, A., 'Domestic Politics and Political Institutions', in *The World History of the Jewish People. 1st series, VI. The Hellenistic Age* (ed. A. Schalit; Jerusalem: Massada Publishing Co., 1972), pp. 255-97.

—*König Herodes, Der Mann und Sein Werk* (Berlin: de Gruyter, 1969).

—'The End of the Hasmonaean Dynasty and the Rise of Herod', in *The World History of the Jewish People. 1st series, VII. The Herodian Period* (ed. M. Avi-Yonah; Jerusalem: Massada Publishing Co., 1975), pp. 44-70.

—'The Fall of the Hasmonaean Dynasty and the Roman Conquest', in *The World History of the Jewish People. 1st series, VII. The Herodian Period* (ed. M. Avi-Yonah; Jerusalem: Massada Publishing Co., 1975), pp. 26-43.

Schneider, G., 'The Political Charge against Jesus (Luke 23.2)', in *Jesus and the Politics of His Day* (ed. E. Bammel and C.F.D. Moule; Cambridge: Cambridge University Press, 1984), pp. 403-14.

Schubert, K., 'Biblical Criticism Criticised: With Reference to the Markan report of Jesus' Examination before the Sanhedrin', in *Jesus and the Politics of His Day* (ed. E. Bammel and C.F.D. Moule; Cambridge: Cambridge University Press, 1984), pp. 385-402.

Schürer, E., *The History of the Jewish People in the Age of Jesus Christ* (rev. trans. G. Vermes, F. Millar and M. Black; Edinburgh: T. & T. Clark, I, 1973, II, 1979).

Schwartz, D., 'Josephus and Nicolaus on the Pharisees', *JSJ* 14 (1983), pp. 156-71.

—'Josephus and Philo on Pontius Pilate', *Jerusalem Cathedra* 3 (1983), pp. 26-45.
—'Viewing the Holy Utensils (P. Ox. V. 840)', *NTS* 32 (1986), pp. 153-59.
Scobie, C.H.H., 'The Use of Source Material in the Speeches of Acts III and VII', *NTS* 25 (1978-79), pp. 399-421.
Segal, P., 'The Penalty of the Warning Inscription from the Temple of Jerusalem', *IEJ* 39 (1989), pp. 79-84.
Sherwin-White, A.N., *Roman Society and Roman Law in the New Testament* (Oxford: Oxford University Press, 1963).
Sijpesteijn, P., 'The Legationes ad Gaium', *JJS* 15 (1964), pp. 87-96.
Simon, M., *St Stephen and the Hellenists in the Primitive Church* (The Haskell Lectures, 1956: London: Longmans, Green, 1958).
Sloyan, G.S., 'The Last Days of Jesus', *Judaism* 20 (1971), pp. 57-68.
Smallwood, E.M., 'High Priests and Politics in Roman Palestine', *JTS* ns 13 (1962), pp. 14-34.
—*Philonis Alexandrini Legatio ad Gaium: Text and Commentary* (Leiden: Brill, 2nd edn, 1970).
—'Some Comments on Tacitus, Annals, XII,54', *Latomus* 18 (1959), pp. 560-67.
—'The Chronology of Gaius's Attempt to Desecrate the Temple', *Latomus* 16 (1957), pp. 3-17.
—*The Jews under Roman Rule : from Pompey to Diocletian* (Leiden: Brill, 1976).
Smith, M., 'Zealots and Sicarii: Their Origins and Relation', *HTR* 64 (1971), pp. 1-19.
—'Palestinian Judaism in the First Century', in *Essays in Greco-Roman and Related Talmudic Literature* (ed. H.A. Fischel; New York: Ktav, 1977), pp. 183-97.
Soards, M.L., 'Tradition, Composition and Theology in Luke's Account of Jesus before Herod Antipas', *Bib* 66 (1985), pp. 344-63.
Sobosan, J.G., 'The Trial of Jesus', *JES* 10 (1973), pp. 70-93.
Stern, M., 'The Herodian Dynasty and the Province of Judaea at the End of the Period of the Second Temple', in *The World History of the Jewish People*. 1st series, VII. *The Herodian Period* (ed. M. Avi-Yonah; Jerusalem: Massada Publishing Co., 1975), pp. 124-78.
—'Sicarii and Zealots', in *The World History of the Jewish People*. 1st series, VIII. *Society and Religion in the Second Temple Period* (ed. M. Avi-Yonah; Jerusalem: Massada Publishing Co., 1977), pp. 263-301.
Sylva, D.D., 'The Meaning and Function of Acts 7.46-50', *JBL* 106 (1987), pp. 261-75.
Tcherikover, V.A., *Hellenistic Civilization and the Jews* (trans. S. Applebaum; Philadelphia: The Jewish Publication Society of America, 1959).
—'Was Jerusalem a Polis?', *IEJ* 14 (1964), pp. 61-78.
Thackeray, H.St J., *Josephus the Man and the Historian* (New York: Jewish Institute of Religion Press, 1929).
Theissen, G., *Sociology of Early Palestinian Christianity* (trans. J. Bowden; Philadelphia: Fortress Press, 1978).
Urbach, E.E., 'Jewish Doctrines and Practices in the Hellenistic and Talmudic Periods', in *Violence and Defence in the Jewish Experience* (ed. S.W. Baron and G.S. Wise; Philadelphia: The Jewish Publication Society of America, 1977), pp. 71-85.
Walaskay, P.W., *And So We Came to Rome* (Cambridge: Cambridge University Press, 1983).
—'The Trial and Death of Jesus in the Gospel of Luke', *JBL* 94 (1975), pp. 81-93.
Walbank, F.W., *Selected Papers, Studies in Greek and Roman History and Historiography* (Cambridge: Cambridge University Press, 1985).
Watson, F., 'Why Was Jesus Crucified?', *Theology* 88 (1985), pp. 105-12.
Weber, W., *Josephus und Vespasian: Untersuchungen zu dem Jüdischen Krieg des Flavius Josephus* (Stuttgart: Kohlhammer, 1921).

Westerholm, S., *Jesus and Scribal Authority* (Lund: Gleerup, 1978).

Williamson, G.A., *The World of Josephus* (London: Secker & Warburg, 1964).

Winter, P., *On the Trial of Jesus* (Berlin: de Gruyter, 1961).

Wolfson, H.A., 'Synedrion in Greek, Jewish Literature and Philo', *JQR* 36 (1946–47), pp. 303-306.

Yadin, Y., 'Pesher Nahum/4Qp Nahum', *IEJ* 21 (1974), pp. 1-12.

Zeitlin, S., 'Did Agrippa Write a Letter to Gaius Caligula?', *JQR* 56 (1965–66), pp. 21-31.

—*Jesus and the Judaism of His Time* (Cambridge: Polity Press, 1988).

—'Synedrion in Greek Literature, the Gospels and the Institution of the Sanhedrin', *JQR* 37 (1946–47), pp. 189-98.

—'Synedrion in the Judeo-Hellenistic Literature and Sanhedrin in the Tannaitic Literature', *JQR* 36 (1945–46), pp. 307-15.

—'The Political Synedrion and the Religious Sanhedrin', *JQR* 36 (1945–46), pp. 109-40.

—*The Rise and Fall of the Judaean State* (2 vols.; Philadelphia: The Jewish Publication Society of America, I, 1962, II, 1967–69).

—*Who Crucified Jesus?* (New York: Harper & Brothers, 2nd edn, 1947).

Ziesler, J.A., 'Luke and the Pharisees', *NTS* 25 (1978–79), pp. 146-57.

INDEXES

INDEX OF REFERENCES

BIBLICAL REFERENCES

OTHER ANCIENT JEWISH WORKS

INDEX OF AUTHORS

JOURNAL FOR THE STUDY OF THE NEW TESTAMENT

9/8/91